the complete book of
road cycling & racing

the complete book of
road cycling & racing

WILL PEVELER

McGraw-Hill

Camden, Maine ▪ New York ▪ Chicago ▪ San Francisco
Lisbon ▪ London ▪ Madrid ▪ Mexico City ▪ Milan
New Delhi ▪ San Juan ▪ Seoul ▪ Singapore ▪ Sydney ▪ Toronto

The McGraw·Hill Companies

Library of Congress Cataloging-in-Publication Data

Peveler, Will.
    The complete book of road cycling and racing / Will Peveler.
        p.   cm.
    Includes index.
    ISBN 978-0-07-148937-9 (pbk. : alk. paper)
    1. Bicycle racing.   2. Cycling.   3. Bicycles.   I. Title.

    GV1049P48   2008
    796.7—dc22   2008002096

2 3 4 5 6 7 8 9 10 11 12 13 14 15 16 17 18 19 20 21 DOC/DOC 1 9 8 7 6 5 4 3 2 1 0

ISBN 978-0-07-148937-9
MHID   0-07-148937-1

Photographs by author unless otherwise noted.
Interior illustrations by Accurate Art, Inc.

McGraw-Hill books are available at special quantity discounts to use as premiums and sales promotions or for use in corporate training programs. To contact a representative, please visit the Contact Us pages at www.mhprofessional.com.

The author and publisher have made every effort to ensure that the information contained in this book was correct at the time of going to press. They accept no responsibility for any loss, injury, or inconvenience sustained by any person using this book or the advice given within it. Consult your physician or health care professional before beginning this or any exercise program. Not all exercise programs are suitable for everyone. Discontinue any exercise that causes you discomfort or pain and consult a medical expert. The instructions and advice presented in this book are in no way a substitute for medical counseling.

This book is printed on acid-free paper.

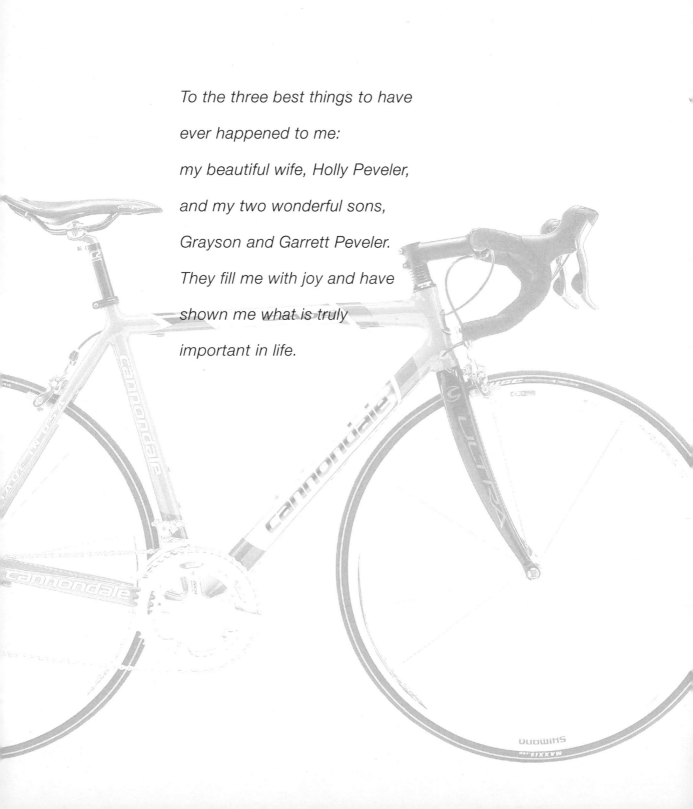

To the three best things to have ever happened to me: my beautiful wife, Holly Peveler, and my two wonderful sons, Grayson and Garrett Peveler. They fill me with joy and have shown me what is truly important in life.

contents

preface

I have been involved in the sport of cycling for a long time, as a bike shop manager, a bike racer, a racing coach, and a researcher specializing in the physiology of bicycling. Because of my diverse experience, I am often approached by friends, students, colleagues, and complete strangers with questions about cycling. These questions cover topics ranging from buying a first bike to fine points of racing strategy to the latest research on nutrition for athletes.

Although there are many great cycling books out there, none of them addresses the whole spectrum of questions that people seem to want answers to. My goal in writing this book was to provide all those answers in a way that everyone can understand.

Of course, it was necessary to impose some limits, because cycling is a huge field. Given the differences between road racing, track racing, cyclo-cross, bicycle touring, mountain biking, downhill racing, enduro, BMX, off-road trials, and freestyle, one could say that cycling is really a number of different sports, just barely related by the fact that they involve two wheels and no engine. This book is about performance-oriented road cycling—both racing and recreational—because that's what I know best, and roads are where most people ride. But within that field, I've attempted to be as comprehensive as possible, to answer all the questions that you, as a rider, are likely to have.

This book was written for those new to performance-oriented cycling and those who have been riding for a while but wish to improve their performance. It assumes that you're past the training-wheel stage—that you know how to stay upright on two wheels and know the basic functions of your gearshifts and brakes. But if you already ride for fitness or pure enjoyment, eventually you're going to want to get better: to ride faster, farther, or more efficiently, or become even fitter. If that's the case, this book is for you.

This book is also for you if you want to make the jump from noncompetitive riding to racing. Once you're a skilled road rider, that desire is almost inevitable, because it's nearly impossible to see the excitement of a road race and not want to be part of it. And if you're already an entry-level bike racer, hopefully this book will help you move up a few notches by showing you how to become a stronger, smarter rider.

That's a pretty diverse group of readers, so I've included all the information I wish I'd had when I began cycling. I hope this book answers all your questions about road riding and racing, and helps you get the most enjoyment, satisfaction, and fitness possible on two wheels.

acknowledgments

My parents have always been a large influence in my life. I would like to thank them for all of their support and teaching as I grew, because without them I could not be where I am today. They taught me the values that have allowed me to become successful in life. I would also like to thank my wife, Holly, for standing by me and supporting me in all of my endeavors. She has had faith in me even when I have not. She is not only the love of my life but my best friend as well. She has also spent many hours reading these chapters and making valuable suggestions.

There are many individuals who have greatly assisted in my ongoing pursuit of knowledge. I would especially like to thank Dr. Frank Wyatt, Dr. Thad Crews, Dr. Matt Green, Dr. Phil Bishop, Dr. Mark Richardson, and Dr. Joe Smith. I would also like to thank my department head, Dr. Mark Bean, and the Mississippi University for Women for allowing me to take a sabbatical to concentrate on this project.

Thanks also to everyone who assisted in providing photos for this book: David Bud (Cannondale); Angela Nock (Hammer); Barbara Dowd, Micah Rice, and Jed Schneider (Jittery Joe's); Nicole Chretien and Sean Sullivan (Mavic); Molly Nygaard (Rudy Project); Charles Herskowitz, Veronika Lenzi, Kathleen Poulos, and Sean Weide (Toyota-United); Nikia Collins (Fuji); and Holly Peveler.

Last but not least, I would like to thank Bob Holtzman, Jenn Tust, and everyone else at McGraw-Hill who made this book possible. Thank you for all of your efforts and your belief in my work.

introduction

Do you remember learning to ride as a child? Do you recall the bike? Mine was a white Huffy with a black banana seat and a race number on the handlebars and frame. I rode that bike until the frame broke and the wheels fell off. My friends and I would race, compete at distance jumping, or just ride and talk for hours.

We still ride together, but now we wear helmets, the bikes cost more, we ride longer distances, and we do not get grounded for leaving the neighborhood. There is something about cycling that makes you feel alive. I think it is as close to flying as you can get without wings.

WHY RIDE?

People take up cycling for many reasons. Some ride for health; some ride for competition; some ride for the social opportunities; and some view their bike primarily as an environmentally clean form of transportation. Regardless of your reasons, we all share the joy of cycling.

Health

Many doctors recommend cycling to patients because of its low impact and numerous health benefits. Endurance exercise lowers the risk of developing cardiovascular disease, type 2 diabetes, and certain types of cancer. Exercise has a positive impact on cholesterol levels, blood pressure, and body composition. Cycling can also improve your psychological well-being by significantly reducing stress.

Competition

Most of us are competitive to some extent. Even cyclists who do not race formally often compete on some level, trying to be the fastest on a group ride or attempting a personal best on a specific route. Whether we test our limits against other cyclists or against the clock, competition pushes us beyond what we would accomplish without it.

The popularity of bicycle racing in the United States has grown exponentially in recent years, and the trend seems likely to continue. With this growth come more and more opportunities

Due to the increased popularity of cycling in general, there has been a large increase in competitive cycling in particular.

to compete locally. In most areas of the United States, you can find many races within a few hours' drive of your home. This has opened up racing to many individuals who may not have considered it previously.

Community

Cycling provides an excellent opportunity to socialize with those of like mind. Joining a local bike club is a good way to meet people and make new friends. If there is no cycling club in your area, start one. It doesn't take an enormous amount of effort, and you'll be surprised by how many cyclists come out of the woodwork when a club appears. My local club began with about fifteen riders and has grown to well over a hundred in just six years.

Cycling can also provide a means for supporting the community through fund-raising. Many organizations stage supported rides to raise money for charity.

Environmental Concern

More and more people are riding their bikes to work to save on gas costs and reduce their carbon footprint. Commuting by bike also allows you to squeeze more training into a normal workday. An extra thirty minutes of riding to and from work adds up. You can also take the long way home to further increase your time in the saddle.

Keep in mind that riding to work requires more planning than does driving. You will need to clean up once you reach your destination. Baby wipes work well if a shower is not available. You will also need to keep a clean set of clothes to change into at work.

BIKE AND GEAR

Whatever your reasons for riding, choosing the right bike and gear for your needs is important. Certain pieces of equipment (such as a helmet) are essential; others are in the nice-but-not-necessary category (such as a heart-rate monitor). When living on a budget it helps to be able to distinguish the essentials from the nonessentials. Part I (The Bike) discusses the bike and gear to help you make educated purchasing decisions, set up the bike to fit you, and learn to maintain it.

RACES AND RIDES

Some people are "into" bicycling because they thrive on competition, whereas others love aspects of the sport that are the antithesis of competition—the friendly, social atmosphere of group rides; the exposure to nature that cycling promotes; the altruism associated with charity rides. None of these noncompetitive attractions, however, are incompatible with riding well and fast; indeed, the better you ride, the more you will enjoy it regardless of your focus. So whether or not you wish to compete, I assume that you have at least some interest in the performance aspects of bicycling. Various types of racing and noncompetitive road riding are briefly described here and are covered in detail in Part II (Riding and Racing), along with the skills needed to do them well.

Racing

The "sport" of road racing is almost a misnomer. There are so many types of races—each with differing demands and rewards, and some requiring significantly different equipment—that it's almost like a family of related sports. Here are the most common types of races:

- Road races. Dozens of riders compete as individuals or teams in these races, which are held on public roads with distances usually from 25 to 130 miles.
- Criteriums. Called crits, these are short, fast races, usually on a flat looped course only 1 to 2 miles long but with many turns. Racers go around the course several times. The turns make the course demanding and technical to ride.

- Time trials. Individuals or teams race against the clock. There are no competing riders (individual time trial) or other teams (team time trial) working with you on the course. Because opportunities for drafting (riding in another rider's slipstream) are reduced compared to road races and crits, special equipment is used to minimize wind resistance. Distances usually range from 5 to 35 miles.
- Stage races. These races combine two or more of the race types listed above and range from two days to three weeks. The Tour de France is a stage race.
- Track racing. Special bikes with no brakes or changeable gears race at high speeds over short distances on a short (200 to 500 meters), round track that is steeply banked to promote high-speed cornering. Because it is a "non-road" event, this type of riding is not covered in detail in this book.

NONCOMPETITIVE RIDING

Organized opportunities for noncompetitive road riding fall into three categories:

- Supported rides. These provide assistance to cyclists such as food, drinks, bathroom facilities, mechanical repairs, and rest areas. Sometimes the course is closed to other traffic. An entry fee is required. Almost all charity rides, in which riders raise money for various causes, are supported rides.
- Nonsupported rides. Most local group rides are nonsupported and are often organized through bike clubs. People simply meet at a given place and time to ride a predetermined route. Riders must be prepared to take care of themselves, carrying their own snacks, tools, and other necessities.
- Touring. Similar to backpacking, bike touring involves carrying all your gear for a period of days or weeks, and usually sleeping in a

tent and cooking on a lightweight stove, or staying in hotels. Touring requires careful planning. You must determine how many miles to travel per day, identify safe roads with as little traffic as possible, and decide where to stop and where to sleep. Some companies provide fully supported tours all over the world, planning the routes, providing gear, and handling logistics. But because maintaining high speeds when loaded with gear is neither an option nor an objective, touring falls outside the focus of this book.

TRAINING AND NUTRITION

Whatever your reasons for riding, training and nutrition are essential. A good training regimen is necessary for success in racing, and greatly increases your performance and health; a poor regimen can lead to a decrease in both, and can be disastrous. The higher the level of fitness or performance you want to obtain, the more carefully crafted the program must be. This subject is covered in detail in Part III (Training and Fitness).

HOW TO GET INVOLVED

Your local bike shop is a good source of information. Most shops have a designated area for event announcements and fliers. However, the most valuable information you receive may be in verbal form from the shop's owner or employees. They can usually provide detailed information about a specific event, including the road conditions and terrain for the course, the usual size of the groups, and how well the event is organized. They can also put you in contact with the event organizers and other local cyclists who may be participating.

Cycling Clubs

The best way to get involved in cycling is to join a local cycling club, which your local bike shop can almost certainly recommend. A good club will provide an enjoyable social and learning environment and a great deal of experience upon which to draw.

Most clubs have a race team whose main focus is to prepare for races. A good club welcomes, encourages, and mentors beginning cyclists. Some clubs have uniforms, coaches, and regular training schedules. Having a qualified coach goes a long way to improving your performance.

If your area has more than one club, visit the different clubs to determine which one best fits your needs. If you are not interested in racing, find a club that emphasizes group events at your level of riding.

Collegiate Teams

The popularity of collegiate cycling is growing, and teams are being developed at more and more schools. Collegiate cycling is unique in that it falls under the jurisdiction of the National Collegiate Cycling Association (NCCA), not the National Collegiate Athletic Association (NCAA).

Because collegiate cycling is a non-NCAA sport, few collegiate cycling teams receive scholarships or substantial financial support from their universities. On the plus side, NCCA cyclists can receive prize money in races without penalty from the governing body, and teams can pursue and accept financial sponsorships. (NCAA regulations prohibit sponsorships and individual compensation for athletic performance.)

For information on universities with cycling teams, visit the United States Cycling Federation (USCF) website (see Appendix) and look under "collegiate cycling." If you are at a university that does not have a team, you can start one through USCF. The process is not difficult or expensive, and most university recreation programs have funds set aside to support "club" sports.

United States Cycling Federation

Virtually all on-road bike races in the United States are sanctioned by the United States Cycling Federation, the road-racing arm of USA Cycling, which is the sport's representative to the U.S. Olympic Committee. All USCF-sanctioned events require a license to participate. USCF sanctioning provides liability coverage to race organizers in case of an accident, and a degree of medical coverage to riders for any injuries suffered during a race. For more information, visit www.usacycling.org and click on the "Road" tab.

Opportunities for the Disabled

A disability need not exclude an individual from cycling. In fact, there are many cycling opportunities for the disabled. Those with prostheses can ride on a regular or a modified bike (one of the fastest cyclists on the Gulf Coast races with a prosthetic leg). Those with limited or no use of their legs can use a hand cycle, a three-wheel bike that is pedaled with the arms. Blind cyclists are able to ride by partnering with a sighted cyclist on a tandem bike. These are just three examples; many other accommodations are possible. For more information, see the Appendix under Organizations for Disabled Cyclists.

the complete book of
road cycling & racing

PART I
the bike

choosing a bike

Locating a good bike shop with a helpful, knowledgeable staff is the first step in selecting your bike and equipment. The staff should encourage you to explain your cycling experience and goals in detail, and should ask many questions. They should have the capabilities to fit you properly on your new bike. If a shop can't or won't provide this level of service, find another shop within driving distance.

Your relationship with the bike shop should be a two-way street. The shop provides valuable services at a fair rate, including objective purchasing advice, mechanical repairs, assistance with warranty issues, advice on riding and racing, and information about local clubs and events. Shops also provide a social atmosphere where cyclists meet and talk about riding. In return, you owe them your loyal business. Give it to them and they'll bend over backward to meet your needs, such as when you need a repair done ASAP.

You may be able to save a few dollars purchasing equipment through online retailers, but they cannot maintain your bike. Of course, you must be guided by your personal economics, and if you have excellent mechanical skills, you may be able to get by largely on your own.

HOW TO BUY

Choosing a bike can be daunting. There are different frame types, materials, and geometries, and different component groups. Your choice will depend on your riding needs, the fit and feel of the bike, and how much you are willing to spend.

Cost and Warranty

A new bike that is appropriate for serious riding with an eye toward performance can cost anywhere from $600 to more than $6,000. You could purchase a $90 bike from a discount store, but I advise against it. Such mass-produced bikes are fine for riding short distances around the neighborhood but will not hold up on long rides. They have a heavy frame and low-end components and do not have sealed bearings. They do not perform well straight off the shelf or over the long haul and are subject to continuous mechanicals (mechanical breakdowns) that will quickly add up to more money than the bike is worth. Keep in mind that you will also need accessories, and they can add up. Go in with a set spending limit and stick to it.

Price and weight are inversely related in bicycles. Making frames and other components light as well as strong involves more precise work and higher-quality materials. The old saying "you get what you pay for" applies, but you do not need to spend a fortune. It is cheaper to lose weight off your body than off the bike, and some bikes in the $600 to $1,400 range offer excellent quality.

Many companies provide a lifetime frame warranty; others offer five- to twenty-five-year warranties. (Parts usually have a one-year warranty.) Warranties typically cover manufacturer defects but not damage due to crashes, although some companies offer a "crash replacement" warranty under which they will replace a crashed frame for much less than its retail cost. In my experience as a bike shop manager, all of the manufacturers were really good about honoring their warranties.

New Versus Used

As with cars, there are pros and cons to buying a used bike. The potential upside, of course, is that you can get more bike for your money. On the downside, you may be buying someone else's problems. Before buying a used bike, have it inspected to ensure that the components are in working order and the frame is not corroded, cracked, or otherwise damaged.

At the high end of the price range, I recommend buying new so you're covered by warranty. Recently, a fatigue crack opened up in one of my high-end frames after four years of riding. The manufacturer replaced the frame with a new model that was better than the original.

If you are in the market for a used bike, here are three good places to look:

- Many bike shops sell used bikes they have acquired through trade or on consignment. They will ensure that the bike is in working order and may back it with a limited warranty.
- Many clubs post classified ads on their websites or pass information by word of mouth.
- Of all the places to buy used bikes on the Internet, eBay seems to have the widest selection and the safest means of purchasing. You will probably not be able to examine the bike before buying it, and you will need to know your frame size in the specific brand you are considering.

Buying a Stock Bike Versus Building Your Own

Most bikes are bought off the showroom floor, but some cyclists dream of buying a bare frame, choosing each component individually, and assembling the bike themselves or having a local shop do it for them. This occasionally makes sense for advanced riders who are familiar with various components and have particular preferences.

For most riders, however, building your own bike is impractical. Bike manufacturers usually do an excellent job of specifying appropriate components for different types of bikes in different price ranges. Because they buy components in large quantities, they receive deep discounts. You would probably add $200 to $800 to the cost of a bike by purchasing the frame and identical components individually. My advice is to buy the stock bike, and have the shop swap out any individual components you want to change.

THE BIKE FRAME

The frame is the heart of the bike and the greatest single determinant of its quality and performance. Although every component can be replaced, if you replace the frame you've got a new bike. No amount of component replacement will make a good bike from a lousy frame (although it's possible to turn a good frame into a lousy bike with poor components).

Frame Geometries

Frame geometry deals with the length and angle of the tubes. It affects the bike's ride quality, steering quickness, and handling.

Road Racing

Racing bikes have a steep head-tube angle, usually between 73 and 74 degrees from the horizontal. This makes the steering responsive and maneuverable. To beginners, this feels "twitchy,"

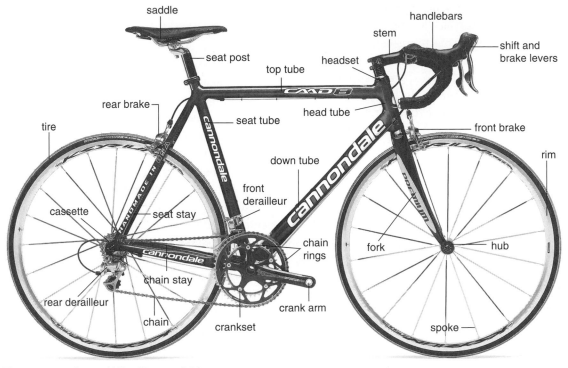

The anatomy of a road bike. (Cannondale)

but given time, most riders become accustomed to the feel. The seat-tube angle is also usually 73 to 74 degrees, placing the rider over the pedals, allowing for efficient transfer of energy, and promoting an aerodynamic position on the bike. These frames are also designed to be stable at high speeds and stiff in a sprint. A short wheelbase also lends itself to increased maneuverability.

Touring

Touring bikes are designed to be stable at slower speeds, to carry gear, and to provide greater comfort than race bikes. With a shallower head tube angle of 71 to 72 degrees, touring frames have slower, more stable steering than race bikes, which makes it possible to attach panniers and carry cargo. The seat tube angle is also 71 to 72 degrees, allowing for a more comfortable upright position. Touring bikes usually have a longer wheelbase than race bikes, which makes for slower steering but increased stability.

Sport

Sport bikes fall between racing and touring bikes. These frames are a little more comfortable than racing frames, have slightly relaxed handling, and promote a more upright position for riders for whom speed is not the sole criterion. The head tube and seat tube angles are 72 to 73 degrees. These bikes are a good choice for beginning riders and riders who are more concerned with comfort than speed but won't be doing extensive touring with heavy gear. Sport bikes usually have a longer wheelbase for stability.

A friend bought a serious race bike with a head-tube angle of 73 degrees, a rake of 45 mm, and a short chain stay. It was a good bike, but he could not get comfortable on it. As a cyclist, his goal is participating in century rides, and he has no interest in racing.

Road-racing frames are designed to be very responsive and maneuverable. (Cannondale)

rake (offset of axle from steering axis)

head tube angle

seat tube angle

Touring bikes are designed to provide a comfortable and stable ride. (Fuji)

He soon sold the racer and bought a sport bike with a head-tube angle of 72 degrees, a rake of 49 mm, and a longer chain stay. The bike positions him in a more comfortable, upright posture that he can maintain for hours. It's not a better bike, but it's better suited to his needs.

Time Trial

Time-trial frames are designed to give an aerodynamic advantage to riders in races where they cannot draft. The seat-tube angle ranges from 73 to 78 degrees, with the steeper angles promoting the most aerodynamic posture.

Steeper, however, isn't always better. Research has shown that cyclists adapt to and perform optimally in one particular position. So if you want to do time trials in addition to other events, choose a time-trial frame with a seat-tube angle similar to the one on the bike you normally ride.

The Union Cycliste Internationale (UCI), the governing body of international bicycle racing, and the United States Cycling Federation (USCF) have strict guidelines for bike geometry. According to UCI rules, the nose of the saddle must be at least five centimeters behind the bottom-bracket spindle, effectively limiting the seat-tube angle to a maximum of about 76 degrees. The UCI also requires that frames be of the conventional double-diamond style, with a seat tube that connects to the bottom bracket.

USA Triathlon (USAT), the governing body of triathlon and duathlon in the United States, has no such specifications. Many triathlon bikes have a seat-tube angle as steep as 78 degrees, and some companies have developed aerodynamic frames that do not have a seat tube that connects to the bottom bracket. Although these bikes are illegal in time trials, they are well accepted in triathlons. If you plan to compete in time trials and triathlons, make sure the bike is time-trial legal.

Traditional Versus Compact Frames

Compact frames are also known as sloping-tube geometries because the top tube slopes down to the rear. (On a traditional frame, it is horizontal.) The head-tube and seat-tube angles are similar in traditional and compact geometries, although compact frames have a slightly smaller rear triangle (formed by the chain stay, seat stay, and seat tube).

Nearly half of professional cycling teams now ride compact geometry. The other half doesn't. So what's the story? Is one better than the other?

In practice, the two geometries produce equivalent results. On both types of frame, you contact the bike at three points—the saddle, handlebars, and pedals—and you set up the bike the same way. With compact geometry you get a larger range of

Time-trial bikes are designed to give an aerodynamic advantage when riding exposed to the wind, outside of a pace line. (Fuji)

Compact-geometry frames differ from traditional frames in that they have a sloping top tube. (Fuji)

adjustment with the seat post. Some manufacturers have responded by producing only three or four frame sizes, which may leave a few riders to fall through the cracks, but most companies produce compact frames in the same range of eight or so sizes comparable to traditional-geometry bikes. (The effective top-tube length of a compact-geometry bike is measured horizontally, not along the tube, and is the same as on a traditional frame.)

Some cyclists claim that the smaller rear triangle of a compact frame makes the bike stiffer, but manufacturers that carefully select good materials can engineer the desired degree of stiffness in either type of frame. It is also claimed that compact frames are lighter, but if you add in the extra weight of the longer seat post, there is no noticeable difference.

Women-Specific Geometries

Recently, companies such as Cannondale, Trek, and Specialized have introduced lines of road bikes designed specifically for women. Recognizing that men and women have different proportions, the companies changed frame geometry and components accordingly. A woman's torso tends to be shorter, so the top-tube length is shorter to make it easier to reach the handlebars. Whereas most road bikes have 700C wheels (see page 15), some of the smaller women's frames come with 650C wheels, for a shorter stand-over height.

Women-specific bikes are designed to better fit the average woman's proportions. (Cannondale)

Handlebars have been narrowed for narrow shoulders and the diameter of the tube is thinner, and the shift levers are shorter for smaller hands.

Not all women need women-specific geometry. Many taller women fit better on bikes with standard geometry, and some men and children fit better on "women's" bikes. The choice of geometry should be determined by your body, not your gender.

Frame Materials

Frames are usually made of steel, aluminum, titanium, or carbon fiber. A few companies build frames using combinations of materials. Each material has advantages and disadvantages, but there can be big differences in quality among frames built from the same material. A $150 steel frame, for example, is much heavier, has a poorer ride quality, and will not last as long as a $1,500 steel frame.

Steel

Modern steel frames are lighter and stronger than their predecessors. The steel lugs that used to hold the tubes together have been replaced with TIG-welded joints, and the walls of the tubes are of varying thickness to eliminate excess weight. Even the metallurgy of the steel itself has improved.

Steel frames have a comfortable ride quality, but they flex during sprints and climbing. Thin-walled tubes have a tendency to dent easily, and steel is subject to rust. To help increase the life of your steel frame, coat the inside with a rust inhibitor on a regular basis. Finally, there is something to be said about the classic feel and look of a steel frame.

Titanium

The most expensive frame material, titanium provides a comfortable ride similar to that of steel, but it's much lighter. It has a longer fatigue life than steel and aluminum, but it tends to flex more than aluminum or carbon fiber during sprints. Titanium does not rust and does not need to be painted; nor does the inside need to be coated against rust.

Aluminum

Aluminum is stiffer and lighter than steel and is the least expensive choice for a lightweight bike of good quality. It's possible to buy a new aluminum-frame bike that weighs 22 to 23 pounds for $600 to $800. Steel-frame bikes in that weight range typically cost 30 to 50 percent more. Although most aluminum bikes cost less than those made of titanium, aluminum is lighter at the same price level. The downside of its stiffness is a rough ride, although this can be partially compensated for by a high-quality carbon fiber fork, seat post, and handlebars. Aluminum frames do not rust and have the shortest fatigue life of any frame material, with a life expectancy of five to ten years.

Carbon Fiber

Early versions of carbon fiber frames used carbon fiber tubing joined by aluminum lugs. Although these were not successful, recent advances have resulted in the lightest, strongest, and most comfortable frames available. Most frames built now use a nearly undetectable carbon fiber lug; others are made in a single piece in molds.

Carbon fiber is the choice of many pro riders; it produces a comfortable ride that is stiff in a sprint. When you apply pressure to the pedals, the bike responds immediately; you can feel it accelerate smoothly and quickly.

Carbon fiber has the longest fatigue life of any frame material. The downside is that carbon fiber frames are expensive.

All frame materials have advantages and disadvantages. I ride a carbon frame, which I think is the most comfortable and responsive material. Other riders prefer steel, saying it allows them to feel the road better. You will need to ride bikes with each material to determine which you like best. Many bike shops have demo bikes that you can use to determine your preference.

Butted Tubes

Conventional metal tubing has a constant wall thickness and is known as plain- or straight-gauge tubing. In steel, aluminum, and titanium frames of higher quality, the inside diameter of the tubing wall varies along its length; the tubing walls are thicker at the ends, where additional strength is needed, and thinner in the middle to save weight. These are known as butted tubes. (As a composite material, carbon fiber lends itself to continuous variation in thickness and reinforcement.)

Tube butting appears in three basic formats:

- **Single butted.** The tube wall is thicker at one end and uniformly thinner throughout the rest of its length.
- **Double butted.** The tube is the same thickness at both ends and uniformly thinner between them.
- **Triple butted.** Both ends are thicker than the middle, but one end is thinner than the other. The middle is of uniform thickness.

Butted tubing is mainly used in the seat tube, down tube, and top tube. The downside to butted tubing is that the middle of the tubes is more susceptible to denting and fatigue. It is also more expensive than plain-gauge tubing.

Frame Aerodynamics

Traditional frames have round tubing and are ideal for climbing or flat stages. Although they lack any aerodynamic advantage, they are much lighter than aero frames and generally more comfortable. When riding in a peloton (a tightly bunched group of cyclists), there is little need for an aerodynamic frame; weight when climbing is a greater concern.

Aerodynamic frames are used during time trials. The seat tube, down tube, head tube, and in some cases the seat stays are "bladed" (foil shaped) to reduce wind resistance. Aero frames are heavier and often less comfortable than traditional frames, but these liabilities are largely negated by the aerodynamic advantages in time trials.

Semi-aero frames combine the best of both types, being lighter than aero frames and more

Traditional tubing is round in cross section. It is strong and lightweight. (Cannondale)

Aerodynamic, or bladed, tubing is foil shaped to provide an aerodynamic advantage. (Cannondale)

aerodynamic than traditional ones. Semi-aero frames are good for flat, fast race stages and up-hill time trials and are beneficial in long breaka-ways during road races.

COMPONENTS AND GROUPS

Component "groups" consist of shifters, derail-leurs, brakes, crankset, and rear cassette. (Sev-eral other components, including the wheels, seat post, and handlebars, are equally important but are not considered part of the "group".) Two main sup-pliers, Shimano and Campagnolo, have dominated the market for high-quality component groups for years, but in 2006 they were joined by a new

company, SRAM, whose line has been meeting with good acceptance. (The Appendix lists web-sites for all companies cited in the text.)

All three companies make good products in a variety of quality and price levels, as shown in the table below. Part of choosing a bike is con-sidering the quality level of the component group you are willing to pay for, and deciding whether you have a preference among the manufacturers. Keep in mind that as long as you have a well-made frame, you can upgrade components later as they wear out or your budget allows. If this is your plan, make sure the frame you buy is worth upgrading later.

COMPONENT GROUPS BY MANUFACTURER				
Price	**Quality**	**Shimano**	**Campagnolo**	**SRAM**
Medium	Good	Sora	Xenon	—
↕↕		Tiagra	Mirage	—
		105	Veloce	—
		—	Centaur	Rival
		Ultega	Chorus	Force
High	Best	Dura-Ace	Record	Red

Components are separated by manufacturer and ranked from good to best. As you move from good to best (top to bottom), the reliability and durability of the components increases. Not all manufacturers produce components at every level; component groups have been lined up with their closest competitors at that level. Note that as quality increases so does the price.

Headset

Headsets contain bearings that hold the fork firmly in place and allow you to steer the bike smoothly.

Headsets vary in diameter. Older bikes have 1-inch headsets, newer ones have 1⅛-inch headsets, and in 2007 a trend started toward headsets that are 1⅛ inches at the top and 1½ inches at the bottom.

New bikes have either external or integrated headsets. External headsets, which were the industry standard until around 2003, have cups designed to accept the bearings, which extend above and below the head tube.

Integrated headsets are becoming the new standard. The bike's head tube is designed to accept one of two basic types of integrated headsets: those with internal cups and those without cups. Internal cups fit inside the head tube; the second type places the bearings directly in the head tube, which is machined to accept the bearings without adding cups.

Older bikes have a third type, in which the top-bearing cup was screwed onto the top end of the fork and clamped the system into place. The newer threadless systems perform much better.

The headset is located at the top and bottom of the head tube and has bearings so the steerer tube can move smoothly.

Stem and Handlebars

The stem connects the fork to the handlebars, which provides two main functions. The obvious one is steering. The second is to support the weight of the rider's upper body. Additionally, the handlebars provide convenient mounting points for brake and shift levers.

A large amount of stress is placed on the handlebars and stem, especially when the rider stands to sprint or climb. Handlebars usually last only three to five years. Check your bar and stem frequently for corrosion and cracks, and replace them after a hard crash involving the front end of the bike. If either fails during a ride, it can be catastrophic.

Handlebars come in different widths, materials, shapes, and diameters. Determining the correct width is covered in Chapter 2 (Fitting the Bike to Your Body). Most high-quality bars are made from aluminum or carbon fiber. Carbon damps road vibration but is more expensive. Different shapes affect hand placement and comfort; the only way to determine what works best for you is to try a variety of styles. Two diameters are common: standard (26.0 mm) and oversized (31.8 mm). The stem clamp and bar diameter must be the same.

Stems also come in different materials, lengths, and angles. The choice of material is based on personal preference. Length and angle are determined by fit, which is discussed in Chapter 2.

Saddle

Choosing the correct saddle can make the difference between a comfortable ride and a ride from hell. The more time you log in the saddle, the more important comfort becomes. No one type of saddle can be recommended for all cyclists, however, because riders have different bottoms, different riding styles, and different ideas of what's comfortable.

One common misconception is that wide, heavily padded saddles are more comfortable. This is usually not the case, because more material between your legs can cause chafe and interfere with the free movement of your pelvis, upper leg bones, and muscles. You may,

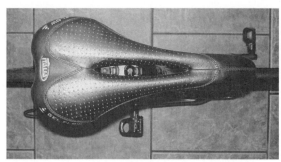

Selecting the proper saddle is essential for comfort. Because no one saddle fits everyone, choose carefully.

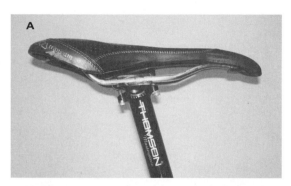

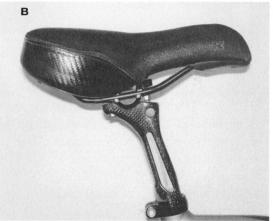

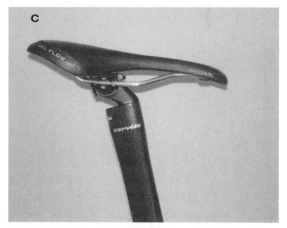

Various types of seat posts: in line (A), setback (B), and aero (C).

in fact, find a relatively hard, thin saddle more comfortable—once you get used to it. Many newer saddles have the middle cut out completely or lowered, creating a channel to reduce the pressure on the nether regions. Buying the wrong saddle can be an expensive mistake; that's why many shops have demo saddles to try.

Seat Post

Most seat posts are made of aluminum, titanium, or carbon fiber. If you are riding an aluminum bike, I highly recommend a carbon fiber post to dampen road vibrations.

Some seat posts position the saddle directly in line with the seat tube; others have a setback. The seat post should allow you to properly adjust your seat fore and aft. The process of fitting your bike (see Chapter 2) will determine which one you need.

Aero posts are designed in a foil shape to decrease drag and improve aerodynamics. Most bikes with aerodynamic seat tubes will come with an aero seat post specifically designed to fit that particular frame. These posts will not be interchangeable from frame to frame.

Pedal Systems and Cleats

Clipless pedals attach your feet firmly to the pedals by means of cleats that are permanently attached to the sole of your cycling shoes. To "lock" yourself in, you simply step down on the pedal; you release your foot by twisting your heel slightly to the outside. Clipless pedals have

entirely supplanted the use of toe clips and straps among serious riders.

Clipless pedals help you pedal more smoothly by allowing you to pull up and through the pedal stroke, decreasing the amount of weight that the

Clipless pedal systems provide a solid connection between the cyclist and the bike.

opposite leg must lift as it pushes down on the other side. Clipless pedals also eliminate any loss of power that might occur due to your foot slipping off the pedal, and they provide a stable connection between your body and the bike, promoting better control in cornering and during high-speed descents.

Many riders who are concerned with bike weight prefer the smallest pedals possible, but I prefer a slightly heavier pedal with a wider platform. This distributes the force over a wider area and eliminates "hot spots" on your feet. SPD (Shimano Pedaling Dynamics) pedals use a cleat that is recessed in the shoe, making for easier walking, but the surface area of the pedal is small; in my opinion they are not appropriate for road bikes. They are, however, an excellent choice for the sport they were designed for: mountain biking.

The first clipless pedals locked the cyclist's feet rigidly in one position on the pedals. This put a lot of strain on the knees and led to many overuse injuries. This problem was corrected in later models by adding "float," a design feature that allows your foot to take a more natural position and move slightly throughout the pedal stroke. Some pedals even allow you to adjust the float to suit your needs.

After you become accustomed to clipless pedals, you will find they are faster and thus safer to get in and out of than straps. They do, however, take some

getting used to. Some new users have a tendency to stop before they are unclipped, and to pull up instead of twisting out of the pedals, resulting in embarrassing falls while stopped. Before you take to the road, practice getting in and out of the pedals by setting up the bike in a stationary trainer or leaning it against a wall. Remember to unclip one foot before you stop the bike by twisting your heel outboard. And lean to the side you are unclipped on.

Crankset

The crankset consists of the chainrings (the front sprockets) and the crank arms (to which the pedals are attached). Cranksets are available with two or three chainrings, and double-chainring cranksets are available in standard and compact versions. Different crank-arm lengths are also available; these are discussed in Chapter 2.

Double cranksets usually come with a large chainring of 52 or 53 teeth and a small chainring of 39 or, more rarely, 42 teeth. Triple cranksets usually come with chainrings of 52 or 53, 39 or 42, and 30 teeth.

With a few exceptions, double cranksets are best. They shift more smoothly, require less adjusting, and weigh less.

The 30-tooth chainring on a triple crankset allows for a lower gear ratio, which makes it easier to climb steep terrain. Triple chainrings are thus

The crankset is an important part of the drivetrain.

worthwhile for young riders, novices, and cyclists who live in mountainous areas.

Compact double cranksets have a 50-tooth chainring (large) and a 34- or 36-tooth chainring (small), which allows for easier climbing than a standard double crankset. Being a double, however, compacts have fewer shifting problems than triples. You will lose some of the higher gear ratios that a standard double or triple provides, but unless you are strongly competitive, this will not greatly affect your riding. If given the choice between a compact and a triple, choose the former.

When compact cranks first emerged, there were compatibility problems with some derailleurs, but these have been eliminated in the newer models. If you are replacing an old standard-size crankset with a new compact, you may need to change your front derailleur for better shifting.

Bottom Bracket

The bottom bracket consists of a spindle (to which the crank arms attach) and bearings (which fit in the bottom-bracket "shell" of the frame and allow the spindle to turn smoothly). Different spindle designs work only with specific cranksets. A new style of bottom bracket has its bearings mounted outboard of the frame, and the spindle is attached to the crankset. This design flexes less, is slightly lighter, and is much easier to install than the conventional style.

Cassettes

The rear cassette consists of 8 to 10 cogs on a ratcheting mechanism; the cassette attaches to the rear wheel hub. Older bikes have eight- or nine-speed cassettes; most newer bikes have ten-speed cassettes. Although eight or nine speeds is adequate, the additional cogs mean smaller steps between cogs, which makes it easier to maintain a steady cadence when shifting gears.

Cassettes come with different combinations of cogs. The most common ten-speed combinations are

Cassette combinations can be changed to suit the terrain where you plan to ride. An 11–21 combination is ideal for flat terrain; a 12–25 combination is better suited for riding in the mountains.

listed in the table on page 14. For example, most 11–21 cassettes (first row of data) have cogs with 11, 12, 13, 14, 15, 16, 17, 18, 19, and 21 teeth.

A 12–23 cassette is a good all-around choice, useful on flat and rolling terrain. A wider 12–25 or 12–27 cassette is beneficial for climbing; a narrower 11–21 or 12–21 cassette is ideal for flat terrain. It is a good idea to own more than one cassette, and to change cassettes to suit the conditions of your race or ride. How to determine gear ratios is discussed in Chapter 4, and how to change cassettes is discussed in Chapter 3.

Derailleurs

The front derailleur is responsible for shifting the chain between the chainrings. The chain passes through a simple metal cage. The mechanism consists primarily of a hinged parallelogram to push the chain left or right while maintaining a roughly constant vertical distance from the chainrings. The clamp on a clamp-on front derailleur fits around the seat tube, whereas the so-called

COMMON CASSETTE COMBINATIONS															
	COGS BY NUMBER OF TEETH														
	11	12	13	14	15	16	17	18	19	20	21	23	24	25	27
CASSETTE RANGE 11–21	•	•	•	•	•	•	•	•	•		•				
11–23	•	•	•	•	•	•	•		•		•	•			
12–21		•	•	•	•	•	•	•	•	•	•				
12–23		•	•	•	•	•	•	•			•	•			
12–25		•	•	•	•	•	•		•		•	•		•	
12–27		•	•	•	•	•	•		•		•		•		•

"braze-on" type attaches with a bolt to a designated tab brazed onto the seat tube. Braze-ons are marginally lighter but are not an option for bikes lacking the mounting tab.

The rear derailleur is attached to a bracket on the right rear dropout (the casting that holds the rear axle at the end of the seat stay and chain stay) and is responsible for shifting the chain between cogs on the cassette. It too uses a hinged parallelogram, but it has a longer throw and incorporates two rollers in a spring-tensioned cage to maintain chain tension and eliminate slack as the chain is shifted onto larger or smaller cogs.

The various brands and models of derailleurs offer different features, but the similarities are greater than their differences. Selection is largely a matter of performance and "feel." Careful adjustment of all models (see Chapter 3) is critical.

The front derailleur shifts the chain between chainrings on the crankset.

The rear derailleur shifts the chain between the cogs on the rear cassette.

Dual pivot brake calipers are common on all newer road bikes.

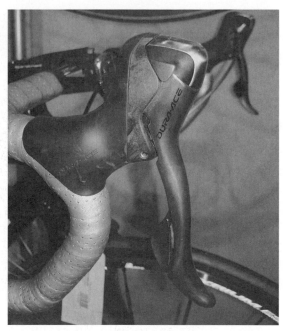

Modern levers serve a dual purpose, allowing you to shift and brake without removing your hands from the levers or the handlebars.

Brakes

Brakes consist of a caliper and two pads. Road calipers with dual pivots provide greater stopping power, although those with a single pivot are lighter. (The old center-pull brakes have disappeared. All high-quality brakes are now of the side-pull style, with the cable coming in on one side.) Single-pivot calipers are usually found on older or low-end bikes, although some serious riders use a good single-pivot caliper on the back wheel, on the grounds that the rear brake is less effective in any case.

Brake cables need frequent adjustment, and brake pads are a regular-wear item that must be replaced frequently. See Chapter 3 for details.

Brake Levers and Shifters

In the past, shifters were located on the down tube, and you had to take one hand off the handlebars to shift gears. Brake levers were on the handlebars, where they were always convenient.

Modern levers combine braking and shifting, so your hands never have to leave the handlebars. The left lever operates the front brake and derailleur; the right lever operates the rear brake and derailleur. (Remember the "R": right, rear.)

Braking is the same on all levers: simply pull back. The method of shifting varies, however. Shimano uses the brake lever and a secondary lever behind the brake lever. To shift to a smaller gear, push the secondary lever inboard. To shift to a larger gear, shift the entire lever inboard. Campagnolo uses a secondary lever and a thumb lever; SRAM uses only a secondary lever. Some levers offer a degree of adjustability to accommodate smaller hands. Try them all to determine which one you prefer.

Wheels

Wheels come in two basic sizes: 700C (the rim will actually measure 622 mm) and 650C (571 mm). Due to the varying sizes of tires, it's rare that a 700C wheel-and-tire combination will measure 700 mm. (Most measure between 680 and 690 mm.)

For this reason, regard 700C and 650C as size designators. The larger 700C wheel is most common on road bikes, while the 650C wheel is mainly used on smaller bikes (such as women's-specific) and some triathlon bikes.

There are three basic types of wheels: training wheels, race wheels, and aerodynamic wheels.

A sturdy wheel for training is known as a training wheel (not to be confused with the outrigger wheels on little kids' bikes). They are heavy but durable and inexpensive. They usually have box-section aluminum rims and 32 to 36 spokes. The hubs may or may not have sealed bearings. (Sealed is better.)

For racing, and especially for racing in hilly or mountainous regions, you want a set of lightweight race wheels. These, too, generally have box-section aluminum or composite rims. The front wheels may have as few as 16 spokes, and the rear as few as 24. (Heavy riders will want higher spoke counts.) Race-quality hubs are lighter than those on training wheels and have sealed bearings. Race wheels are expensive; most are not durable enough for everyday training.

Lightweight wheels are designed for racing, but they may not be durable enough for everyday riding. (Mavic)

Training wheels are designed to take the rigors of everyday riding, but they're heavier than race wheels. (Mavic)

Aerodynamic race wheels are designed for situations where you cannot draft, as in time trials. These wheels vary from a deep-dished aluminum or carbon fiber rim to a 3-spoke design made from composites to a full disc wheel. The deeply dished and disc-style wheels are slightly heavier than similarly priced non-aero race wheels, but most are still lighter than any training wheel and some midrange lightweight wheels. The downside

Aerodynamic race wheels are designed to cut through the wind, giving the rider an aerodynamic advantage. These wheels come with deep-dished rims (right) or as a full disc, which is used only as a rear wheel (left). (Mavic)

to deep dished or disc wheels is that they play havoc on bike control in strong crosswinds. They are also expensive and produce a harsh ride.

The ideal situation is to have a wheel set in each category. If you can afford only one set, it should fall between training wheels and lightweight race wheels in terms of weight and durability; ideally it will have a V-section rim for decent aerodynamics.

Spokes may have a traditional round cross section or a "bladed" foil shape. Bladed spokes decrease drag and improve aerodynamics; round spokes are stronger. Bladed spokes can be difficult to true because you have to keep the blades facing the right direction. My advice is to choose

traditional spokes for your training wheels and bladed spokes for your racing set.

Tires

The type of bike tires that you grew up with as a kid, with a separate inner tube, are known as clinchers. They are inexpensive, durable, easy to repair and replace, and appropriate for training-wheel sets. The maximum pressure typically ranges between 110 and 120 psi.

Tubular tires, also known as glue-ons, sew-ups, or, bizarrely, tubeless tires, are the main choice of professionals. They are light in weight and can be inflated to extremely high pressure

(130 to 170 psi), which decreases rolling resistance. With a perfectly round cross section, they present a larger contact patch than clinchers at steep angles of lean and therefore provide better cornering grip. Furthermore, tubular rims are lighter than clincher rims.

The downside to tubulars is their cost and the difficulty of installation and repairs (see Chapter 3). They are literally glued to the rim, and in case of a flat they must be pulled from the rim to reach and cut the stitches that hold them together. This reveals the very thin tube inside. After you patch the tube, you have to sew the tire back together with needle and thread and reglue it to the rim, then wait for the glue to dry before using the wheel. (Tufo, a Canadian tire manufacturer, has formulated a glue tape that works better than any glue I have used, somewhat simplifying the process.)

The process is so time consuming that it's essential to carry a spare tire when you ride tubulars. In contrast, a clincher repair takes just a few minutes, and the patch kit weighs just ounces. Bottom line: Train on clinchers for practicality, and race on tubulars for performance.

True tubeless tires, similar to tubeless automobile tires, have recently been introduced to road cycling. (They have been around for a while in mountain biking.) It can be difficult to get the bead to seat against the rim with an airtight seal, but once you get it, you can inflate these tires up to 180 psi.

OTHER GEAR

Sorry, but you're not done spending money yet—not by a long shot. There is a whole pile of additional gear, most of which you wear, required to ride safely and comfortably.

Helmet

While writing this book, I went down at 28 mph in a group ride. During a sprint, the rider directly in front of me clipped the rear wheel of the man directly in front of him and went down. My front tire hit his bike. I flew over the handlebars, and the back of my head bounced off the pavement a few times before I came to a stop. While slightly dazed, I was able to ride away from the accident.

I was, of course, wearing a helmet, without which I would have been more than just dazed. It may not seem like a long fall from a bike, but it is enough to crack your skull and cause brain damage.

A helmet is one of the most important accessories you can buy. Helmets have evolved over the past ten years and are now much lighter and not as hot.

When choosing a helmet, make sure it fits comfortably yet firmly. A helmet must be worn properly, with the straps snug and the front low enough to protect your forehead. Select one you like the looks of; if you think it makes you look dorky, you may not wear it.

If a helmet makes contact with the ground or other object during a crash it should be replaced. Even if the helmet appears to be undamaged the structural integrity may be compromised. Many helmet makers offer substantial discounts in what are known as crash replacement programs.

Helmets range in price from about $25 to $200. Both meet the government safety standards,

The wrong way to wear a helmet—pushed too far back on the head.

When the helmet is worn correctly, it covers a good portion of the forehead.

but better helmets usually have a hard molded covering, lacking on the cheapest models, that offers better protection. As prices go up, weight goes down and ventilation improves. All of that said, even the cheapest helmets go a long way toward keeping your head in one piece.

Until recently, time-trial helmets were designed only to improve the aerodynamics of the rider's head. Now, however, the USCF requires that they also provide crash protection.

Shoes and Socks

Comfort and fit are the most important considerations when buying a pair of cycling shoes. If they do not fit properly, you're in for a world of pain, and you can forget optimal power output.

Shoes should have stiff soles. The stiffer the sole, the greater the force that is transferred to the pedal and the less that is lost to flex. A flexible sole increases stress to the ligaments and tendons on the bottom of the feet, causing discomfort known as a "hot spot" and possibly leading to overuse injuries. The stiffest and longest-lasting sole material is carbon fiber. Nylon soles can be as stiff as carbon fiber initially, but they will eventually start to flex.

Uppers can be made from real or synthetic leather. Synthetic leather does not stretch and holds up much better to weather than real leather. Strap closures are better than shoestrings, and

Aerodynamic helmets reduce drag while protecting the head during a crash. (Rudy Project)

When choosing cycling shoes, comfort is just as important as performance. Select a comfortable shoe with a rigid sole and three closure straps. (Cannondale)

three straps are much better than two. Mechanical ratcheting strap closures allow for a firm, comfortable fit, so the shoe will not slip.

Shoe soles are drilled to hold the cleats that clip into the pedals. A three-bolt pattern is becoming standard, so most shoes are compatible with the majority of pedal systems on the market. Some shoe companies sell adapter plates to accommodate other patterns. Ask before you buy, though, to make sure the shoe is compatible with your pedals.

Cycling is a non-weight-bearing activity, so you don't need socks with heavy cushioning on the sole; it only holds moisture. Choose a lightweight, breathable sock that wicks moisture away from your foot.

Clothing

Clothing for cycling has come a long way over the last twenty years. New materials such as CoolMax wick moisture away from the body and do not become heavy with sweat or rainwater. These materials keep you cooler and are more aerodynamic and more comfortable than wool shorts and jerseys.

Cycling jerseys are made from material that wicks moisture away from the skin; the jerseys are designed to have a tight fit to reduce wind resistance. (Cannondale)

Jerseys

A cotton T-shirt is a poor choice for cycling. Cotton traps and holds moisture, which makes the shirt heavy and causes chafing, and a standard T-shirt cut is baggy and catches the wind. Cycling jerseys wick moisture away from the skin and fit tighter to cut wind resistance. Cycling jerseys have rear pockets that are handy for carrying snacks, money, small tools, or a cell phone.

Shorts

A good pair of cycling shorts is a must. Cycling shorts are designed for wicking, aerodynamics, and comfort in the saddle. A patch of synthetic chamois in the crotch area provides padding and helps prevent chafing. (Shorts are rarely made with real chamois leather anymore.)

A good pair of riding shorts can make the difference between an enjoyable ride and a miserable day in the saddle. Note the patch of padded "chamois" material. (Kathleen Poulos, Toyota-United)

The price of shorts ranges from $25 to $200. Spend enough to get a pair with flat, smoothly sewn seams (bulky seams can chafe) and sufficient padding.

Gloves

Cycling gloves add padding between your hands and the handlebars. This is important because constant pressure against the ulnar nerve, which passes along your palm, can cause your hand and fingers to go numb. The padding also damps road vibration, which can feel annoying.

The leather palms of the gloves also protect your hands in the event of a crash. Most people have a tendency to land on their hands when they crash, and you can lose a lot of skin from your palms if they are not protected. You typically want fingerless, mesh-backed gloves for warm weather.

Outerwear

Riding in cold or wet weather can be miserable. There are a few articles of clothing you should have to improve your riding experience in adverse conditions. (Other aspects of riding in cold are discussed in Chapter 5.)

◘ The speed of cycling creates windchill, making a warm day seem cooler and a cool one cold. A wind vest is worn when it is too cold for just a jersey and too hot for a jacket. Wind vests feature a windproof front and a mesh back that allows heat to escape.

Cycling gloves serve two purposes: they provide padding to increase comfort and reduce numbness in the hands, and they offer protection to the palms in a crash. (Cannondale)

Carry a rain jacket when riding on overcast days—a lightweight one for warmer temperatures and a heavier one for colder days. (Veronika Lenzi, Toyota-United)

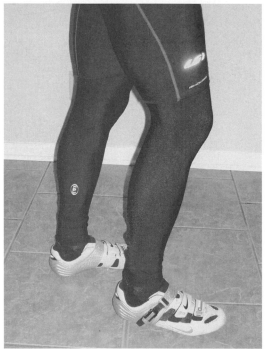

Arm warmers and leg warmers are easily removed after you warm up while riding in moderately cold temperatures.

A wind vest provides relief from the wind on moderately cold days.

◘ Many times you start a ride cold but warm up as you go. Leg and arm warmers keep your extremities warm when you're wearing a short-sleeve jersey and cycling shorts. Arm warmers fit underneath your short-sleeve jersey and are easily removed by sliding them down and off your arm. Leg warmers fit underneath your cycling shorts and have a zipper located at the ankle that allows easy removal over your shoes.

◘ Assume that you will get wet when you ride in overcast weather, and carry a light, breathable rain jacket. A nonbreathable jacket retains most of the heat that you produce while riding, which will cause you to become soaked anyway, but with sweat. Clear vinyl rain jackets with vents are good for cooler days.

- A cold-weather jacket and cold-weather tights are necessities when the temperature drops.
- In cold weather, it is important to stem the loss of heat through your scalp. Wear a hat in cold conditions. Make sure the hat fits underneath your helmet, and adjust the chin strap accordingly. During *really* cold weather, wear a balaclava to protect your face as well.
- Winter gloves should be warm, block the wind, and not have so much padding that they interfere with your ability to shift gears. Blocking the wind seems to be more important than insulation; as long as you keep the wind off your fingers, you can go with thinner gloves in most conditions. In extremely cold weather, you may need to give up a little mobility, in which case three-fingered gloves and mittens are warmer than five-fingered gloves.
- Most cycling shoes are designed for maximum airflow, to keep your feet cool. In cold weather, wear winter shoe covers, which block the wind and keep your feet warmer. Designed to fit over your shoes, they have an opening that allows your cleat to fit through for easy connection to the pedals. Some shoe covers slide over the shoe, while others have zippers located at the heel.

CYCLE COMPUTERS

A cycle computer is a valuable yet inexpensive training aid that tells you how far you've traveled, helps you keep track of mileage, enables you to

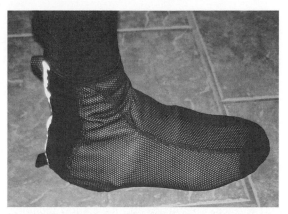

Most cycling shoes are well ventilated to keep your feet cool, but this is undesirable in wintertime. Shoe covers prevent wind from entering through ventilated areas.

record ride times, and monitors current and average speed. Prices start at about $30 and go up as the number of features increases.

I strongly advise buying, for $10 to $15 more, a cycle computer that also records cadence—the speed at which you turn the pedals, measured in

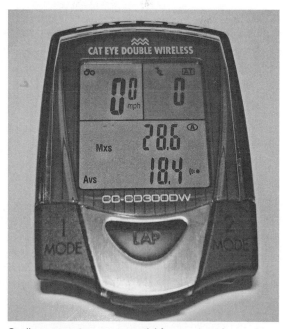

Cycling computers are essential for anyone who wants to train seriously.

rpm. Cadence is a critical measure of your economy of effort; it is discussed in detail in Chapter 4. If you live in a mountainous region, consider buying a cycle computer with an altimeter function that records changes in elevation.

Most cycle computers have wires running to sensors on the front fork to measure speed, and on the chain stay to measure cadence. Wireless computers have sensors in the same locations that send coded signals to the base unit. The absence of wires makes the bike look less cluttered, but wireless computers still have a few technical hitches, and many units can be unreliable. They also drain batteries much faster than wired computers, require two batteries instead of one, and cost about three times as much.

Garmin, a manufacturer of global positioning systems (GPS), recently introduced a combination GPS–cycling computer. In addition to having standard cycling computer features and measuring heart rate, it can automatically map your route and help you find your way back again if you get lost. Another benefit is that at the end of a ride you can download your workout for analysis using the Garmin Training Center. The unit is expensive (about $300), and because it tracks your position from space, it does not read sudden changes in speed. At steady speeds, however, it is extremely accurate.

Polar and Ciclosport make cycle computers that measure heart rate and have the capability to download ride data for an analysis of your performance.

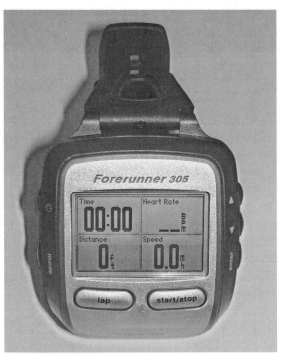

The Garmin Forerunner 305 functions as a cycle computer, a heart-rate monitor, and a GPS.

fitting the bike to your body

Proper bike fit is important for optimal performance and injury prevention. When cycling, you are in a fixed position, and your legs turn over continually in that position. If your position is incorrect, you may impose inappropriate stresses on your body that can lead to overuse injuries. The body cannot effectively be adjusted to fit the bike, so the bike must be adjusted to fit the body.

The bike can be adjusted by altering saddle height, fore and aft position of the saddle, saddle tilt, stem length, handlebar height, and cleat position on the shoe.

When determining a bike setup, start with the lower body and work your way up. It is important to wear your normal cycling gear when setting up the bike, to ensure that you are in your normal riding position and to make it easier to find the necessary landmarks located on the body.

Although the following procedures result in a good "fit" for most people, they do not work for everyone. They do, however, give everyone a good place to start. If you find that certain aspects of the fit don't correspond to your individual biomechanics, make adjustments in small increments.

PERFORMANCE VERSUS COMFORT

A technically proper setup may put you in the perfect aerodynamic position, but if you are uncomfortable in that position you will not be able to perform optimally. One way to overcome this is to adjust your bike's fit in small increments over time, so your body can adapt to a better position without discomfort. If you are not interested in racing or otherwise achieving peak performance, an aggressive racing position may not be necessary, and adjusting your bike for greater comfort may be entirely appropriate.

Altering your bike to a more favorable setup may lead to a temporary decrease in performance. Your body has adapted to the position that you currently ride in; when you switch to a new position, it takes time for your body to readapt. If you have changed your position due to an overuse injury, it may take a while for your symptoms to diminish or disappear.

FRAME SIZE

Ensuring that you have the correct size frame is the first step in bike fitting. If the frame is too small or too large, you will be unable to achieve a proper bike fit regardless of adjustments to the components. To ensure that the frame is the correct size, you need to step through the fitting procedures.

Road frame size may be measured in two ways. The first, called center to top, measures from the center of the bike's bottom bracket to the top of the top tube. The second, called center to center, is from the center of the bottom bracket to the centerline of the top tube. On a traditional-style frame, there is usually about a one-centimeter difference between the two: for example, a frame that measures 56 cm center to top will measure 55 cm center to center, but this varies with the size and profile of the frame tubing. Furthermore, some manufacturers measure their frames differently; one manufacturer, for example, measures from the center of the bottom bracket to the top of the seat-tube collar.

CRANK-ARM LENGTH

The next step is to determine crank-arm length. Stock bikes are equipped with crank arms sized proportionally to the frame; because of this, most cyclists skip this step. In fact, it is rarely necessary and often not cost-effective to alter the crank-arm length on a new bike. Nevertheless, it is important to confirm that the crank-arm length is appropriate to your needs.

The crank-arm length ranges from 160 to 185 mm (measured from the center of the pedal axle hole to the center of the bottom-bracket hole), with the most common lengths being 170, 172.5, and 175 mm. The length is usually engraved on the back of the crank arm.

A longer lever arm provides more leverage, but in practice this does not necessarily translate into greater power production with each stroke. More torque is required to spin a longer crank arm, and your body may not be capable of producing that amount of torque at an efficient cadence over a long period of time. A too-long crank arm also increases knee flexion (bend in the knee), which can lead to overuse injuries.

The crank-arm length is usually determined first by the rider's height or inseam (that is, leg length), then adjusted for the style of riding or type of event. Because height alone does not account for variations in leg length among individuals, inseam length is a better starting point.

To measure your inseam, you will need an assistant, a book, and a measuring tape that reads in centimeters (the latter can be purchased in fabric and hobby shops). Place your back against a wall with your feet about five centimeters apart. Place the book between your legs, with the upper edge tight against your groin and the back edge flush against the wall. Have your assistant measure from the top of the book to the floor. Make your initial crank-arm-length determination based on the table below.

Inseam	Crank-Arm Length
<70 cm	160 mm
70–73 cm	165 mm
73–81 cm	170 mm
83–86 cm	172.5 mm
86–89 cm	175 mm
>89 cm	175–185 mm

Longer cranks are recommended for time trialing and climbing, and shorter cranks are recommended for track racing and criteriums. Cyclists who prefer to push larger gears at lower cadences usually like longer cranks; those who prefer to "spin" (maintain a high cadence) tend toward shorter cranks.

For optimal performance, the crank-arm length should allow you to maintain a cadence of 90 rpm or greater with a smooth pedal stroke. (See Chapter 4 for more information on cadence.) A crank arm that is too long will cause an obvious glitch in your stroke as it passes through the top of the circle. A too-long crank arm also increases the risk of clipping the ground with your pedal while cornering.

If you do choose to change the length of the crank arm, it will take some time for your legs to adapt to the change. Be especially careful if you increase the length because it will increase the torque placed on the knee. Refrain from hard workouts until your body has adapted to the new length.

CLEAT POSITION

If you are using clipless pedals, you need to position the cleats properly on your shoes. The fore and aft position of the cleats is easy: you want the cleats positioned so that the ball of your foot (the metatarsophalangeal joint) is directly over the pedal spindle. To accomplish this, place masking tape on the inside of the shoe so it covers the ball of the foot. Through palpation, find the center of the ball of the foot and mark it with a line on the masking tape. Adjust the cleat fore and aft until this line is centered on the pedal axle. Cyclists with larger feet (more than size 10½ U.S.) should place the ball of the foot slightly in front of the pedal axle to reduce stress on the Achilles tendon.

The next step is to determine cleat rotation. Sit on a table and let your feet dangle. Give your legs time to relax, then observe the natural position of your feet. Because modern clipless pedals have enough float to allow the foot to find its natural position, the majority of riders should have the cleats face straight forward. If your feet point too far out or in, you may need to adjust the rotation of the cleats for a more natural position.

Some pedals have adjustable float. Beware of dialing in too much float, which forces the muscles of the ankle and leg to work harder to stabilize the joints and can lead to injury as easily as with too little float.

Inversion and eversion are misalignments of the feet. In inversion, the soles of the feet rotate toward each other, as though you were standing on the outside edges of your feet. Eversion is the opposite, with the soles rotated away from each other. Cycling when either condition exists can lead to overuse injuries. Cleat wedges, which fit between the cleat and your shoe, will enable you to compensate for inversion or eversion by bringing your feet closer to neutral. Cleat wedges can also be stacked to compensate for slight leg-length discrepancies. Although you can make these adjustments on your own, you should seek professional advice before making alterations to compensate for eversion, inversion, or leg-length discrepancies.

SADDLE ADJUSTMENTS

Saddle Tilt

In most setups, the saddle should be leveled before adjusting the height and fore-aft position. You can use a bubble level to check this. If the saddle

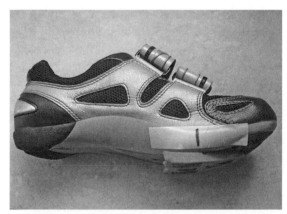

Locate the ball of your foot. Mark the position on the shoe on masking tape with a pen, then align the pedal cleat accordingly.

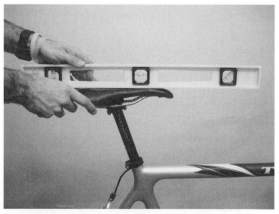

Adjust the saddle so it's level, then make small adjustments up or down as needed.

is tilted up at the front, it will make for an uncomfortable ride and can lead to numbness and chafing of sensitive regions. If the saddle is tilted down, it creates a tendency for the rider to slide forward, causing more weight to be placed on the hands and arms. This can lead to a sore upper back, shoulders, and neck and numbness in the hands. It also places extra weight on the front of the bike, which negatively affects handling. If you are using aero bars, the required hip angle might call for a saddle with the nose tilted slightly downward.

Saddle Height

Research that I conducted determined that a saddle height that sets the knee at an angle of 25 degrees when the pedal is in the six o'clock position is optimal for power output and efficiency. Other research indicates that anything over 35 degrees may have negative consequences for knee health and stability. There are four common methods for adjusting saddle height, but I recommend using only the Holmes method, which provides the best results for injury prevention and performance. (Because the other three methods are mentioned frequently in cycling literature, they are discussed as well.)

The Holmes Method

To set the saddle height using the Holmes method, you will need a goniometer (a device consisting of two arms fixed around an axis used to measure the angle of a joint), which you can purchase from any medical supply store for about $12. Select one with long arms, which make it easier to line up the required landmarks on the body. You'll also need an assistant, some visible tape or colored sticky dots from an office supply store, and a stationary trainer.

Place your bike in the stationary trainer and pedal for a few minutes to find your "comfort" spot on the saddle. Once you are comfortable, stop pedaling with one foot at the six o'clock position. The assistant should check that you have not pushed

The most accurate way to determine the correct saddle height is with a goniometer, which allows you to adjust the knee angle to 25 to 30 degrees.

your heel down or shifted in the saddle when you stopped pedaling. The assistant then places the axis of the goniometer on the lateral femoral condyle at the knee, and aligns the lower end of the device with the lateral malleolus of the ankle; he or she aligns the upper end with the greater trochanter at the hip. Before aligning the goniometer, find these spots using palpation, then place tape or the sticky dots on these three spots to ensure that the same place is measured each time. Because these boney landmarks will move under the skin if the saddle height is changed drastically, check that the tape remains over the landmarks before the knee angle is measured again. It is imperative to find the correct boney landmarks and align the goniometer accordingly. Move the saddle up and down to produce the desired angle. Once

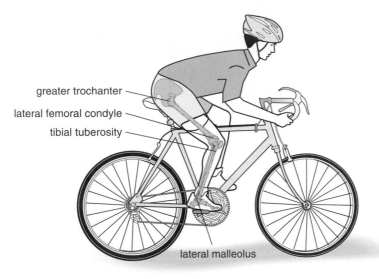

greater trochanter

lateral femoral condyle

tibial tuberosity

lateral malleolus

These are the "boney landmarks" used in the Holmes method for measuring the knee angle with a goniometer.

you have the saddle height set, pedal again, then stop for another measure. Do this two to four times to ensure the same measurement.

Using the Holmes method gives you a starting point; from there you may make minor adjustments from 25 degrees to dial in the height that works best for you. I recommend staying between a 25- and 30-degree knee angle; to prevent overuse injuries, you should never go beyond 35 degrees.

When you think you are finished, mount up again and have the assistant watch you from behind. If your hips are rocking from side to side, the saddle is too high. If your knees are pointing out and not centered over the pedals, the saddle may be too low. Also have the assistant watch from the side. If your knees are locking out at the bottom of the stroke, the saddle is too high. Watch for too much bend in the knee at the top of the stroke. This may be due to a crank arm that is too long rather than a saddle height that is too low.

It may take two to four weeks for your body to adapt to a new saddle height, during which time you may experience a decrease in performance. But once your body adapts, performance should improve.

Other Methods

There are three other common methods for setting the saddle height, none of which I recommend. I describe them here so that, if your bike shop or a colleague recommends them, you'll recognize and know why to avoid them.

To use the Hamley method, measure your inseam and multiply by 1.09. Use the resulting number to set the saddle height by measuring from the center of the pedal axle to the top of saddle, with the pedal at the bottom of the stroke and the crank arm in line with the seat tube. Measure the saddle at the point where your ischium (your "sit bones") contacts the saddle.

To use the LeMond method, measure your inseam as before and multiply by 0.883. Use the product to set the saddle height by measuring from the center of the bottom bracket to the top of the saddle.

Both of these methods rely on formulas that do not take individuals' differing body proportions into consideration—that is, longer or shorter femurs, longer or shorter tibias, larger or smaller feet. The LeMond method also takes no account of crank-arm length. Half of the time, these methods produce results that fall outside the recommended 25- to 35-degree knee angle, sometimes by a large amount.

The last method is the heel-toe method. Set up the bike in a stationary trainer and place your heel on the pedal with your knee locked out. Adjust the saddle so you are just sitting on it when your leg is straight. Pedal backward with your heels on the pedals, making sure that your hips do not rock back and forth; your heels should just about come off the pedals. Ideally, then, when you place the ball of the foot over the pedal spindle, you will have the proper bend in your knee. Unfortunately, this is often not the case, and it frequently produces saddle heights outside the recommended 25- to 35-degree knee-angle range.

Saddle Position Fore and Aft

Now that you have set the saddle height, you need to determine its fore and aft position. You will

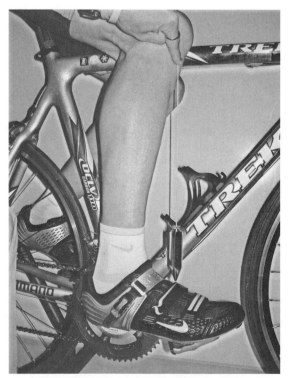

Use a plumb line to adjust the saddle's fore and aft position so the knee is aligned with the pedal axle.

need a plumb line, which you can buy at any hardware store.

Ride for a couple of minutes with the bike on a stationary trainer and get comfortable in the saddle. Stop with the crank arms parallel with the floor. Place the plumb line right at the tibial tuberosity on the forward leg, where the patella tendon attaches to the tibia, and let the weight hang straight down. For climbing specialists, it is recommended that the line should drop 1 to 2 cm behind the center of the pedal axle. Cyclists have a natural tendency to shift to the back of the saddle while climbing. For this reason it is not necessary for the majority of us to shift the saddle back. For sprinters and time-trial specialists, the plumb line should fall 1 to 2 cm in front of the pedal axle. The majority of cyclists, however, should have the line fall directly over the center. Aligning the axis of the knee over the pedal spindle places the line of power directly through the pedal. Adjust the saddle fore and aft until you accomplish this. You will need to pedal for a couple of minutes each time you adjust the saddle to ensure that you are sitting in the same spot.

When you are finished adjusting the saddle fore and aft, recheck the saddle height, because moving the saddle forward lowers it and moving the saddle aft raises it.

HANDLEBAR ADJUSTMENTS

Handlebar Width

Now that you have the lower half of your body dialed in, it's time to look at the upper half. The first consideration is the width of your handlebars, which should equal the width of your shoulders. Too narrow makes for an uncomfortable ride; too wide makes you catch a lot of wind unnecessarily.

Stem Length

Of all the steps in the setup, stem length is the one that will be most personalized based on comfort. You need to place your bike in a stationary trainer and use a plumb line.

Use a plumb line to determine stem length.

Pedal for a few minutes to get comfortable, with your hands in the drops (lowest portion of the handlebars) and your head up, duplicating the position of looking down the road. Have your assistant hold the plumb line to the end of your nose. The weight should fall somewhere between the centerline of the handlebars and 1 cm aft of the handlebars. This places your elbows at an optimum angle between 15 and 20 degrees and provides the necessary 1 to 2 inches of clearance between your knees and your elbows.

Adjusting the stem length so that the plumb line falls one centimeter behind the handlebar will stretch you out just a little more and improve aerodynamics. Beginners may find this uncomfortable, however, and may wish to use a shorter stem.

Adjust the stem length by changing the stem. For proper bike handling, the stem length should be between 90 and 120 mm. If you can't achieve a good setup within that range, you should look for a different-size bike frame with an appropriate top-tube length.

Handlebar Height

Racers and other performance-oriented riders should set their handlebar height so that when they are in the drops, their back is flat when viewed from the side. For most riders, this means the top of the handlebars should be 1 to 3 inches lower than the top of the saddle. This optimal position is not practical for all riders, however. If you are not very flexible, it may take a while to work into this position; if you have a bad lower back, you may need to ride in a more upright position permanently.

You can change the height of the handlebars by adjusting the stack height or changing the angle of the stem. The stack height is adjusted by adding or removing spacers between the top of the headset and the bottom of the stem. Lower the stack height in small increments and get accustomed to changes over a period of a few weeks until you achieve the position that you find to be optimal, keeping in mind that comfort is of primary concern on this aspect of bike setup. Do not cut the steerer tube until you are completely satisfied with the position; if you cut it too short, you'll have to buy a new fork. Some manufacturers of all-carbon forks set limits on stack height to prevent fatigue to the steerer tube. You can also purchase an adjustable-angle stem to raise or lower the height of the handlebars.

If you have a threaded headset and fork system, you can adjust the height by raising or lowering the stem. When adjusting a threaded system, always check the *quill* (the section of stem that inserts into the headset and steerer tube) for the insertion limit mark. It is unsafe to have this mark showing above the headset.

If you drastically change the stem height, you will need to recheck the stem length.

TIME-TRIAL SETUP

The lower half of the body is positioned the same for time-trial and traditional setups, with saddle tilt being the only possible exception. You may need a slightly nose-down tilt on the saddle due to the rotation of the pelvis. Even so, keep the saddle as level as possible.

The big difference in the setup on a time-trial bike is in the positioning of the upper body; the objective here is to reduce the rider's wind resistance by bringing the arms close together, further flattening the back, and lowering the chin. Professional cyclists use a wind tunnel to optimize their time-trial position. This isn't practical for most of us, so a simpler procedure is used.

To improve aerodynamics during a time trial, aero bars are used; they decrease the frontal area of the rider that is exposed to the wind. However, aero bars do not magically improve aerodynamics. If your arms are set wide apart and you're sitting high, aero bars are of little use. Set aero bars so your arms are as close together as possible while still maintaining comfort and control.

Change the stem as needed, so a plumb line dropped from the front of the shoulder runs through the back of the elbow. The stem in a time-trial setup should be long enough to place the elbows at an 80- to 95-degree angle.

The handlebars should be low enough to allow for a flat back but still retain a couple of centimeters' clearance between the quadriceps (upper surface of the thighs) and your abdomen when you're at the top of the pedal stroke. Have an assistant observe your position, and confirm that your pelvis is tilted forward. If your back is rounded, you may be sitting upright on the saddle and just bending forward to get into the aero bars. This places unnecessary stress on the lower back, which will decrease performance and can lead to lower back injury.

Many cyclists find it difficult to achieve a flat back at first. Start with a higher stem height, then lower it incrementally as your flexibility increases. The position should always be comfortable and allow for good control of the bike.

Use a power meter (see page 149) to determine whether a new position has improved or diminished your power output, but do not compromise comfort too far to achieve additional power.

In the proper aero position, the pelvis is rotated forward and the back is as flat as comfort allows.

Position the aero bars as close together as comfort and safety allow.

RECORDING YOUR SETUP

It can take a long time to dial in your bike to where you are really comfortable and efficient. Because of this, it's a good idea to take measurements and record them so you can set up your bike the same way in the future. The seat post has a tendency to slip over time, but if you have recorded the height, it will be easy to readjust without going through the whole measurement routine again. Measurements also allow you to set up two bikes the same way. You can use a table similar to the one below to keep your data organized.

Measure the saddle height from the center of the pedal axle to the top of the saddle. To determine the saddle's fore-and-aft position, use a plumb line and a ruler to measure the horizontal distance from the nose of the saddle to the center of the bottom bracket. Use a long bubble level and a ruler to measure the drop from the nose of the saddle to the top of the handlebars.

BIKE MEASUREMENT RECORD	
Date	
Make	
Model	
Year	
Frame size	
Top-tube length (center to center)	
Head-tube angle	
Seat-tube length (center to top)	
Seat-tube angle	
Stem length	
Handlebar width	
Crank-arm length	
Pedal axle to top of saddle	
Nose of saddle to center of bottom bracket	
Drop from top of saddle to handlebars	

bike maintenance

Even the most complicated bike repairs are relatively easy compared to working on automobiles. Any mechanically inclined person can perform all of the regular maintenance required to keep a bike running smoothly. Learning how will allow you to keep your bike on the road without excessive downtime and will save you money.

This chapter is designed to give you the information you need to take care of your bike on a day-to-day basis and perform minor repairs on the road; it's not meant to be a complete guide to bicycle repairs. For this type of comprehensive treatment, I recommend *Big Blue Book of Bicycle Repair* by C. Calvin Jones.

BASIC MAINTENANCE PRINCIPLES

There are numerous opportunities to learn bike maintenance and repair. Many bike shops run clinics and classes. You can learn on your own from books. Most component manufacturers provide detailed installation instructions with their products and post maintenance procedures on their websites. Many technical schools offer professional training that may lead to certification as a bike mechanic.

Cleanliness and Orderliness

Keep your work area clean and orderly. Bike parts are often coated with grease or oil and can pick up dirt and debris, both of which increase friction and wear. Keep your tools organized in a designated toolbox or on a pegboard so you can find what you need when you need it. (A pegboard allows quicker access; a toolbox is more convenient for travel.) After every work session, take a few minutes to clean your work area and put away the tools.

Tools and Supplies

Bike maintenance requires generic mechanics' tools such as wrenches and screwdrivers, and cycle-specific tools that are designed to work on a particular component and for which there are no practical alternatives. You can equip yourself with the basics for $200 to $300, which will pay for itself quickly compared to the cost of professional maintenance. You can start by buying the generic tools, and add the specialized ones as you need them. For example, you won't have to buy a bottom-bracket tool until you need to remove the bottom bracket.

Specialized tools are usually not interchangeable among manufacturers. For example, if you have a Campagnolo bottom bracket, you'll need a Campy tool. Likewise with Shimano. Even within the same company's line, there may be different bottom brackets that require different tools, so it's essential to know the make and model of your components before you buy.

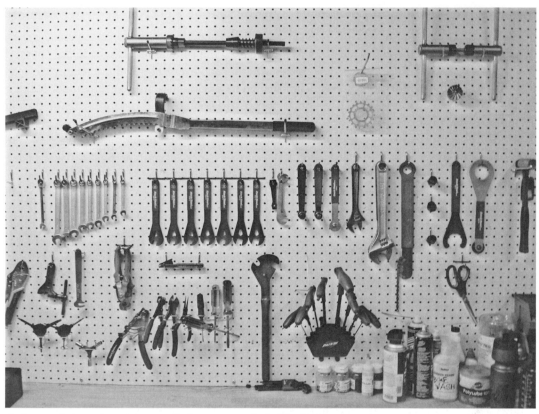

A clean, orderly work area ensures that you can easily find the tools you need.

PRICES OF BASIC BIKE-SHOP TOOLS

Floor pump	$20–$80	Bottom-bracket tool	$15
Set of hex wrenches	$10–$30	Chain wear indicator	$10
Chain tool	$15	Tire levers	$5
Cassette tool	$5	Wheel truing stand	$50–$200
Chain whip	$15	Spoke wrench	$5
Adjustable wrench	$15	Spoke tension meter	$60
Crank puller	$15	Work stand	$80–$300
Pedal wrench	$15–$30	Cone wrenches	$20–$40
Screwdriver set	$10–$40	Torque wrench	$30–$200
Wire cutters	$10	Cassette brush	$5
Housing cutters	$30	Magnet bowl for small parts	$6

A few parts and supplies are needed so regularly that you should keep spares in your shop:

- brake pads
- brake cables and housings
- shifter cables and housings
- cable and housing ends
- chain
- chain master link
- tubes
- tires (an old one is OK for emergency replacement)
- rim tape
- spokes
- bar tape
- shoe cleats
- chain lube
- grease
- electrical tape

Tighten/Loosen

With few exceptions, nuts and bolts on bikes (and everywhere else) tighten by turning clockwise and loosen counterclockwise. Clockwise-tightening fasteners have what are known as "right-hand" threads. Some people find the saying "righty tighty, lefty loosey" a good way to remember: if you picture a nut or a bolt head as a clock, the top of the clock, at twelve o'clock, tightens to the right. Make sure you're looking at the nut or bolt from the correct direction: if you approach it from the back, clockwise and counterclockwise (and left and right) are reversed.

The only parts with left-hand, or *reverse*, threads are the left pedal and the drive side (the side with the chainrings) of English-style bottom brackets. Right-hand threads are so common that it requires careful attention to work with reverse threads.

Every bolt has a specific torque established by the manufacturer to keep it from being stripped by overtightening or coming loose due to undertightening. To measure torque, you need a torque wrench.

Check Your Work

After completing a maintenance procedure, check that all the bolts are tightened to the appropriate torque and everything is in proper order. Inspect the bike while it's still on the stand. Make sure that the cables are routed properly so they don't bind and everything moves as it should. Some problems may not appear on the stand and do not become apparent until the bike is placed under the stress of riding, so take the bike for a short, nondemanding ride to ensure that everything is in working order before really pushing it on a long ride.

CLEANING

Although many people think of cleaning the bike as a cosmetic job, it's really about preservation. As we ride, the sweat rolls off our bodies and onto the bike. Sweat has a tendency to corrode just about any metal part it comes in contact with and can even remove the protective coating from a paint job.

After every ride, wipe down your bike with a damp cloth to remove sweat and grime, and wash the bike about once a week. All you need is soapy water, a sponge, a soft brush, a hose, and dry rags. Start by wetting down the bike with a little water. Do not use the high-power spray on your hose nozzle, and *never* wash your bike at a car wash with a high-pressure sprayer; this could force water into the bearing sets, displacing the grease and leading to premature bearing wear. Even with a gentle flow, do not spray water directly into the bottom bracket, seat post, headset, or wheel hubs. Wipe down the frame with a soapy sponge and rinse everything clean. Use a soft-bristle brush to reach areas that the sponge cannot reach. After washing the bike and cleaning the drivetrain (discussed next), wipe away any excess water with a dry cloth.

Cleaning the chain, chainring, and cassette every week or two will greatly extend the life of the drivetrain. The oil that is used on the chain to reduce friction between moving parts picks up

Use a cassette cleaning brush to remove grime wedged deep between the cassette cogs.

Cleaning your bike not only keeps it looking good, it washes away sweat (which can cause corrosion) and road grime (which can cause wear to the drivetrain). (Kathleen Poulos, Toyota-United)

debris that, over time, actually increases friction, causing accelerated part wear. Because cleaning the drivetrain is messy, you may want to tackle it before the rest of the bike.

To do this, you will need degreaser and a brush. Bike-specific degreasers are available, or you can use liquid dish soap. Purchase a cassette brush with long, stiff bristles to get between the cogs. An old toothbrush works well for cleaning the chain.

Mix the degreaser with hot water, then use the brush to scrub the chain, chainrings, rear cassette, and pulleys on the rear derailleur. Rinse clean the drivetrain as you scrub, then remove the excess water with a dry cloth and apply fresh chain oil (see the upcoming "Chain" section).

AFTER RAIN

It is inevitable that you will be caught in the rain from time to time. Riding in the rain can be a valuable training tool because eventually you will have to compete in it. But it's not good for your bike, because water and grit picked up from road spray get into the moving parts. After riding in heavy rain, some preventive maintenance is in order. (You may also want to consider these steps if you were overzealous with the water hose while washing your bike.)

Wipe any excess water from the bike, then lubricate where necessary. Water has a tendency to enter the bike frame at the seat post, so remove the post, drain the water, and allow the frame to dry before replacing the post. If you pour out an excessive amount of water, pull the bottom bracket, clean and dry the bottom-bracket shell, and clean, dry, and re-lube the bottom bracket. Water may also get into the headset, which should be removed, cleaned, dried, and re-greased. All of these procedures are discussed below.

MAINTENANCE PROCEDURES

Bikes are, happily, somewhat generic (although less so now than a few years ago), with generally similar engineering across various makes and models and common dimensions and threads for many parts. This makes many parts interchangeable and most maintenance procedures broadly applicable to most bikes. (In contrast, just try putting a Chevrolet wheel on a Ford axle.) Nevertheless, some companies produce proprietary products that require special tools and procedures. The following procedures are therefore somewhat genericized. The best source of detailed instructions for specific components is often the manufacturer.

Removing and Replacing Wheels

The first step to removing either wheel is to open the brake caliper so the tire can slip between the brake pads. On Shimano and SRAM brakes, lift the quick-release lever on the calipers; on Campagnolo brakes, use the pin on the shift/brake levers.

Next, open the quick release on the skewer. You may have to loosen the knurled nut on the opposite end of the skewer; in most cases, the wheel should then just fall out. If not, you have retention tabs on your fork, so loosen the nut on the side opposite the quick-release lever until the wheel is free.

To release the wheel from the bike, open the skewer by pulling out on the skewer lever. (top shows the lever in the closed position; bottom shows the lever in the open position).

Lift the quick-release lever on the brake caliper to open the calipers and allow the wheel to slide free.

Reinstall the front wheel with the quick-release lever on the left side of the bike. Slide the axle into place on the fork dropouts and make sure it's centered, then close the quick-release lever, making sure it faces the back of the bike. The quick release should feel firm when you close it. If you had to loosen the nut to remove the wheel, you need to retighten the nut until the lever feels firm as it closes. Once the wheel is in place, close the brake's quick release to move the calipers

When removing the rear wheel, open the skewer and gently pull back the rear derailleur to allow the wheel to drop out.

When removing the rear wheel from horizontal dropouts, pull the chain straight back to release the wheel.

back into position. Spin the wheel to make sure it's centered between the brake pads.

The steps for the back wheel are the same with a minor exception. Before attempting to remove the rear wheel, shift the chain onto the smallest rear cog and the small chainring. (Cross chaining such as this is to be avoided when riding, but it's OK now because there's no stress on the components.) This will minimize chain tension and move the chain to the "outside" at the rear of the bike, out of the way. After opening the quick-release lever, gently pull the rear derailleur straight back so it's not beneath the cassette, then allow the wheel to drop down. If you have horizontal dropouts, you need to pull the chain back as you pull the wheel back.

To reinstall the rear wheel, place the chain on the small cog, then push the wheel into place in the dropouts. (Make sure you haven't changed the derailleur setting in the meantime.) The rest of the steps are the same as for the front wheel.

Brakes

Inspect the brakes often. Adjustments must be performed frequently, and cables and shoes need regular replacement.

Adjustment

The calipers must be centered, with equal gaps on both sides of the rim. First, make sure the wheel is true and placed correctly in the dropouts. If the calipers need centering, start by simply gripping the caliper and moving it one way or the other. Test it by squeezing the lever. If it doesn't stay centered

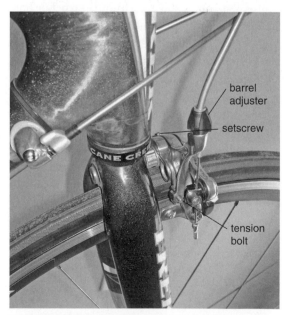

Center the brake calipers by adjusting the setscrew. The barrel adjuster is used to alter the distance between the brake pads and rim.

or otherwise function properly, or if it was loose and moved too easily, move on to the second method. Use a cone wrench (a narrow wrench designed to adjust wheel-bearing cones) to hold the caliper centered while tightening the mounting bolt on the opposite side. The last method involves adjusting the setscrew located on most dual pivot brake calipers. Tightening or loosening the screw will move the caliper left or right.

Once the brakes are centered, check the distance from the brake pads to the wheel rim. The recommended clearance is about three millimeters on each side. If the clearance is too wide, braking power is greatly impaired; too tight, and they may drag on the rim if the wheel becomes even slightly off center or out of true. Small adjustments can be made by screwing the barrel adjuster on the brake caliper in or out to create or remove slack in the cable. If you have to screw the barrel adjuster all the way out, the cable is too loose, in which case you should screw the barrel adjuster back in and adjust the cable itself. Loosen the nut on the cable anchor bolt, hold the caliper at the desired clearance, pull the slack out of the cable, and retighten the anchor bolt. (A tool called a third hand can be used to hold the calipers at the proper distance while you work on the cable.) Work the brakes a few times to make sure the clearance is right and the cable doesn't slip.

Shoe Replacement

Brake pads are "consumables," designed to wear out so your rims don't. Examine the brake pads once or twice a month. Some pads have wear lines to indicate when it's time to replace them. With others, just watch the grooves and replace the pads when the grooves start to disappear. Riding on worn pads can damage the rims and negatively affect braking. Always replace brake pads in pairs.

Some brake pads are integral with the shoes and must be replaced as a unit. Others mount in reusable shoes, and only the pads need to be replaced when worn. With either type, remove the brake shoe from the caliper by removing the

mounting nut. With the single-unit pad and shoe, just discard and replace. For brake shoes with replaceable pads, loosen the small bolt on the shoe to free the pads; these fit snugly and may require the use of pliers to remove and insert. Replacement pads must be installed into the shoe in a specific direction. Most are marked with an R or L for "right" or "left." When reinstalling shoes with replaceable pads, ensure that they are installed on the correct side. If you install the shoes on the incorrect side, the pads will be facing in the wrong direction and will rip out during braking.

Refasten the shoes to the caliper tight enough so they stay in place but loose enough so you can move them. Depress the brake lever gently so the pads make contact with the rim. Locate one shoe

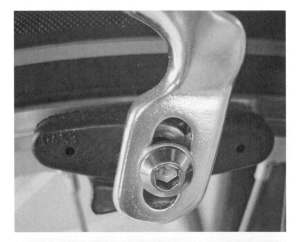

Brake shoes come in two styles: disposable shoes (top) and shoes with replaceable pads (bottom).

When replacing the brake pads, make sure the new ones line up with the rim and that shoes with replaceable pads are facing in the correct direction.

at a time against the rim, making sure the shoe doesn't hang below the rim, extend above it, or take a tipped-up or tipped-down attitude. Apply force to the brake lever to hold the shoe firmly in place, and tighten the mounting nut. (You may need to hold the shoe steady with pliers to prevent it from turning.) Apply the brakes and make sure that the pads are engaging correctly on the rim.

If your brakes make excessive noise when you ride, clean the rims with rubbing alcohol and a rag,

Do not allow the shoes to tip up or down (as shown) when replacing them.

and use sandpaper to remove a thin surface layer from the brake pads. If this doesn't correct the problem, examine how the pads make contact with the rim as you activate the brakes. If the back end of the pad makes contact first, you need to toe in your brake pads so the front end makes contact first. Loosen the shoe mounting nuts and angle the shoes so the back edge of the pads is about half a millimeter off the rim when the front end just touches, then retighten the nuts. If you have old brake shoes that lack this adjustment capability, replace them with a new model.

Another common cause of squealing brakes is cheaply made or worn-out calipers that vibrate when in use and can't be stabilized. The only fix for these is replacement.

Cable Replacement

You should replace brake cables when they become corroded or frayed. Replacement procedures vary slightly from bike to bike, so these are just the basics.

If you notice that the brakes stick a little or are slow to disengage, there may be a buildup of gunk inside the housing. Lubricate the cable by squirting chain lube into the housing. If this doesn't correct the problem, the cable is corroded or you've got impacted gunk and need to replace the cable. In either case, you should replace the housing as well. I recommend brake housings that are coated with PTFE (that is, Teflon) because they offer very low friction.

Loosen the cable bolt at the calipers and cut the lower end of the cable end so it can be pulled through the bolt. Next, pull and release the brake lever a couple of times. This should pull the head of the brake cable out of its socket in the lever so it can be gripped and the cable pulled free. Check the ends of the cable housing to make sure they aren't corroded. If the housing is fine, insert the new cable, feeding it through the socket at the lever end and rerouting it through the housing down to the brake caliper. Run the cable through the anchor bolt between the caliper arm and the cable retention plate, pull out all the slack, adjust the brakes accordingly, and tighten the anchor bolt. Work the brakes a few times to make sure that all the slack is out and the adjustment holds. If it doesn't, loosen the cable bolt and readjust. Things have to seat themselves firmly, especially if you replace the housing, so it usually requires a couple of times before you get the correct distance. Next, cut the end of the cable with cable cutters (use good ones to prevent fraying), leaving ½ to 1 inch extra. Place an end cap on the bare end of the cable and crimp it in place to prevent fraying.

If you need to replace the housings as well, do one brake at a time so you remember the proper route of the cable along the frame. Start by removing the bar tape from the handlebars, then remove the cable. Next, remove the tape holding the brake housing to

After routing the cable behind the cable retention plate, adjust the brake calipers to the desired distance, pull out all the slack in the cable, and tighten the cable bolt.

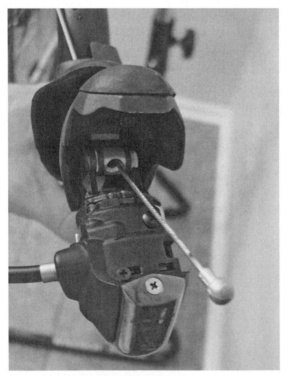

After releasing the brake cable, pull the brake lever a few times until the head of the cable protrudes far enough to be grabbed.

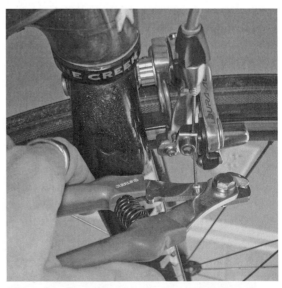

After cutting the cable, place a cable end cap over the end of the cable and crimp the cap in place to prevent the cable end from fraying.

the handlebars. If the old housing is the correct length, save it as a guide for cutting the new housing.

The housing for the front brake runs from the lever, along the handlebars, and down to the front caliper. Two pieces of housing are needed for the back brake: one from the lever and along the handlebars, then to a housing stop on the top tube. The cable runs bare along the top tube to another housing stop near the back of the top tube, then enters the second piece of housing, which runs to the back brake caliper.

Cut the housing to length so it takes a smooth curve without excessive slack. If in doubt, cut it a bit long. Hold it in place, then trim it shorter as needed. Use cutters designed specifically for cutting housing, and make sure the ends are cut clean. Don't use regular cable cutters, which will smash the ends of the housing. And don't cut cables with your housing cutters: it will ruin the cutting edge.

Here's the process using the front brake as an example. When the housing is ready, thread the cable through the lever and pull out the slack. Run the cable through the housing, and seat the upper end of the housing in the lever. Thread the cable through the barrel adjuster and the cable retention plate on the caliper, and seat the lower end of the housing into the barrel adjuster. Pull the slack out of the cable and anchor it at the caliper. Make sure the lever actuates the brake smoothly and the housing doesn't hang up on anything when you turn the headset. If either problem is present, you may need to adjust the length of the housing or play with the routing. Tape the housing to the handlebars with electrical tape along the same route that was used previously and check brake actuation again. Adjust the brakes and cut off the excess cable.

The rear brake follows the same procedure, with obvious accommodations being made for the different cable routing and the two-part housing.

Other Brake Maintenance Issues

Levers are usually trouble free, requiring only a bit of lube on the pivots and an occasional check

for corrosion. If the brake lever feels wrong (explained next), the problem is usually elsewhere.

If a brake feels mushy or you can pull the lever all the way to the handlebars, there is too much clearance between the brake pads and the rim. First, make sure you closed the caliper's quick release after reinstalling the wheel. If the cable hasn't slipped through the anchor bolt and if brake shoe wear isn't excessive, you need to adjust the caliper clearance.

If the brake is slow to return to its normal position after braking, there may be a kink in the housing or cable, or the housing is gunked up or corroded, or the caliper's return spring has fatigued. Check the first two scenarios first; both require replacing the cable and housing. The last requires increasing the spring tension in the caliper. On some newer calipers, there is a tension bolt for increasing spring tension. On calipers without this feature, you can attempt to increase tension by bending the springs outward. You'll have to disassemble the calipers to access them, and you'll still end up with fatigued springs, but it might resolve the problem for a while. A better solution is to replace the caliper.

Shifters and Derailleurs

Poor shifting due to misadjusted derailleurs is a common occurrence. To avoid this problem on the road, check your shifting before you leave home. If everything is in proper order, most adjustments on the road can be made quickly and easily, usually with no tools at all.

Shifters

As with the brakes, when there is a problem shifting it is rarely in the levers; more than likely it is in the cable, housing, or derailleur. When they occur, most lever problems must be solved by replacement. Some shift levers can be serviced, but this is complex and beyond the scope of this chapter.

Adjusting the Front Derailleur

Before making any other adjustments, make sure the front derailleur is mounted correctly. Shift or push the derailleur over the large chainring; there should be a 1 to 2 mm gap between the bottom of the derailleur cage and the chainring teeth, located on the large chainring. If adjustment is necessary, shift to the small chainring, loosen the cable retention bolt, loosen the binder bolt on the mounting bracket, and move the unit up or down as needed. Retighten the bracket, then the cable anchor, and recheck for height.

Next, look at the derailleur from ahead to make sure the cage is parallel to the chainrings. Follow the same steps as above to change the angle if necessary.

Limit screws on the derailleur body restrict the distance that it travels in and out. If travel is insufficient in either direction, the chain will not shift onto the desired chainring, but at least you can

The low- and high-gear limit screws are designed to limit the outward and inward movements of the derailleur.

still keep pedaling on the present one. If derailleur travel is too great, the chain will be "thrown" past the desired chainring and you'll be out of business. The limit screws—marked L and H for low gear and high gear—prevent the cage from moving the chain too far inward or outward, respectively.

I hope it goes without saying that you can't shift the chain unless you're pedaling forward, so you'll have to support the bike on a stand, with the rear wheel off the ground, for derailleur adjustments. Pedal at sufficient speed to mimic riding: 50 to 60 rpm will do.

Start by setting the lower limit. Shift the chain to the small ring in front and the largest cog in back. You do not want tension on the derailleur, so release the cable by loosening the anchor bolt. If necessary, tighten or loosen the L screw so there is about one millimeter of clearance between the chain and the inner plate of the derailleur cage. Pull the slack from the cable and retighten the anchor bolt. While turning the crank by hand, shift to the large ring and back down again. The chain should drop smoothly onto the inner chainring. If the chain falls off to the inside, tighten the L screw and try again. If it is slow to drop, loosen the L screw and check the gap again. Most adjustments to the limit screws should be small—typically one-eighth to one-quarter turn at a time.

When the front derailleur is adjusted properly, there is a 1 to 2 mm gap between the top of the large chainring and the bottom of the cage. It will vary. The gap will be larger near the back portion of the derailleur. You measure at the top of the chainring.

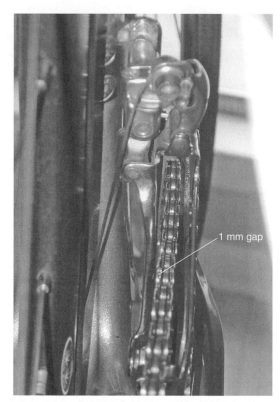

Adjust the low-gear limit screw until there is a 1 mm gap between the small chainring and the inner front derailleur plate.

Adjust the high-gear limit screw until there is a 1 mm gap between the large chainring and the outer front derailleur plate.

Next, set the high-gear limit. Shift to the large ring in front and the smallest cog in back. Manually pull the cable tight to ensure that the derailleur is firmly against the limit screw. Turn the H (for high gear) limit screw to set a 1 mm gap between the outer derailleur plate and the chain. Shift back and forth between the chainrings as before, and readjust as needed.

Now that the limit screws are properly set, you need to adjust the shifting. Shift to the small ring in back and the large ring in front. If the derailleur cage contacts the chain, increase the cable tension by turning the barrel adjuster until you have the appropriate 1 mm clearance. The chain should now shift smoothly. If the barrel adjuster can't take out all the slack, loosen the anchor bolt, pull out the slack, and retighten, then check the shifting again.

Adjusting the Rear Derailleur

As with the front derailleur, make sure the rear one is mounted correctly. First, ensure that the mounting bolt is tight. When shifted into the lowest gear, the top pulley, known as the jockey wheel or guide pulley, should be as close to the largest cog as possible without interference. This usually translates to about six millimeters of clearance to allow room for the chain in between. If necessary, tighten the B (for body) screw to tilt back the derailleur body and increase the clearance, or loosen the screw to tilt the body forward and reduce the clearance.

The spring-loaded cage on the rear derailleur is designed to keep tension on the chain as it moves between cogs on the rear cassette.

Next, set the limit screws. The low-gear (L) limit screw prevents the derailleur from shifting into the spokes, and the high-gear (H) limit screw prevents the chain from being thrown off the cassette to the outside. The limit screws are *not* used to adjust shifting from cog to cog.

Start with the high-gear limit, placing the chain on the large ring in front and the smallest cog in back. Loosen the cable bolt and release the cable tension. The guide pulley should be directly under the smallest cog. If necessary, turn the H screw until the pulley and the cog are aligned perfectly. Pull the slack from the cable and tighten the anchor bolt. Shift to the next largest cog on the cassette and back down again. The chain should move smoothly.

Set the low gear limit next. Shift the bike to the small chainring and the largest cog. Grip the derailleur cable and pull, or push the derailleur by hand to ensure that the derailleur is against the lower limit screw. The guide pulley should line up perfectly with the largest cog, and the derailleur should not touch the spokes. Adjust the L screw as needed, and check shifting between the largest and next-largest cogs.

Now adjust the shifting between cogs by changing the cable tension at the barrel adjuster

The body screw is used to set the clearance between the rear derailleur and the cassette.

Adjusting the low- and high-gear limit screws on the rear derailleur prevents the chain from traveling into the spokes or becoming wedged between the cassette and the frame.

When the high-gear limit screw is properly set, the rear derailleur guide pulley should line up directly below the smallest cassette cog.

When the low-gear limit screw is properly set, the rear derailleur guide pulley should line up directly below the largest cassette cog.

on the rear derailleur. First remove any slack from the cable at the anchor bolt. Place the chain on the large ring in front and the smallest cog in back. Shift from the smallest to the next-largest cog. If the chain hesitates while moving to the next gear, increase the tension by turning the barrel adjuster counterclockwise. If the chain tries to move beyond the next cog, decrease the tension by turning the barrel adjuster clockwise. After making these adjustments, try the next two or three cogs. If the chain shifts smoothly, move on to the next step. Shift the chain into the small ring in front and the largest cog in back. Shift from the largest cog to the next one down. If the chain hesitates or will not shift down, decrease the tension. If it tries to go too far, increase the tension. Check shifting up and down and make adjustments accordingly.

The barrel adjuster on the rear derailleur can be used to fine-tune shifting by increasing or decreasing cable tension.

Replacing Cables

Smooth-running cables facilitate quick and precise shifting. Corroded cables and gunked-up housings should be replaced. If you replace cables, replace the housings as well.

Access to the upper end of the shift cable differs by manufacturer. For Shimano, you need to pull the brake lever to gain access. For Campagnolo, the entry point is on the side, below the thumb lever. Access on SRAM levers is on the side, beneath the rubber hood.

The front derailleur cable starts at the left shift lever. Shift the chain onto the small chainring, loosen the cable anchor bolt on the derailleur, and cut off the end of the cable so it can be pulled through. Push the cable so its end fitting comes out of the shift lever. Grip the fitting and pull the cable free. Remove the old housing and use it to measure the new housing. Cut the new housing with housing cutters, then add the housing ends.

Route the housing from the left lever to the barrel adjuster on the left side of the down tube. Thread the new cable through the lever, through the new housing, through the barrel adjuster, through the cable guide on the underside of the bottom bracket shell, between the chain stays, and up to the derailleur. Pull out the slack and

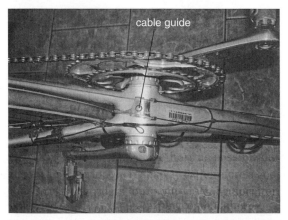

cable guide

The cable guide, located on the underside of the bottom-bracket shell, ensures that the cables are routed along the correct path. The guide also protects the frame from cable rub.

anchor the cable in place, then cut the cable with wire cutters, leaving about an inch extra, and crimp an end cap in place. Adjust the derailleur as described earlier. As you ride, you may need to increase tension in the cable a few times before the housing has completely seated itself.

Procedures are nearly identical for the rear derailleur cable and housing. Work with the chain on the smallest cog, and route the top section of housing from the lever to the barrel adjuster on the right side of the down tube, and the second piece from the housing stop on the chain stay to the barrel adjuster on the rear derailleur. Run the new cable through the lever, the first piece of housing, down alongside the down tube, through the cable guide under the bottom-bracket shell, along the right chain stay, through the second piece of housing, and to the anchor bolt on the derailleur.

Chain

Worn chains wear down the rest of the drivetrain and tend to break easily. Keeping the chain clean and lubed will greatly prolong its life. You should replace the chain every 1,000 to 2,000 miles, depending on its quality and how well it is maintained.

Lubing

Depending on your local weather, you can choose a wet or dry chain lubricant. Dry lube picks up very little debris, but it washes off easily in wet conditions. Wet lube picks up more debris but can withstand wet conditions. Only use bicycle lubes: many other popular lubricants (such as motor oil) attract excessive amounts of debris and should be avoided.

Before lubing, remove any old lube and debris by wiping down or thoroughly cleaning the chain, as needed. Apply new lube to the rollers (the side plates don't need it) and let it soak in. Remove any excess with a rag. This will help prevent an immediate buildup of debris.

Replacement

If the chain is skipping on the cassette, a replacement is overdue. Before you get to that point,

Use a chain gauge to determine whether the chain is worn and needs to be replaced.

To determine chain length, route the new chain over the large chainring, through the front derailleur, over the smallest rear cog, and through the rear derailleur. Pull the two ends of the chain together beneath the chain stay until the rear derailleur pulleys are lined up vertically.

you can use a chain gauge to determine whether the chain is worn, comparing your measurement against the manufacturer's specifications. If a new chain skips on the rear cassette when under strain, you waited way too long and the cassette will need to be replaced as well.

Choose the correct chain. Eight- and nine-speed chains are wider than ten-speed chains and are not interchangeable. To remove (or "break") the old chain, place it in the chain tool and turn the handle until the pin falls free. Clean the rest of the drivetrain before you install the new chain.

Before installing the new chain, it must be sized, or broken to the proper length. If the old chain was the correct length, you can use it as a guide. Because it has elongated from use, you can count links or line up the two chains side by side and match them link for link. If you don't have the old chain or if its length was incorrect, route the new chain over the large chainring, through the front derailleur, over the smallest rear cog, and through the rear derailleur. Pull the two ends of the chain together beneath the chain stay until the rear derailleur pulleys are lined up vertically. Mark the chain and remove the excess, making sure you end up with a roller at one end and a pair of side plates at the other. The exception to this is if you will use a master link (discussed later), in which

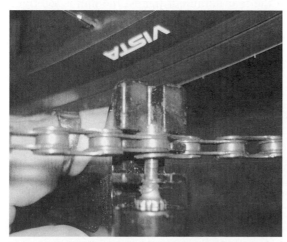

Use a chain tool to push the connecting pin through the link to break the chain for removal.

When joining two ends of a chain with a connecting pin, make sure you have a pair of side plates at one end of the chain and a roller at the other end.

case cut the chain one plate short so you have two roller ends.

There are two ways to join the ends of the chain. First, here's the method utilizing a chain tool and the connecting pin that's included with all new chains. Shift the front derailleur to the small chainring and remove the chain to the inside so it's draped over the bottom-bracket shell. This will release all tension from the chain, making it easier to work with. Bring the two ends together and place the pin, pointed end first, through the pin hole in the near side plate. Fit the two ends into the chain tool and screw down the handle, forcing the pin through the roller and into the far side plate. You will feel the pin ends snap into place. Remove the chain tool and use pliers to snap off the pointed end of the pin, then wiggle the newly joined link up and down to ensure that it moves freely. If a seven-, eight-, or nine-speed chain does not move freely, wiggle the link from side to side to loosen the connection. Do not use this method with a ten-speed chain; it is too thin and the plate may come loose from the pin.

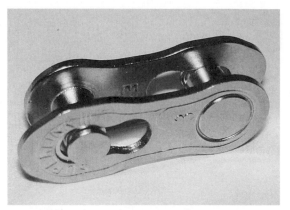

Using a master link instead of a connecting pin makes it easy to install and remove a chain.

Because of the difficulty of joining a ten-speed chain with a pin, I recommend using a master link instead. A master link also makes it easy to remove the chain for maintenance. Master links are designed to connect two roller pin ends by the use of pins connected to the plates of the master link. The master link consists of two plates that are designed to connect two roller ends of a chain. Each plate has one pin that is designed to fit through the roller and connect to a slot on the opposite plate. After connecting the chain, turn the pedals and watch the rear derailleur for any catches as the chain passes through the pulleys. If the rear derailleur jumps, the link is too tight and not operating smoothly. Loosen the link and repeat the installation.

Tires

Inspect your tires before every ride. Make sure no debris is lodged in the treads or is cutting into the rubber because it can work its way through into the tube.

Check the tire pressure. Cycling tubes are permeable and lose as much as 10 to 20 psi overnight. When the tire pressure is low, the sidewall can be compressed by a bump in the road, causing a pinch flat. Low tire pressure also negatively affects handling and speed.

connecting pin

chain tool

Use the chain tool to push the new connecting pin through the chain until it seats.

If your tire has a slow leak, do not ignore it because it will eventually become a large leak. Take the time to replace the tube in the comfort of your home before you ride.

Flats are a common occurrence in cycling, and tires wear out with fair regularity. It is not practical to run to the shop every time, so learning how to fix flats and change tires is a must. Clincher and tubular tires require different procedures.

Clincher Repair and Replacement

Remove the wheel from the frame, and remove the valve cap from the valve stem. There is no need to take the entire tire off the rim to fix a flat, so unless you're replacing the tire, you'll need to free only one side of the tire. You will need two or three tire levers. Place one tire lever between the tire and the rim. Being careful not to pinch the inner tube, pry the lip of the tire over the rim, levering the tool all the way down so you can clip the other end around a spoke and hold it in place. Repeat with the other tire levers until you have freed a sufficient amount of the tire bead from the rim so you can free the rest by hand. Grip the tube and pull it out of the tire, feeding

the valve stem through the rim last. Inspect the tube and look for the hole. You want to determine where and how the puncture occurred; if the flat was caused by a tack or a bit of glass lodged in the tire, you've got to find it before it causes another instantaneous flat.

If you can't see the puncture easily, inflate the tube. If the hole is still not obvious, hold the tube next to your ear and rotate it bit by bit until you can hear or feel the leak. If you still can't find it, place the tube under water in a sink, a few inches at a time, and watch for bubbles. When you find the puncture, mark it with a grease pencil.

Punctures from sharp objects are usually small pinholes. (In contrast, pinch flats are usually oval shaped and often come in closely spaced pairs.) In case of a sharp-object puncture, determine whether the object is still embedded in the

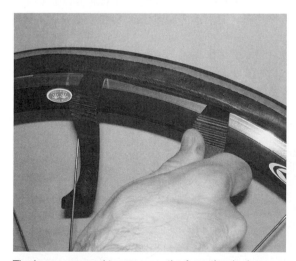

Tire levers are used to remove a tire from the rim by prying the tire bead up and over the rim wall.

You can locate a small hole in an inner tube by inflating it, submerging the tube in water, and watching for bubbles.

tire. Inspect the tread, then *carefully* run your fingers along the inside of the tire to feel for any debris or protrusions. Remove any objects you find.

Check the rim tape that protects the tube from the spoke nipples. Make sure it's still in place and no spoke ends or burrs are projecting through. If a spoke projects through the nipple, file it down before reinstalling the tape.

You have the option of patching small holes or using a new inner tube. Large holes and holes located around the stem cannot be patched. I recommend using a new tube when possible, and saving patches for emergency road repairs.

There are two types of patches: self-adhesive and vulcanizing. Self-adhesive patches are easier to use and take up less space in your road kit. Vulcanizing patches, which come in a kit with a tube of glue, are more reliable.

To use the latter, rough up the area surrounding the hole with the abrasive found in the patch kit. This is usually sandpaper, but if it's a metal nutmeg-grater-like device, be careful about roughing up the tube *too* much. Clean the roughed-up area with alcohol and let it dry. To use a glue patch, apply the glue to the area, then affix the patch. Make sure that the edges are adhering, and hold the patch in place firmly

Once you replace the tube, work the tire back onto the rim. Be careful not to pinch the tube between the tire and the rim, and make sure the bead seats against the rim.

with your thumb for 30 to 60 seconds. To affix an adhesive patch, just peel off the backing and apply as above.

If you're replacing the tire as well as the tube, place the tire halfway onto the rim—with one bead all the way on and the other hanging off the side. If you're simply fixing a flat, that's exactly where you left the tire when you removed the tube. From this point, the procedure is the same whether you're using a new tube or a patch.

Inflate the tube just enough so it begins to take shape. Place the valve stem through the hole in the rim, then push the rest of the tube into the tire all the way around. Start working the tire back onto the rim, starting with both hands at the twelve o'clock position and pushing with your thumbs or the heels of your hands. Work to the left and right with both hands simultaneously until you get the tire bead all the way inside the rim. If there is too much air in the tube, it will get in the way, so let a little out if necessary. Do not use tire levers to force the tire back onto the rim; this can easily pinch and damage the tube. Check that the tube is not pinched between the tire and the rim, then inflate the tire to the pressure marked on the tire sidewall.

Tubular Repair and Replacement

It takes a little more time and effort to change a tubular tire. Remove the old tire from the rim by

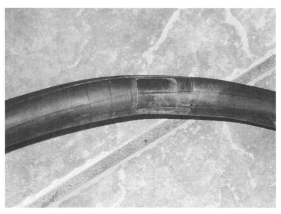

Once you find the hole in the tube, you can repair it with a glue patch or a self-adhesive patch.

hand, and remove any clumps of remaining glue from the rim with acetone and a plastic scraper. Acetone is hazardous, so wear goggles, a respirator, and plastic (not latex) gloves. Acetone will also remove the decals from your wheels, so apply the acetone carefully to avoid the decals. You do not want to remove all the glue from the rim, just the clumps of glue.

You can patch tubular tires, but patches are not as reliable as new tires. I advise against using patches on a race wheel: it's not worth risking a race to save money.

To patch a tubular tire, you need a special tubular patch kit, which will have almost everything required. Remove the tire from the rim, inflate it, and place it in water. Mark the tire where bubbles are coming out, then remove the base tape an inch above and below the mark. Cut the stitches that hold the tire together, using a seam cutter from a sewing kit. Pull a length of tube out of the tire and locate the hole. Repair the hole with the patch from the kit. Apply talcum powder to the tube, push it back into the tire casing, and sew up the tire with a needle and thread. If possible, use the original holes to stitch the tire back together. Once you finish sewing, glue the base tape back in place.

If you're installing a new tire, you should stretch it first. Place the wheel on the ground with

With the casing open, the tube is exposed and ready to be patched.

After patching the hole, sew the casing shut and glue the base tape back down.

Once you locate the hole in the tube of a tubeless tire, use a seam cutter to cut the thread and open the casing.

the valve-stem hole at the top. Place the stem through the hole and work the tire onto the rim, moving your hands downward on both sides at once. When you get near the bottom of the wheel, pick up the wheel and roll the last section of tire onto the rim. Inflate the tire to full pressure and let it sit a few minutes to a few days. The longer you let it stretch, the easier it will be to work with.

Next, deflate the tire and remove it from the rim. If the base tape on the inside of the tire has a PTFE (that is, Teflon) coating, abrade it gently with a file. This will give the glue something to grab onto. Inflating the tire until you can rotate the bottom side out will make this easier. Always

When placing the tubular tire back on the rim, start at the top and work your way to the bottom.

ensure that the rim is clean before you begin the gluing process. Any dust, dirt, or debris could hinder bonding of the glue. Apply a thin layer of glue to the rim and the base tape of the tire with an acid brush or a toothbrush. Make sure the glue extends all the way to the edge of the rim's mounting surface. Allow the glue to dry overnight. Repeat this process one to two more times. You can cut this process short, but you may run the risk of the

tire separating from the rim. Finally, apply another thin layer of glue to the rim and let it sit for 10 to 15 minutes. Mount the tire to the rim using the same method you used to stretch a new tire, being careful to keep the glue off the sides of the rim. (If you get glue on a metal rim, clean it with acetone. If you have composite rims, consult the manufacturer for cleaning procedures.) Inflate the tire and place the wheel in a truing stand. Rotate the tire and check that the treads are centered, moving the tire one way or the other as required. Allow the tire to sit for at least 24 hours before riding.

Pressure-sensitive glue strips, produced by Tufo tires, are less messy and easier and faster to use than regular glue, and I recommend them highly. Follow the same steps for removing the old tire and preparing the new one. Wrap a glue strip around the rim, then cut a hole for the valve stem.

Inflating the tubular off the rim causes it to turn inside out, making it easy to abrade the base tape with a file.

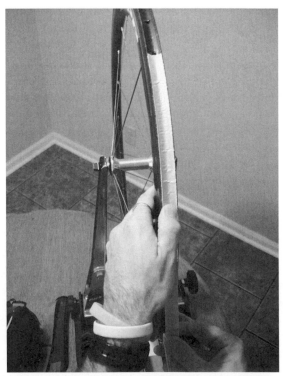

When applying a glue strip, make sure the rim is clean. A truing stand makes the job easier.

Leave the backing on the glue strip, but bend both ends of the backing so they will protrude between the tire and the rim. Install and center the tire on the rim, then pull out the ends of the backing, making sure the tire stays centered. Inflate the tire fully. You can begin riding immediately, but go easy for the first 5 to 10 minutes, avoiding sharp corners and steep descents until the glue sets. There has been some concern about glue strips causing carbon fiber to separate when removing the tire. If you have composite rims, check with the manufacturer before using the glue strips.

Wheels

Properly functioning wheels enhance performance and produce an enjoyable ride. A wheel that is out of true and rubbing the brakes, or a hub with pitted bearings, greatly increases the amount of energy required to pedal.

Hubs

Hubs are designed to rotate on bearings around the axle as the wheel spins. To minimize friction and wear, the bearings are packed with grease and enclosed from the elements. But over time the grease breaks down and moisture and dirt work into the bearings. Hubs need to be serviced every year or two, depending on the frequency and conditions of your rides.

Hubs also loosen with use, so you should check for play on a regular basis. Hold the frame steady with one hand and the wheel with the other. If you can move the wheel from side to side or hear any movement, you need to tighten the hub.

Although hub adjustment and overhaul are not difficult, the procedures vary greatly by make and model, putting them beyond the scope of this book. Consult the manufacturer for procedures and any special tools required.

Truing

When a wheel is out of true, you feel a noticeable wobble when riding, and it becomes impossible to adjust the brake calipers close enough for good braking performance. Wheel truing is not difficult; if you ride frequently you should consider investing in a truing stand. You can make passable truing adjustments with the wheel on the bike, but the process is not as accurate or convenient as when using a stand. The following description assumes that the wheel is in a stand.

Remove the wheel from the bike and place it in the truing stand using the quick-release mechanism. Spin the wheel and slowly move the truing calipers (or pointers) toward the rim. When you hear the caliper scrape the rim, stop and locate the spot where it makes contact. Loosen the spoke on that side of the wheel with a spoke wrench, and tighten the spoke on the opposite side. Make small adjustments, turning the spoke nipple one-quarter to one-half turn at a time. Counterclockwise tightens and clockwise loosens—if you view the spoke nipple from the end of the spoke, not from the inside of the rim. You might need to adjust several spokes on each side to straighten a wide section of rim that's out of true. Spin the wheel to see if it clears. If the caliper does not clear, repeat the process. If it does, tighten the calipers and repeat until the wheel is true. Keep in mind that wheels are never perfectly in true; a variation of 1 mm is usually acceptable.

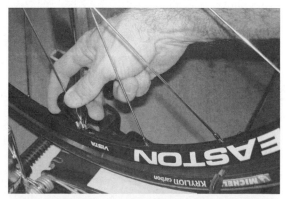

Make small adjustments when truing a wheel, turning the spoke nipple one-quarter to one-half turn at a time using a spoke wrench.

Changing the Rear Cassette

You will need to change the rear cassette from time to time to adapt to the terrain in which you are riding. Two special tools are required: a chain whip and a cassette tool.

Remove the wheel from the bike, extract the rear skewer, and lay the wheel flat with the cassette facing up. Wrap the chain whip around the cassette in the direction shown so you can apply clockwise pressure to the cassette. Place the cassette tool, which is splined and designed to fit into the lockring in the cassette and insert the quick-release skewer through it, tightening the quick release to hold the cassette tool in place. Hold the cassette tool with a big adjustable wrench, and unscrew (counterclockwise) the cassette lockring. It is normal to hear loud clicking as the lockring releases. Lift the cassette off the freehub. Remove the old grease from the hub body with a rag and apply new grease before you replace the cassette. The cassette is "keyed" specifically to one wide spline and can go on only one way. If the individual cogs are not bolted or riveted together, make sure that the side that is stamped with the number of teeth faces out when reinstalling the cogs on the freehub. Once the cassette is in place, use the cassette tool to retighten the lockring. When you're finished, there should be no play between the cogs.

Wrap the chain whip around the cassette so it holds the cassette in place.

With one hand, hold the cassette in place with the chain whip. With the other hand, loosen the cassette lockring, using a large wrench placed on the cassette tool.

Crankset

Removing a crankset is easy if you have the right tools. There are three basic methods to remove a crankset, determined by its style.

The first method, used mainly on older bikes, involves a crank puller designed for your crank. Begin by placing the chain on the large chainring. It may be necessary to apply a large amount of

To remove the cassette, first remove the skewer.

With a screwdriver, remove the dust cover from the crank arm to expose the crank-arm bolt.

force to the wrench. If your hand slips, the chain will protect it from the chainring's teeth. Pry or screw out the dust cover and back out the crank bolt with a socket. Make sure the push pin is backed all the way out in the crank puller, then screw the crank puller into the crank arm by hand. Turn the handle clockwise on the crank puller; as it begins to tighten, it will bear against the spindle

After removing the crank-arm bolt, back the crank arm off the spindle using a crank puller.

and push off the crank arm. Follow the same procedure for the other side.

To reinstall the cranks, begin by cleaning the bottom-bracket spindle. Splined spindles should be greased; square tapered spindles should be left dry. With square tapered spindles, align the crank arms at 180 degrees from each other. If the spindle is splined, make sure the splines are aligned correctly between the spindle and the crank arm, or you may ruin both. On keyed spindles (Shimano OctaLink or the ISIS standard drive), one spline is larger than the rest; make sure this spline lines up correctly with the appropriate notch in the crank. Apply grease to the bolts, and tighten the crank arms with a torque wrench. Lastly, replace the dust cap.

The next method involves cranksets with self-extracting bolts. This type of crankset has a dust cover with a hole in the center to allow a

Some cranksets have self-extracting bolts and don't require a crank puller.

Use a pin spanner to remove the dust covers before reinstalling the crank arms.

After loosening the crank-arm bolts, remove the crank-arm retention cap.

hex wrench access to the crank-arm bolt. Insert the hex wrench and loosen the crank bolt. As the bolt loosens it presses against the dust cover and backs off the crank arm.

For installation, remove the dust covers from both crank arms using a pin spanner. Remove the crank-arm bolts. Clean and lube the threads on the crank arms, the dust covers, and the crank-arm bolts. Line up the crank arms and tighten the crank-arm bolts, then reinstall the dust covers.

Most newer bikes have integrated cranksets with the spindle attached to the drive-side crank arm

instead of the bottom bracket. This type is the easiest to remove and install. Loosen but do not remove the clamp bolts on the left crank arm. Remove the crank-arm retention cap and pull off the left crank arm. Next, slide off the drive-side crank arm.

drive-side crank
arm and axle

WRENCH\FORCE

Once the nondrive crank arm is removed, slide the drive-side crank arm and axle free from the bottom bracket.

Loosen the clamp bolts on the nondrive side.

Clean and lubricate the spindle prior to reinstallation. Take the drive-side crank arm and slide the spindle through the bottom bracket until it bottoms out. The left crank arm is keyed so it goes on only one way. Slide on the left crank arm and fasten it in place with the retention cap, turning the cap only hand tight or with a torque wrench if specified. Tighten the clamp bolts on the crank arm by alternating between the two bolts.

Bottom Bracket

There are different types of bottom brackets, and we will look at only the two main types: cartridge style and outboard bearing bottom brackets. Both types of bottom brackets are manufactured with either English or Italian threads. English-threaded bottom brackets are reverse threaded on the drive side, so you must turn the bottom-bracket cup clockwise to loosen. Italian-threaded bottom brackets are "normal" threaded on both sides. If you have a proprietary bottom bracket, contact the manufacturer for detailed maintenance instructions. You will need a bottom-bracket tool designed for your specific bottom bracket.

Cartridge-style bottom brackets are manufactured with either splined or tapered spindles. To remove a cartridge-style bottom bracket, first remove the crankset. Next, remove the bottom bracket by loosening and removing the right side first. Next, remove the left-side bottom-bracket cup. Clean and grease both the bottom bracket and the shell.

The bottom-bracket cups are marked *right* and *left*. Insert the left cup halfway, then insert the right side and tighten it. Return to the left side and finish tightening the left cup. Check that the spindle rolls smoothly, then reinstall the crankset.

Outboard bearing bottom brackets do not have a spindle and are designed to accept the spindle on integrated cranksets. Removal and installation follow the same procedures as cartridge bottom brackets.

There are three basic styles of bottom brackets—from left to right: outboard bearing, cartridge-style splined, and cartridge-style tapered.

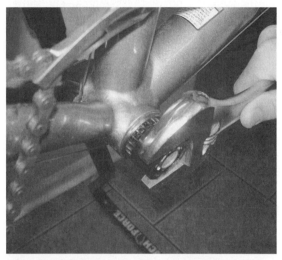

With a cartridge-style bottom bracket, remove the bottom bracket by loosening and removing the right side first.

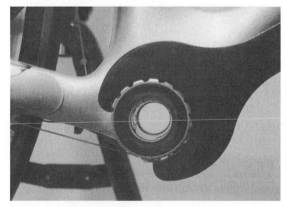

Bottom-bracket tools are specific to each type of bottom bracket. This is an outboard bearing bottom bracket.

Headset

Keeping the headset bearings clean and lubed prolongs their life. Due to the different styles of headsets and the specialized equipment necessary to remove the cups, service and inspection are covered here, but not removal and installation. When servicing your headset, pay close attention to where each part goes as you remove it.

To service the headset you must first remove the stem. Start by completely removing the top cap and bolt, loosening the stem bolts, and pulling out the stem. Assuming that the brake and shifter cables are still installed in the levers, place a rag on the top tube to protect against scratching the finish when you rest the stem and handlebars on the top tube. Push the fork down 1 to 2 inches, then push it back up. The compression washer and cover should come back up with it; remove them from the fork, then pull out the fork. If the fork is stuck, tap it out with a rubber mallet, or place a block of wood on top of the steerer tube and tap it out with a hammer, using caution if the fork has a carbon fiber steerer tube. Inspect the upper and lower bearings for wear. (If the bearings are pitted, the

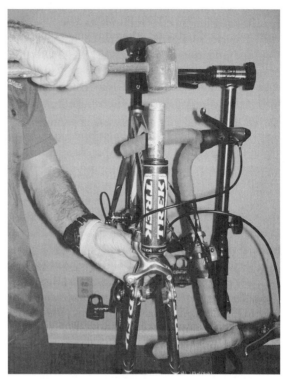

Remove the fork by gently tapping on the steerer tube with a rubber mallet.

To remove the stem, remove the top cap and loosen the stem bolts.

headset must be replaced.) Clean the old bearings with degreaser and allow them to dry.

To reinstall, repack the bearings with grease. Place the lower bearings and seal on the fork and insert the fork back through the head tube. Place the upper bearings, compression ring, and top cover on the top of the head tube, then replace the spacers and the stem. The top of the steerer tube should be just slightly below the top of the stem. Then replace the top cap and bolt.

It is important to understand how these parts interact. Although the top cap pulls up on the star nut or compression plug inside the steerer tube, you still need a gap between the top of the steerer tube and the stem so that pressure from the top cap is applied to the stem. In turn, pressure from the stem is applied to the spacers, down through the bearing races and to the bearings. Tighten the

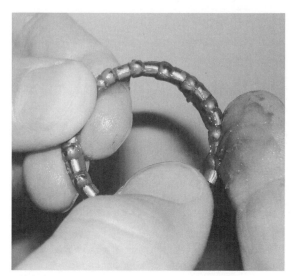

After cleaning the headset bearings, pack them with grease before replacing.

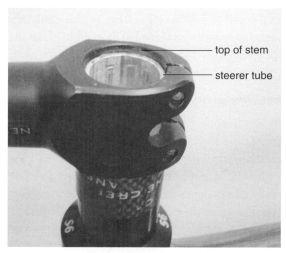

— top of stem

— steerer tube

There should be a slight gap between the top of the stem and the top of the steerer tube.

top bolt until it feels snug. You want the top cap tight enough to hold the fork in place with no play but loose enough to allow the handlebars and fork to steer smoothly. Next, ensure that the stem is straight, then tighten the bolts on the stem.

Check that you have the top cap tightened an appropriate amount. The handlebars should rotate from side to side smoothly and easily but with no play whatsoever. If necessary, loosen the bolts on the stem, then back off or tighten the top-cap bolt. Retighten the stem bolts and test again.

Handlebars

Inspect the handlebars on a regular basis for corrosion or damage and replace them at the first sign of problems. Although extremely light aluminum bars are nice, they fatigue faster than thicker, heavier bars. Most sources recommend replacing your bars every one to four years, or after any crash.

Bar Tape

Change the bar tape regularly. Bar tape soaks up sweat, which promotes the growth of bacteria and mold. Sweat also corrodes the metal under the bar tape, and you need to remove the tape to inspect for corrosion and cracks.

Remove the end caps, then unwrap the bar tape from the top down. Although you will install new end caps, keep the old ones to replace lost caps down the road. Remove the short pieces of tape directly below the shift/brake levers, then clean and inspect the handlebars (see photos next page).

Peel back the rubber hoods on the levers, then replace the pieces of tape below the levers. Start wrapping the tape from the end of the handlebars, leaving enough extending over the end to be tucked into the bar later. Begin wrapping at an angle so the tape overlaps itself by one-third of its width on each turn, keeping it tight and rolling directly from the roll around the bars as you go. If the tape has a peel-and-stick backing, remove it as you wrap. Work your way up the bars and around the lever. Push the hoods back down to ensure that the bars are covered by the hoods or the bar tape. When you reach the point where you wish to end, cut the bar tape at an angle so it ends evenly. Secure the cut end with the tape provided or with electrical tape. I prefer electrical tape: it seems to hold better. Finish by installing the new end plugs.

Peel back the hoods on the levers and replace the short pieces of bar tape under the hoods.

To loosen the pedal, turn the pedal wrench toward the back of the bike; to tighten the pedal, turn the wrench toward the front.

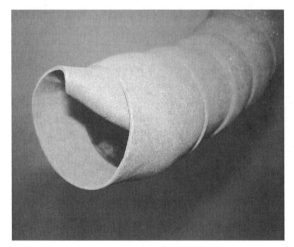

Leave enough tape protruding beyond the bar end so it can be tucked inside and held in place with the end cap.

Changing Pedals

The left pedal is reverse threaded; the right one is normal. To keep it simple, remember that turning the wrench to the back of the bike loosens the pedal; turning it to the front tightens it; this is true on both sides. Most pedals require a pedal wrench, although some newer pedals use a hex wrench on the pedal axle. After removing the pedals, wipe the threads clean and apply fresh grease. During installation, tighten the pedals by

hand as far as possible to prevent cross threading. The pedal should go on smoothly. If it does not, you may have cross threaded or need to clean the threads. Finish tightening the pedal using a pedal wrench.

Seat/Post

Before removing the seat post, mark it with electrical tape so you can easily replace it at the correct height. Loosen the clamp bolt and pull the post free. When working with a carbon post, do not rotate the post back and forth while removing; this can score the carbon and weaken the post.

When installing a metal post into a metal seat tube, always apply grease. This prevents the post from seizing in the seat tube and helps keep moisture out of the frame. Never apply grease if the post or the seat tube is made of carbon fiber. Use a torque wrench and the manufacturer's recommended torque to tighten the clamp bolt, and beware of overtightening, especially when using a carbon post. Seat posts are marked with an insertion limit line. If the limit line is showing, the post is too high and could break. Insert the post farther into the tube, or replace the post with a longer one.

REPAIRS ON THE ROAD

"Mechanicals" on the road are inevitable. It's essential to know how to repair the most common problems, if only to keep from having to hike many miles back home several times each season. This section addresses most breakdowns and is designed to get you rolling again if you experience one.

Road Tools and Spares

To avoid carrying excess weight, you need tools designed specifically for repairs on the go. Most cyclists carry these in an under-the-seat pouch. Your kit should include the following:

- Small multi-tool. These include most hex wrenches you'll need, plus a chain tool.
- One to three tire levers. The less skilled you are, the more levers you'll need.
- Spare inner tube *and* a patch kit. Murphy's Law says that if you flat once, you'll flat again. If you're riding tubulars, take a spare tire with dried glue on the base tape.
- Master link for the chain, or an extra chain pin. I prefer a master link, which works even if a link is broken; not so a spare pin.
- Spoke wrench for minor wheel truing.
- Tire pump.

You have three basic choices when choosing a pump. A frame pump allows you to inflate your tires to high pressure, but it is relatively heavy and, being so long, it must be mounted on brackets beneath the top tube. A mini pump is lightweight and fits into an under-the-seat pouch or a jersey pocket, but achieving high psi with it is difficult. A carbon dioxide (CO_2) pump, which uses a compressed-CO_2 cartridge, is lightweight, fast, and small enough to fit into a jersey pocket, but you need a new cartridge for each use. If you flat more than once, this could be a problem.

Shifting Problems

Front derailleurs are usually less troublesome than rear derailleurs, but both may need adjustment on the road. If you're having difficulties moving to a larger chainring or a larger cog in the back, adjust the appropriate barrel adjuster on the down tube to increase the cable tension. If you're having trouble going to a smaller chainring or cog, decrease the tension. You can make these adjustments without stopping. If this does not correct the problem, pull over and make adjustments using the barrel adjuster located on the derailleur, as described earlier.

If the chain is being thrown off the chainrings, the limit screws are not properly adjusted.

Be prepared if you're stranded by having a well-stocked road kit.

When riding, use the barrel adjusters on the down tube to make minor adjustments to shifting.

Normally, you would pull over and manually replace the chain, but during a race you may be able to reengage the chain without stopping if it is not lodged. If the chain is thrown while you're moving to the smaller chainring, stop pedaling and adjust the front derailleur as if you were shifting to the large chainring. Resume pedaling slowly; the chain should be picked up by the small chainring, at which point you can resume pedaling normally. If the chain is thrown to the outside, simply shift to the smaller gear while pedaling slowly forward; the chain should reset itself. This procedure does have the potential to damage components and the frame, so if you're not racing, don't risk it. Pull over to manually set the chain.

Tire Repairs

One of the most common problems you will experience on the road is a flat. During a supported race you do not have to fix a flat; you will be handed a whole new wheel for a quick change. Everyday riding, however, requires fixing your own flats. I recommend practicing field repair of flats in the comfort of your home before you need to do it on the road.

Move a safe distance off the road if possible. If you must make a repair on a narrow shoulder, face the oncoming traffic so you can move quickly if necessary. Stabilize the valve stem when using a hand pump; moving it back and forth with each stroke may cause the stem to tear at its base.

Chain Repairs

Breaking a chain can be scary. It usually occurs when a large amount of force is placed on the pedals during sprinting or climbing. All of a sudden the chain snaps; there is no resistance on the pedal, you fly forward, and your heart jumps into your throat. Hopefully both tires will stay rubber side down.

Most of the time the break will be simple, with only one or two links damaged. Remove any damaged links, reroute the chain, and connect the two ends with the master link from your tool kit. Losing some links from the chain when it breaks is possible although uncommon. Before you connect the chain, make sure you have the entire length.

When you get home, inspect the chain to see whether it is salvageable; if the chain is fairly new, look for any damaged links. (If the chain is old, don't even bother to inspect it; just buy a new one.) In 90 percent of the cases, the chain should be replaced. If in doubt, replace it.

Wheel Problems

Most wheel deformities are caused by hitting potholes, encountering debris in the road, running off the road, and crashing. Wheels can also come out of true due to insufficient spoke tension. Make a habit of regularly checking spoke tension before you ride.

If a wheel goes just slightly out of true while you're riding, you can probably just open the brake calipers a bit so the rim does not hit the brake pad, and wait until you get home to true the wheel. You can also use a spoke wrench to bring the wheel back into true, although it may be difficult to get the wheel in perfect alignment without a truing stand.

If a spoke breaks, tape it to or wrap it around an adjacent spoke so it does not hit the fork or frame as the wheel rotates. If you're riding a race wheel with a low spoke count, however, you may not be able to ride with a broken spoke.

If you're not racing, avoid high speeds when riding a wheel that is out of true or missing a spoke. Travel back to your starting point by the shortest route at a leisurely pace. If you doubt the stability of the wheel, call someone to pick you up or bring you a spare wheel.

DURA-ACE

PART II
riding and racing

riding skills

This chapter covers the skills necessary to become a competent cyclist—basic skills that are important for performance and safety. You will learn proper pedaling, gear-shifting, and braking techniques as well as how to position your body for efficiency and comfort and how to handle your bike in a variety of situations. Racing-specific skills are covered in Chapter 8.

POSTURE/POSITION

Your upper body position on the bike should be based on comfort and aerodynamics. Most riders find it comfortable to keep their hands on the top of the handlebars or the hoods. This results in an upright posture that creates a great deal of wind resistance, which is OK when aerodynamics are not important, such as drafting, climbing, or on easy rides with no training objectives. When riding in the draft of other cyclists, keep your hands on the hoods and not on the top bar so they remain near the brake levers.

When riding unsheltered and when time matters, you should move your hands to the drops for improved aerodynamics. Aero bars are used in time trials to put the rider in an optimal aerodynamic position. Aero bars are designed specifically for time trials; you should not go into the aero position when drafting or are otherwise in close proximity to other riders because the bars position your hands too far from the brake levers for quick braking response.

Aerodynamics

To appreciate how position affects aerodynamics and performance, try the following experiment when the wind is blowing between 10 and 15 mph. Sitting as tall in the saddle as you can, ride directly into the wind for 5 to 10 minutes. Pay attention to your speed and your heart rate, using a cycling computer and a heart-rate monitor, and to your perceived effort. Then get as low as possible into the drops and ride for another 5 to 10 minutes, keeping your heart rate and perceived effort the same. You will notice a significant increase in speed.

Much research has been done on the aerodynamics of cycling, and professional cyclists spend a lot of time in wind tunnels looking to improve performance. Cyclists can reduce their time-trial times by minutes by using aero equipment and riding with aero bars in an aerodynamic position.

Turbulence (or drag) is generated as air travels over the surface of an object. Turbulence creates an area of low pressure behind the object and an area of high pressure in front of it. Air moves from an area of high pressure to an area of low pressure, creating force against the leading edge. The faster an object moves, the greater the drag, and its effect are much greater on a cyclist traveling at 25 mph than on one traveling at 15 mph.

There are two main types of drag in effect during cycling. The first is surface drag. The rougher a surface and the larger the surface area, the greater the

These three photos demonstrate how the rider reduces his frontal surface exposed to the wind when he goes from riding upright, to riding into the drops (top right), and by using aero bars (bottom).

turbulence. Cycling jerseys and shorts are therefore made mostly of smooth materials and fit the body tightly. Time-trial riders wear special "skin suits," which are cut to fit without wrinkles or gaps when the rider is in an aero posture. Some companies use dimpled material on the arms of jerseys to improve aerodynamics. The dimples cause a specific type of turbulence that causes the boundary layer to "stick" closer to the arm and reduce the turbulence at the trailing edge.

Form drag deals with the shape of an object. A traditional round frame tube creates a large amount of turbulence at its trailing edge, whereas on an aerodynamic frame air flows more smoothly around the foil-shaped or bladed tubing (see illustration next page). This reduces the pressure differential between the leading and trailing edges, so the cyclist expends less energy overcoming turbulence.

Cyclists talk a lot about aerodynamic equipment, but the surface area of the rider is much greater than that of the bike. The cyclist's body accounts for 70 to 80 percent of the total drag of the bike and rider. Aero bars are used in time trials

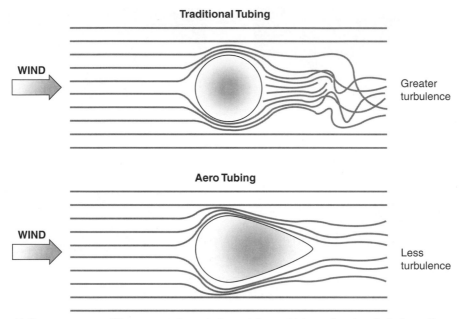

Air flows more smoothly over aerodynamic frame tubes, which produce less turbulence than traditional round frame tubes.

to reduce the frontal surface area of riders by making them adopt a streamlined posture, with the torso nearly horizontal and the arms pulled close together in the front. Moving from an upright position to an aero position with the use of aero bars decreases a rider's workload by about 9 to 10 percent. When riding a road bike without aero bars, you can reduce the frontal surface area by getting into the drops and assuming a low posture. Moving from an upright position with your hands on the hoods to a lower position with your hands on the drops will decrease your workload by about 5 to 6 percent.

PEDALING

Now that you're positioned on the bike, let's start pedaling. It's not as simple as just pushing the pedals, however. Proper pedaling mechanics, cadence, and gear selection all affect efficiency and performance.

Pedaling Mechanics

Coaches and cyclists often advise riders to "pedal in perfect circles." What does that mean? Cranksets are concentric within the bottom bracket, and crank arms do not change length, so the pedals always travel in a perfect circle. I prefer to tell cyclists to work on "pedaling smoothly," which more accurately describes the ideal pedal stroke.

Pedaling smoothly is neither easy nor intuitive because the direction in which you apply force to the pedal changes throughout the stroke. From the twelve o'clock position to about the three o'clock position, force is applied down and forward by the right leg. From three o'clock to six o'clock, it is down and back. From six o'clock to about nine o'clock, the force is up and back, and from nine o'clock to twelve o'clock, it is up and forward. Due to the muscles involved, the angles of the joints, and a little help from gravity, more force is applied between the two o'clock and four o'clock positions than anywhere else in the stroke. The least amount of force is applied between nine o'clock and twelve o'clock. The total amount of applied force varies through the rotation of the crank.

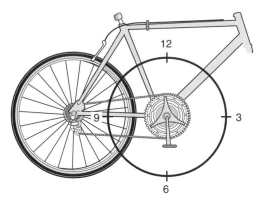

If the pedal stroke is pictured as a clock, the right leg applies its greatest power when it's pushing almost straight down (between two o'clock and four o'clock) and the least power when it's pulling up and forward (between nine o'clock and twelve o'clock).

Both legs must work together. As one leg pushes down, the opposite leg lifts. By pulling up between the six o'clock and twelve o'clock positions, you are not adding a noticeable amount of force, but you are decreasing the weight that the opposite leg must lift during its downstroke.

This may seem awkward at first. Your legs will oppose each other and your pedaling will be jerky and inefficient. With training, though, neuromuscular adaptations occur that will enable the leg muscles to fire in proper sequence. Your pedaling will become better synchronized, and your economy will greatly increase.

The best way to assess your pedaling economy is to ride on a set of trainers or rollers. If you are not pedaling smoothly, you will feel and hear the flywheel speed up with every downstroke. If you are pedaling smoothly, the flywheel will roll smoothly, with no noticeable lunges.

Cadence

The number of revolutions your pedals make in one minute is cadence. It is important to keep your cadence between 90 and 100 rpm. There are some exceptions to this rule (explained later).

A cadence of 90 to 100 rpm is far faster than most nonserious riders use, but it pays off in economy of energy expenditure. Assuming that you maintain the same speed over the ground, a lower cadence (70 to 80 rpm, for example) means that you are using a larger gear combination and putting more force into each pedal stroke. This requires the use of more intermediate- and fast-twitch muscle fibers, both of which produce more force but fatigue much more quickly than the slow-twitch fibers, which do more of the work at higher cadences. The trade-off needed to maintain the higher cadence is an increased aerobic requirement. (See Chapter 10 for details on muscle physiology.)

When the muscles in your legs contract, they push the blood through the veins and back toward the heart, helping the heart overcome gravity. It is theorized that at high cadences, more blood is pushed to the heart, which may result in an increase in stroke volume—the amount of blood expelled from the heart and sent out through the body on each beat—thus supplying more oxygen-rich blood for increased aerobic performance.

Because of the increased aerobic requirements associated with higher cadence, it may feel as though you are working harder. It will take about two weeks of riding for your body to adapt. Once you adapt, you will become more comfortable and will be riding more economically, which will translate into improved performance.

The exceptions mentioned earlier deal with time trials, sprints, and climbing. To be competitive in a time trial, it is necessary to produce maximum sustainable power. The best way to do this is by increasing cadence to around or above 100 rpm, not by selecting a higher gear ratio. Sprinting during attacks (a swift acceleration designed to separate a rider from the pack), responding to attacks, and sprinting for the finish line follow the same basic principle.

Climbing requires a different approach. On long climbs, good riders tend to drop their cadence to around 70 rpm. Maintaining a high cadence while climbing may tax the aerobic system too much and require dropping to a lower cadence. Climbing cadence will vary with the rider. The heavier the rider, the greater the power required to overcome gravity and climb at a given speed. The greater the cyclists' aerobic capacity, the higher their cadence may be. Those with lower cadences will be pushing larger gears to keep the same pace, and in most cases they will fatigue much faster.

Monitoring cadence will help improve your performance. If you are having trouble maintaining a certain speed at your desired cadence on flat terrain, change the gear ratio, as described in the next section.

In the past, cyclists had to count revolutions per minute to monitor cadence. Now, cycling computers with a cadence function are available for less than $40—well worth it if you care about performance.

Gear Selection: Cranksets and Cassettes

Cranksets and rear cassettes are designated by their number of teeth. A 53/39 crankset has chainrings with 53 and 39 teeth each. An 11–21 cassette has 11 teeth on its smallest cog and 21 on its largest. Gear combinations are expressed as the product of the two—53 × 11, for example.

The larger the chainring, the farther you go per pedal stroke and the harder it is to pedal. It's the opposite on the rear cassette; the larger the cog on the cassette, the shorter the distance you travel per stroke and the easier it is to pedal. A 53 × 11 combination therefore produces the fastest speed per pedal revolution, but it also requires the largest power output. A 39 × 21 combination is easy to pedal, but slower.

Gear combinations are determined by the number of teeth on the chainring and the number of teeth on the cassette.

Gear development describes the distance the bike travels as a function of gear ratio and wheel size. The bike's speed, therefore, is a function of gear development and cadence. The formulas for determining gear development and speed are as follows:

Step 1.
Gear development (in.) = (chainring ÷ cog) x wheel size (in.) x 3.14

Step 2.
Gear development (ft.) = gear development (in.) ÷ 12

Step 3.
Speed (mph) = gear development (ft.) x rpm × 0.0114

Example:
Scenario: Gear ratio of 53 × 11, cadence of 90 rpm

Step 1.
Gear development (in.) = (53 ÷ 11) × 26.5 × 3.14 = 400.92 in.

Step 2.
Gear development (ft.) = 400.92 ÷ 12 = 33.41 ft.

Step 3.
Speed = 33.41 × 90 × 0.0114 = 34.28 mph

The table on the next page shows the speed obtained using different gear ratios while pedaling at 90 rpm. Here's how to determine the chainring and cassette combinations that best suit your needs:

1. Find the number of teeth on the chainrings and rear-cassette cogs you are using or thinking of buying. The number is usually stamped on them. If you can't locate the numbers, just count the teeth. Mark the first tooth with a marker so you know where you started.

2. Photocopy the table and highlight the appropriate chainrings and cassette cogs, along with the corresponding speeds. This will allow you to compare gear ratios between the various combinations.

3. Create your own table using the formulas above to accommodate different cadences, wheel diameters, or chainring and cassette cog sizes.

SPEED AS A FUNCTION OF GEAR COMBINATION

(Speed in miles per hour. Based on a 700C wheel and a cadence of 90 rpm.)

		REAR CASSETTE COG													
CHAINRING		27	25	24	23	21	20	19	18	17	16	15	14	13	12	11
	30	7.90	8.54	8.89	9.28	10.16	10.67	11.23	11.86	12.55	13.34	14.23	15.25	16.42	(17.73)	(19.40)
	34	8.96	9.68	10.07	10.32	11.52	12.09	12.73	13.44	14.23	15.12	16.13	17.78	18.61	(20.15)	(22.00)
	36	9.49	10.24	10.67	11.14	12.20	12.80	13.48	14.23	15.07	16.01	17.07	18.79	19.70	(21.34)	(23.28)
	39	10.27	11.10	11.56	12.06	13.21	13.87	14.60	15.41	16.32	17.34	18.50	19.82	21.34	(23.12)	(25.22)
	42	11.07	11.95	12.45	12.99	14.23	14.94	15.73	16.60	17.58	18.68	19.97	21.34	22.99	(24.90)	(27.16)
	50	(13.17)	(14.23)	(14.82)	(15.47)	(16.94)	17.79	18.72	19.76	20.92	22.23	23.71	25.41	27.36	29.64	32.34
	52	(13.70)	(14.80)	(15.41)	(16.08)	(17.62)	18.08	19.47	20.55	21.76	23.12	24.66	26.43	28.46	30.83	33.63
	53	(13.97)	(15.08)	(15.71)	(16.39)	(17.96)	18.85	19.85	20.95	22.18	23.57	25.14	26.93	29.01	31.42	34.28

(Gear combinations in parentheses are not recommended due to cross chaining.)

The exact method of shifting is determined by the type of shift levers on your bike. The differences between each company's shift levers are discussed in Chapter 2. Through practice you will develop a feel for your specific type of lever. However, the concepts of shifting remain the same regardless of the shift system you use.

Never shift unless pedaling; it puts your chain and derailleur in a bind that could damage the drivetrain when you apply pressure to the pedals. This is especially true if you shift over more than one cog at a time.

Avoid *cross chaining* when choosing a gear combination. Cross chaining occurs when you're in the large ring in the front and the larger cogs in the back, and when you're in the small ring in the front and the smaller cogs in the back. Either way puts too much of an angle on the chain and can lead to damaged or broken links. Gear combinations to avoid, due to cross chaining, are shown in parentheses in the table on page 71.

By selecting gear combinations appropriately, it is possible to produce the same speed on either the large or small chainring. For example, at 90 rpm a 39×14 combination will produce a speed of 19.82 mph, and a 52×19 combination will produce a speed of 19.47 mph—in other words, pretty darn close. The combination you decide to use will be dependent on the type of riding you're doing. If you're racing, using the large chainring will make it easier to respond to any accelerations from the group. On a recovery day, you should be in the small chainring. Another consideration is the average speed you intend to maintain. For speeds of 20 mph or greater, use the large chainring; below 20 mph, use the small one.

There will be times when you'll need to shift both front and back gears. Don't shift both simultaneously or the chain may drop off the chainring. When you begin a climb, you'll want to drop from a difficult gear combination to an easier combination. To avoid losing too much momentum, start by shifting down two or three gears (smaller gears) in the back, then immediately shift from the large to the small chainring. If you shift to the small chainring first, you'll lose momentum as you shift the rear to the appropriate cog.

Once you top the hill and begin to descend, move back to the large chainring. If you move to the large ring in the front without adjusting the back, you may be overgeared and it may be difficult to pedal. To prevent this, shift up one or two cogs (larger cogs) on the back immediately before shifting to the large ring.

Always attempt to anticipate shifting requirements. When traveling into a curve that requires you to slow, shift to easier gears as you enter the curve. Otherwise you may be overgeared as you come out of the curve. If you can pedal through the curve, adjust based on feel. Gear down as you come to a stop as well, so you are not overgeared when you take off.

BRAKING

Braking is not as complicated a topic as pedaling, but it too calls for good technique.

Although the front brake has considerably more stopping power than the rear brake, you don't want to slam on the front brake while going downhill at thirty-five miles per hour. This might fulfill your childhood dream of flying, but you will eventually land on the hard, unforgiving asphalt. Through practice and "feel," you will learn to feather both brakes with an appropriate amount of force to stop quickly and smoothly.

When braking hard or on a downhill, shift your weight to the back of the bike. This comes so naturally that many cyclists shift back without even realizing what they're doing. Not only does this decrease your risk of flying over the handlebars, but also it shifts weight to the rear wheel, giving it more traction and making the rear brake more effective.

No matter how quickly you need to stop, don't lock up the brakes. If the wheels aren't spinning, you have no steering control. Maximum braking effectiveness occurs just before the point of lockup, when the wheels are turning slowly and the tires are still gripping the road surface.

If you change brakes or wheels, you must adjust to a new "feel" when braking. When I built my first time-trial bike, I installed single-pivot brakes to save weight. Going down a steep hill during my first ride on the new bike, I started braking where I usually did before the stop sign, but the bike did not slow down at the rate that I expected. In spite of panic pressure on the levers, the stop sign came and went before I finally came to a stop in the middle of the intersection. Luckily there was no traffic at that moment. I learned that the single-pivot brakes were not as strong as the double-pivot brakes on my road bike, so I knew that I had to start braking sooner.

Likewise, braking in wet conditions requires more time and distance than in dry conditions. Water interferes with the grip of the brake pads on the rims, and traction is reduced between the tires and the road. This makes it harder to lock up the brakes against the wheel, but easier to skid nonetheless.

STEERING

There are three common methods for taking curves and turns. The best method for most wide- and moderate-radius curves involves leaning the bike into the curve with the inside pedal up and your weight shifted to the outside pedal. Keep your center of gravity low to increase your stability. At higher speeds it's advisable to get into the drops to further lower your center of gravity. Keep your head up and focus on your path of travel through the turn. This method of steering does not involve any noticeable turning of the handlebars.

When making sharp or slow turns, rotate the handlebars in the direction you wish to travel, and do not lean. By keeping your weight centered over

There are three basic methods of steering; leaning the bike through a turn is the most common. (Charles Herskowitz, Toyota-United)

the contact points of the tires, you limit the risk of sliding, especially when there is water or debris on the road.

The last method, called countersteering, is used to change directions quickly—for example, to take a sharp turn at speed or to avoid an obstruction right in front of you. Begin by slightly twitching the handlebar in the direction opposite the one you want to go, but keep your weight centered over the bike. Let's say you're making a quick turn to the right. Twitch the bars to the left, and the bike will begin moving in that direction. If you don't lean, your body will continue moving straight ahead due to momentum. This will quickly place your body mass to the right of the contact point of the tires on the road, which will cause a quick lean to the right; the result is that the bike will travel in the intended direction. Practice this in a safe, traffic-free environment before attempting it at high speeds on the road.

Point of Focus

Have you ever swerved to miss something and ended up riding right at the edge of the road, then had a hard time not drifting into the roadside ditch? By focusing your attention on the ditch, you make it that much harder to avoid.

Your bike tends to travel where your vision is focused. The trick is to focus on where you want your bike to travel instead of where you don't want it to go. In this case, turn your attention back to the pavement and away from the ditch, and you'll almost certainly recover.

Looking over your shoulder to see what's behind you involves a lot of head-turning. Many cyclists drift a great deal when checking for overtaking cars, sometimes moving right into their path. As long as you're aware of that natural drift, you can train yourself to compensate for it. Another method is to look back underneath your arm, which limits the amount of head-turning. Its practicality depends upon your riding position and the length of your arms.

Affixing a mirror to your handlebars helps you keep an eye on the traffic behind you. This is not recommended for racing. Avoid using mirrors that attach to your helmet or glasses; both of these can interfere with your vision.

CORNERING

Cyclists who cannot hold their line while cornering put themselves and others at risk, whereas those who can will make up time on their rivals.

The bike's cornering limits are set primarily by the bike's geometry and the traction of the tires. These limits become clear only through practice. Always keep the outside pedal down while cornering. If the inside pedal is straight down, you risk clipping it on the road, which can lift a wheel and cause a crash. I have hit the ground on more than one occasion while attempting to pedal through a corner. The feeling of the bike skipping when the pedal hits the pavement makes your hair stand on

When cornering, it's important to keep the inside pedal up and to lean through the corner. (Charles Herskowitz, Toyota-United)

end. If this occurs, just do your best to get the bike under control.

Through practice and experience, you will learn your and your bike's cornering limits. As your confidence grows, you'll be surprised how far you can lean. The greater the speed maintained through a corner, the farther you will need to lean the bike. Keep your center of gravity low by placing your hands in the drops. Always brake before entering a curve. When you brake in a curve, your bike will attempt to go straight and you could lose control.

Practice cornering in a grassy field to give yourself a good idea of how far you can lean your bike over without going down. Keep in mind that traction on grass is less than on asphalt. This drill is designed for beginners to become accustomed to leaning through a curve. Once you're comfortable with this drill, move to a large parking lot that is free of obstacles and continue to practice cornering. Once you're comfortable in the parking lot, you're ready for the road.

There will be times when you'll need to pedal through a curve to maintain contact with the group. Through trial and error you'll be able to determine at which angles you can pedal and at which ones you cannot. Being able to accelerate through a curve will give you the opportunity to put distance between you and your opponents.

Riding beyond your ability has a tendency to produce two different outcomes, sometimes simultaneously. The first is that your riding will improve; the second is that you will crash. Learn from your mistakes as well as your successes. If you do not push your limits, you'll never know what you're capable of.

CLIMBING HILLS

Some people love to climb; others don't. The difference is usually based on whether or not they *can* climb.

Love it or not, climbing is a large part of cycling, and you should not avoid hills in training just because you don't like them. Train on climbs in order to improve. If you live in an area that doesn't have a lot of hills, find a long one and climb it repeatedly. The alternative is that hills will steal your energy and wreck your enjoyment on rides outside of your area, and you'll drop off the back of the pack in every race.

Those who have difficulty climbing are deficient in cardiovascular fitness, power-to-weight ratio, or both. The first problem area is simple to overcome: ride! The second will take a little more work. Power-to-weight ratio is simply your power

Learning to climb is a good way to increase your overall performance. (Barbara Dowd)

output at a given load in watts divided by your weight in kilograms. The higher the number, the better the rider. Power-to-weight ratio is discussed in detail in Chapter 11.

When climbing, place your hands on the hoods. This puts your back in a more upright position and your hands will be in the right place when the time comes to stand. Although many coaches recommend that you scoot back on your saddle when climbing, I don't think this is always appropriate. Your bottom will naturally move to the most efficient position on the saddle, and some riders find optimal power in their normal position.

Climbing out of the saddle demands increased energy, so find your rhythm and stay seated for most of the climb. There are times when it's necessary to stand, however: to initiate or respond to an attack; to alter position in order to relieve aching legs; or when the climb is steep enough to demand it.

When you climb out of the saddle, the bike will move back and forth as you pedal. This movement assists you in pedaling and moving the bike forward, but keep the movement small. Exaggerating it wastes energy.

When shifting from a seated position to standing while climbing, your revolutions per minute will drop and you'll need to go up one or two gears to maintain speed. A loss in momentum can interfere with your rhythm and cause you to slow down. When you stand, your weight shifts forward, changing the center of mass and causing a significant negative acceleration. To offset this loss of momentum, shift just before you stand and keep tension on the pedals as you stand.

ROAD CONDITIONS

One second of inattention to road conditions can be disastrous. When cornering, keep an eye out for potholes, puddles, uneven pavement, gravel, glass, dirt, and sand. When approaching a turn, choose a line that's free of debris. If that's not possible, take the turn slowly and carefully.

Wet roads change how a bike handles. It's helpful to become accustomed to these changes. (Charles Herskowitz, Toyota-United)

Cross railroad tracks at a 90-degree angle so your front wheel doesn't get caught in a groove. If the tracks do not cross the road at 90 degrees, slow down on the approach and angle the bike accordingly. To prevent a pinch flat or wheel damage, shift your weight to the back wheel, allowing the front to lightly cross the tracks. Once the front wheel crosses, shift your weight to the front and allow your back wheel to cross.

Rain changes the characteristics of the road surface. Running water can move mud, sand, and other debris onto the road. Lane-marking paint is slippery when wet, and rain can bring oil to the surface of a road. Decrease your speed and do not lean as far into turns. Assume that any standing water hides a pothole and avoid it.

RIDING IN TRAFFIC

We all grew up hearing "Don't play in the street. It isn't safe" from those who loved us, and "Go play in traffic" from those who didn't. I wish I could say otherwise, but road riding is inherently dangerous, and you need only read the newspaper for a few weeks to find numerous reports of cyclists hit by motor vehicles.

Bicycles are like any other road-legal vehicle under the law. Riders have the same rights and generally must follow the same rules. The main difference is that you must stay to the far right, giving other vehicles room to pass on your left. There are times, however, when you need to move from the right side of the road and interact more directly with traffic. If the lane is too narrow for cars to safely pass you, move to the left and claim your place in the lane to avoid being squeezed off the road. In preparation for a left-hand turn, move into the center of your lane or into the left-turn lane. When approaching a stop sign or a traffic light, move over and take your place in line with other traffic. This makes you more visible to cars and establishes your place in line through the intersection.

Do not ride alongside cars stopped at an intersection, and be cautious when passing cars parked on the side of the road. Watch for cars that may be leaving a parking place, and assume that any car door may open unexpectedly. Watch also for pedestrians who may step out from between parked cars. Moving slightly toward the center of the lane will reduce all of these dangers.

Many motorists don't realize that bikes are considered vehicles, and they're unsure how to interact with cyclists. Indicate your intentions clearly. Do not use the right-turn arm signal that you used when learning how to drive a car; few motorists understand it. Instead, extend your right arm and point right. If you are turning left, extend your left arm and point left. If you are merging with traffic, point to the gap you are moving into while making eye contact with the driver behind you.

Cyclists need to be predictable. When you approach an intersection and are not required to stop, do not stop. If it's your turn at a four-way stop, proceed. Drivers will know how to respond if you ride decisively when in traffic, do not hesitate, and move as though you are a vehicle.

RIDING IN A GROUP

A cyclist must be completely comfortable riding alone before attempting to ride in a peloton. If you cannot hold your line on your own, you will endanger yourself and those around you in a group.

Beginners usually lack the skill to ride comfortably in a group; if you try before you're truly ready, you may hear disparaging remarks from members of a club that you may be thinking of joining. Do not get discouraged or allow others to ruin your enjoyment. Stay out of the peloton until you're more confident. Ride more, get better, and try again.

For experienced riders, remember what it was like when you began riding. When new cyclists attend a group ride, welcome them and try to turn them into assets for your club. Rather than muttering about the newbies' skill level, take the time to teach them how to ride safely in a group.

Learning to ride safely in a group is extremely important. Cyclists must be confident in their bike-handling abilities before moving from solo riding to group riding. (Veronika Lenzi, Toyota-United)

RIDE LEVELS FOR A LARGE CLUB		
Group	**Average Speed (mph)**	**Level**
A	24+	Advanced
B	20–23	Advanced
C	18–20	Intermediate
D	16–18	Intermediate
E	<16	Beginner

Do not take beginners on an unfamiliar route, then drop them because they're riding too slowly. For each ride, designate a sweeper who will stay with the beginners, allow them to set a pace they can maintain, and be on hand to help with any problems. Rotate sweepers so one person doesn't get stuck with the job all the time. If the club is large enough, you'll have to ride sweep only a few times a year, which should not affect your training.

You can also designate "hard" and "easy" rides, which will help new riders find their own level and give them targets for improvement. A large club might have five levels, as shown above.

Smaller clubs may be able to field only two or three levels, but the principle is the same. Lower levels are not only for novices. This method allows experienced riders to choose a ride based on their training goal for that particular day.

Communication

The key when riding with other cyclists is communication. It is accomplished verbally, through hand signals, or a combination of both. When using verbal communication, make sure you are heard: shout! When signaling, make sure you can be seen. Always repeat signals up and down the line, so everyone receives the message.

Following are widely accepted protocols for common situations. If your club uses different protocols, go with them instead.

- Signal your intentions when approaching a turn. For a left-hand turn, point your left arm to the left. For a right-hand turn, point your right arm to the right.
- If you intend to slow down or stop, yell "slowing" or "braking." You can also signal by dropping your arm and pushing your hand to the rear, with the palm facing backward. I like yelling better because it allows you to keep both hands on the brakes.
- When you stand to climb or accelerate, your bike will decelerate momentarily. If the rider behind you is maintaining a constant speed, the gap between your back wheel and his or hers will close quickly. Also, while you're standing, your bike will shift from side to side, possibly endangering someone beside you. Yell "standing" so everyone knows what to expect.

When slowing for any reason, always signal the riders behind you by dropping your arm and pushing your hand back, with the palm facing toward the rear.

When approaching obstacles in the road, it's the lead rider's responsibility to point them out. The signal should be passed down the line by the other riders.

Drafting behind other cyclists can reduce your workload by 30 to 40 percent.

- The lead riders are responsible for pointing at obstacles such as potholes, uneven pavement, or debris on the road. This signal is relayed down the group to the last cyclist in line. If the lead riders swerve around an obstacle without signaling, somewhere down the line a cyclist will hit it.
- When a car is coming up from behind, yell "car back." When a car is coming from ahead, yell "car up."

Drafting

Riding in the area of low pressure that occurs behind a rider reduces drag, so the workload is reduced 30 to 40 percent compared to riding alone. For any performance-oriented rider, drafting is an important skill.

For the draft to work, you have to ride 4 to 12 inches behind the wheel of the rider in front of you. This is a potentially precarious situation. You need to pay attention to the wheel in front of you, but not to the exclusion of the road ahead and the riders around you. It is essential to ride smoothly and predictably, holding a steady line and avoiding swerving and frequent speed changes. If you begin to overtake the rider in front of you, do not apply the brakes. Instead slip into the wind, slow your cadence, or stop pedaling. Making drastic changes in speed creates a yo-yo effect, and you and all the cyclists behind you will have to work harder than necessary.

If you notice riders who cannot hold a line, do not complain under your breath. They may not realize the problem. Instead, politely explain the problem and offer tips on how to develop the skill.

When riding in a crosswind, the area of low pressure is not directly behind the rider. If the wind is coming from the right, drift to the left of the cyclist in front of you until you feel the wind resistance decrease. If it is coming from the left, do the opposite.

weather and altitude

Weather has a huge influence on the cycling experience. It's summer as I'm writing this in Alabama and the temperature exceeds 100° F almost daily. However, I can ride in comfort throughout the winter. If you live in higher latitudes, you may experience more pleasant summers than I, but your winters may be brutal.

There are various ways to make cycling in adverse conditions tolerable, if not always comfortable. But it's more than just a matter of comfort: the riding environment also affects performance and can have serious implications for your health.

RIDING IN THE HEAT

The human body performs best when its core temperature stays within a small range anchored around 98.6° F; it becomes stressed even a few degrees outside that range. When we exercise, our bodies produce heat as a metabolic by-product. Typically 30 to 40 percent of the energy we produce generates movement, and 60 to 70 percent is dissipated as heat. Should anything interfere with the dissipation of heat, our core body temperature will increase, with potentially serious health consequences.

Due to increased temperatures during exercise, blood flow to the skin is greatly increased to aid in cooling the core. Plasma, the fluid part of the blood, is an ideal medium for heat transfer due

Take precautions when riding in a hot environment. Failure to do so can have severe health consequences. (Barbara Dowd)

to its high water content. The blood absorbs heat from the body's core and carries it via capillaries to the periphery of our bodies, where the heat dissipates at the skin. The blood, now cooled, then returns to cool the core and absorbs more heat to be carried back to the skin. For this process to work, the skin must remain at a lower temperature than the core.

The body relies on two main strategies to achieve this optimum core temperature: evaporation and convection. When you exercise you sweat, which keeps your core temperature at a manageable level. The more heat that is generated through metabolism and the hotter the environment, the more you sweat. For sweat to cool the body, it must evaporate on the skin. Any sweat that rolls off the body rather than evaporating is wasted.

Relative humidity has a large effect on sweat evaporation. (Relative humidity is a measure of the percentage of air that is saturated with moisture.) If the relative humidity is 40 percent, the air can absorb 60 percent more moisture. If the relative humidity is 90 percent, evaporation will be slow and much of the sweat will roll off the body. Cycling aids evaporation by continually moving air that is not completely saturated over the skin.

Convection also plays an important role in keeping a healthy core temperature. The act of air passing over the cyclist allows for heat dissipation through transfer from the rider to the air. The heat from the body transfers to the boundary layer of air that surrounds it. When cycling, this boundary layer is continually being replaced with cooler air, allowing for greater heat transfer from the body to the environment.

Dehydration has a strong negative effect on the body's ability to cool itself. A cyclist's body temperature is negatively affected by a fluid loss that is equal to about 2 percent of body weight. (This assumes that the cyclist was fully hydrated at the start of the ride.) Many cyclists who ride in hot, humid conditions stay chronically dehydrated.

To make a long and complicated story short, sweat is basically filtered plasma. If you sweat a lot and don't replace the liquid through an adequate hydration program, you will experience a significant drop in plasma volume, meaning less fluid available for heat exchange. There will also be a drop in blood pressure due to a decrease in whole blood volume, which will further reduce the circulation of blood flowing to the skin to promote cooling. The core temperature will then increase significantly. Dehydration can also lead to an electrolyte imbalance, which can cause mental confusion and cardiovascular complications.

Heat-Related Illnesses

If left untreated, heat-related illnesses can lead to serious complications or death. It is imperative to know the symptoms of the two main categories of heat-related illness: heat exhaustion and heatstroke. Heatstroke is a life-threatening condition that must be treated immediately. Some of the symptoms of heat exhaustion, which are listed below, cross over from one category to the other, and heat exhaustion can quickly turn into heatstroke.

Heat Exhaustion
- headache
- tingling sensation in the skin
- chills
- feeling of weakness
- dizziness
- pale, moist skin
- rapid, weak pulse

Heatstroke
- core temperature greater than or equal to 104° F
- headache
- chills (This may occur if the body's thermoregulatory system is askew and behaves as though the body is cold. This will cause the body to attempt to further raise the temperature instead of cooling itself.)
- confusion
- hot, dry reddish skin
- cessation of sweating
- rapid, strong pulse

If a heat-related illness is suspected, stop training and move to a cool environment. Do not attempt to keep pushing on: your condition will only get worse. Use wet towels, ice, or a cold shower or bath to reduce body temperature. Drink plenty of water to restore proper hydration levels. If you cannot get your core temperature down or if it continues to rise, seek medical attention immediately. If heatstroke is suspected, go straight to the emergency room.

Prevention of (and Acclimatization to) Heat Stress

If possible, avoid riding in the hottest part of the day (usually between noon and 3 P.M.). Beat the heat by riding as early in the morning as possible. This will take dedication on your part, but it beats frying like an egg.

Acclimatization is the body's process of adapting to heat stress. A lack of acclimatization plays a key role in many heat-related illnesses. It takes about ten days of riding in the heat to become fully acclimatized. Do not ride hard during this period. Start slowly and work up to your normal training schedule.

If you live in a region where summers aren't excessively hot but you're planning to race somewhere really hot and humid, you should acclimatize before the event. If possible, travel to the event at least three days prior, giving yourself that much time to adapt. If that's not possible, try one or more of these methods to acclimatize before you travel:

- Wear an extra layer of clothing while riding in your normal environment. This will create a microenvironment under the clothing, simulating increased heat and humidity.
- Build a heat chamber for training in your garage or a work shed, adding heat lamps as necessary to increase the temperature. You might have a hard time convincing your significant other to allow you to build such a chamber in the house itself. Sitting in a sauna may help, but it will not be as effective as a more active method.

When using either of these methods, be extra careful to avoid a heat-related illness. Do not become overzealous in your training. The idea is to slowly adapt to a hot, humid environment. Use common sense and listen to your body.

Specific adaptations occur in the body during acclimatization that help the body remain healthy and perform better in the heat. You will begin to sweat earlier than normal, before your core temperature rises significantly. You will also sweat more, and sodium levels within the sweat will decrease to assist in sodium retention and electrolyte balance. Training in the heat increases glycogen use, which will deplete energy stores much faster compared to training in cooler environments. This effect will be minimized once you acclimatize to the heat, which will spare energy. (See Chapter 10 for more on the physiology of glycogen production.)

Hydration

Even though the importance of hydration is well known, athletes who train in hot environments have a tendency to stay chronically dehydrated. This places them behind the curve before they even begin their training day. Many cyclists use thirst as a marker of hydration, but it is a poor indicator. If you're thirsty, you are already dehydrated and performing suboptimally.

You can monitor hydration levels by tracking changes in body weight. Record your weight, in the buff, before and after you ride. The difference in weight is the water loss from your ride. If you are two pounds lighter, you need to replenish that difference. This process requires a reliable scale that produces the same weight rating when you step on and off it repeatedly.

Clothing

To promote evaporation, clothing must be breathable to allow heat to escape and air to come in contact with sweat. Clothes should also be light in color to reflect sunlight, not absorb it and convert it into heat, as dark clothes do.

Unfortunately, almost all cycling shorts are black, and they become extremely hot in bright sunlight. On the other hand, I do not recommend white cycling shorts. You can see skin through them, and they show permanent grease marks, whereas black ones don't.

RIDING IN THE COLD

When the weather turns cold, you can still ride outdoors; you just need to take proper precautions to ensure a safe and tolerable, if not entirely comfortable, ride.

When evaluating cold weather, check the temperature and the windchill factor. Windchill—a combination of temperature and wind speed—measures how cold it actually feels. Some weather stations report windchill as the "feels like" temperature. For example, a temperature of 40° F and a wind speed of 10 mph feels like 28° F.

The principle of convection applies to cold weather as well as hot weather. Your skin gives up heat to the surrounding air. If the air is not moving, convection results in a boundary layer of warmer air forming around your body. If the air is moving (as in windy conditions) or you are moving through the air (as when riding), the boundary layer is continually replaced with cooler air; this prevents the warm boundary layer from forming, so your skin cools more rapidly.

The body is inclined to maintain a steady internal temperature. In cold weather, the blood cools through convection through the skin, then circulates back to the body's core, where it tends to bring the temperature below the preferred 98.6° F. The body reacts by narrowing the blood vessels (a process known as vasoconstriction), which limits the circulation of blood to the periphery of the body and concentrates it in the core, where it will stay warmer. Although this helps maintain the body's metabolic processes and keeps internal organs

When riding in cold conditions, pay close attention to the windchill and the type of clothing and number of layers you wear. (Barbara Dowd)

functioning, it has two negative consequences. Leg and arm muscles are deprived of the oxygen-rich blood they need to generate power, reducing cycling performance. And the extremities and skin are deprived of warm blood, increasing the risk of frostbite (the freezing of body tissues) in extreme conditions. Thankfully, however, only rare circumstances will cause you to ride in temperatures that could lead to frostbite.

A second mechanism helps keep the body warm: its metabolic rate can be cranked up to increase internal heat production. This is accomplished in two ways. As the body's core temperature begins to lower, the body starts to shiver. This rapid, repeated flexing and unflexing of the muscles generates heat. There is also evidence that the body reacts to cold temperatures by automatically increasing its metabolism even with no increase in muscular movement.

As mentioned earlier, about 60 to 70 percent of energy production is dissipated as heat during exercise. Although this is not economical, and it creates a problem in hot environments, it can be useful in cold environments.

Cold-Related Illnesses

Hypothermia occurs when the body's core temperature drops below 95° F. Here are the symptoms:

- shivering (begins before core temperature reaches 95° F)
- weakness
- confusion
- impaired speech
- loss of dexterity and coordination
- pale gray-tinged skin

As hypothermia progresses and the body's core temperature continues to drop, symptoms worsen in this order:

- increasing mental confusion
- stiffening of muscles; sluggish movement

- slowing of heart rate and breathing
- loss of consciousness
- pulmonary edema, in which fluid accumulates in the lungs due to a significant decrease in the depth and frequency of breaths
- cardiac arrest

If hypothermia is suspected, get into a warm environment immediately. Dry, warm blankets or a hot bath or shower are good ways to bring the body's temperature back to normal. If a warm environment is not readily available, at least find shelter from the wind. Even after you have moved to a warm environment, wet clothing will continue to lower your core temperature, so change into dry clothes as soon as possible. If you are stranded on the road, take off your clothes long enough to wring the moisture out of the inner layer, then put them back on immediately. (This assumes your clothing is soaked with sweat.) This will eliminate some of the water next to the skin and keep you slightly warmer. You can also huddle together with friends for increased warmth. In severe cases, which entail a strong possibility of cardiovascular complications, seek medical attention immediately.

Though extremely rare in cycling, severe hypothermia can occur in stranding situations. When riding in remote areas in cold weather, it is a good idea to ride with a buddy, carry a cell phone, or let someone know your exact route and when you will return.

Training in a cold, dry environment can trigger an asthmatic episode. Cyclists with asthma need to be aware of this and take precautions, as described in Chapter 15.

Prevention of (and Acclimatization to) Cold Stress

The body does acclimatize to cold stress, but not to the dramatic extent it does when subjected to heat stress. Individuals who are acclimatized to a cold environment start shivering much later than those who are not acclimatized. It is theorized that this occurs due to a slight increase in resting metabolism and increased blood flow to the extremities. Because of the limited adaptations that occur, however, the prevention of cold-related illnesses must focus on clothing selection and riding strategies.

Clothing

Layering is the key to riding in the cold. At least three layers are usually required. The innermost, base layer should be a wicking material (such as CoolMax or polyester) to move moisture away from your skin. Do not wear a cotton or wool base layer: both retain moisture and lead to rapid cooling. The outermost layer should be wind- and waterproof but must also allow the dissipation of excess moisture that would otherwise accumulate underneath the fabric. It does so by means of vents designed into the clothing or through the fabric itself, as in the case of materials such as Gore-Tex, which allow moisture to pass in only one direction—away from the body.

The layers in between provide insulation, trapping the warmth given off by your body through convection to create a cozy microclimate. The type and number of insulating layers are determined by the air temperature and your ability to move freely. Lightweight or heavyweight polyester fleece (depending on the temperature) is a good choice for an insulating layer. All insulating layers should be breathable, so that moisture wicked by the base layer can continue to travel away from the body and out through the outer layer's venting system. Be careful not to overdress, which will restrict your freedom of movement and lead to the production of more moisture (sweat) than your clothes can dispel. Layering provides you with the opportunity to remove garments when riding if you become too hot.

Do not ignore your extremities when preparing for a winter ride. Cover your head and face to block the wind and retain heat. Arm warmers and leg warmers are good choices because you can peel them off if you become too hot. Gloves should be windproof and water resistant. Cold, wet feet will make for a miserable ride, so use shoe covers over your normal cycling shoes or buy a pair of winter cycling shoes.

Do not base your clothing choices on what someone else is wearing because people respond differently to the cold. Cyclists with a high body fat index are typically able to tolerate cold temperatures better than cyclists with little body fat. Older cyclists typically feel the cold more than younger adults due to a blunted thermoregulatory response. In cold environments children lose heat at a much faster rate than adults, due to a larger surface area in relation to their body mass.

The best way to determine what to wear in cold weather is to create a chart listing windchill and clothing. For each ride keep a log of the windchill and the clothes you wear. After the ride, record whether the clothing was too much, not enough, or just right. Note the clothing that works well at a given windchill. It will probably take you most of one winter to develop a reasonably complete chart, but thereafter you can refer to it for years to easily determine what you should wear. You should begin a ride feeling somewhat cool. If you are warm before you start, you will be drenched in sweat within the first two miles. During short rides you can actually overheat if you are overdressed. On long rides, excessive sweating can lead to rapid cooling as the ride progresses.

Ride Strategies

The distance traveled, the length of time exposed to the environment, and the speeds traveled all make cycling unique among sports. During the winter it is a good idea to ride shorter routes and/or consecutive loops rather than riding long out-and-back or one-loop routes. Although it may sound boring to ride a 25-mile loop four times, it is better than riding a 100-mile loop or a 50-mile out-and-back route because you'll never be more than 12½ miles from home. If the weather takes a turn for the worse or you suffer a mechanical breakdown or you begin to get hypothermic, you'll return home that much quicker. Even if you can call someone to pick you up, the shorter route will allow a quicker response.

Limit the frequency and duration of stops when riding in cold weather. When you stop, although the windchill diminishes, your core temperature remains elevated for a brief period, which can promote increased sweating, which leads to rapid cooling of the body. In addition, your metabolism rate drops when you rest, resulting in lower heat production. The longer you stop, the more heat you lose, and you may be unable to maintain core temperature for the rest of the ride.

RIDING AT HIGH ALTITUDES

Racing and training at altitude is an important issue for cyclists. As altitude increases above 5,000 feet, its physiological effects increase accordingly. Traveling from sea level to train or race at altitude has a negative impact on performance and possibly health. However, training at altitude does have potential ergogenic benefits. (Ergogenics are any outside factors with a positive influence on performance.)

Many people think that there is less oxygen in the air at high altitudes, but this is not the case. Air contains 20.93 percent oxygen at sea level as well as atop Mount Everest. The issue is oxygen availability, which depends on the barometric pressure and the partial pressure of oxygen at any given altitude.

Barometric pressure can be thought of as the "weight" of the atmosphere. As you move up in altitude, there is less atmosphere above you, hence less "weight" pushing down. This translates to lower air pressure.

The partial pressure of oxygen (PO_2) is the pressure of oxygen at any given barometric pressure.

TYPICAL PARTIAL PRESSURE OF OXYGEN BY ALTITUDE

Altitude (ft)	Barometric Pressure (mm Hg)	PO_2 (mm Hg)
0	760	159
5,000	632	132
7,000	586	123
10,000	522	109

Because the percentage of oxygen in the atmosphere does not change, the formula is simple:

$$\text{barometric pressure} \times 20.93\% = PO_2$$

Barometric pressure at sea level is typically about 760 mm of mercury (mm Hg), therefore:

$$760 \text{ mm Hg} \times 20.93\% = 159 \text{ } PO_2 \text{ (mm Hg)}$$

When examining the table above, you will notice that as altitude increases, barometric pressure decreases, with a corresponding decrease in PO_2. Gas diffuses from high to low pressure. Oxygen diffusion from the lungs into the blood is affected by its partial pressure in the atmosphere in relation to its partial pressure in the blood. The greater the pressure differential between the two, the better the oxygen transfer. A lower PO_2 creates less of a pressure differential and has a strong negative effect on oxygen absorption into the blood.

At altitude, hemoglobin saturation drops significantly due to lower PO_2 values. The pressure gradient between the arterial blood and the tissues also drops at altitude, so less oxygen is transferred into the tissues. This puts the body into a hypoxic state, in which oxygen delivery to the tissues is significantly decreased. At altitude, because less oxygen is being delivered to the tissues, such as muscle, an unacclimated body usually feels weak. It is common to feel fatigued and unable to ride at your normal intensity.

Your body will attempt to compensate for a low PO₂ by increasing the rate and depth of breathing. At high elevations and exercise levels, it may seem as though you are hyperventilating. Through a series of biochemical reactions, increased ventilation will ultimately impede your body's ability to buffer lactic acid during high-intensity work, resulting in a decrease in performance at or above threshold.

Altitude-Related Illnesses

Altitude sickness is common in individuals who travel from sea level to high altitudes. The severity of altitude sickness varies among cyclists, as does the altitude at which it occurs. The faster you change altitudes, the more pronounced the symptoms. But until you have experienced high altitudes, you will not know how your body will respond. Symptoms of altitude sickness include the following:

◘ decreased ability to breathe at a normal rate and depth
◘ headache
◘ nausea and vomiting
◘ weakness
◘ mental confusion
◘ insomnia

Two other more serious conditions can occur, but usually only above 9,000 feet. Pulmonary edema is a condition in which fluid accumulates in the lungs. It is marked by wheezing, skin discoloration, weakness, and coughing up pink phlegm. Cerebral edema is excess pressure on the brain, caused at high altitudes by an increase in fluid volume in and around the brain. Cerebral edema is marked by neurological symptoms such as loss of coordination, mental confusion, slurred or confused speech, and fatigue. Pulmonary and cerebral edema can lead to serious complications and death. If any of these symptoms occur, move to a lower altitude and immediately seek medical attention. Thereafter, acclimatize by increasing your altitude by about 1,000 feet a day as long as you remain asymptomatic.

Prevention of (and Acclimatization to) Altitude Stress

To participate in an event at high altitude, it would be ideal to show up two to three weeks early to acclimatize. Or you can use training equipment that simulates a hypoxic (low oxygen) state to elicit the same response as training at altitude. This is accomplished by lowering the percent of oxygen available in an enclosed space as opposed to altering pressure to affect oxygen saturation. The enclosed space can be anything from an oxygen tent to a converted room.

Although these adaptation strategies are beneficial, they will not allow you to achieve the level of performance that is normal for you at a significantly lower altitude. They reverse themselves two to three weeks after you return to sea level. Nevertheless, there may be some positive effects to altitude training, as described on page 88.

Hydration

Dehydration can occur quickly at altitude due partly to excessive water loss through respiration. Air at high altitudes tends to be dry, so as we breathe in, the lungs transfer a lot of moisture into the air, which is then exhaled. (Less moisture transfer occurs when breathing humid air.) Because breathing greatly increases at altitude, there is an increase in water loss due to respiration. Urination also increases significantly at altitude. This situation leads to a greatly reduced plasma volume, leading to a higher heart rate at any given submaximal intensity (or, any physical exertion below maximal effort). To counter these effects, it is important to stay adequately hydrated.

ALTITUDE AS AN ERGOGENIC AID

Using altitude to increase performance seems like a good idea. A number of adaptations occur that will increase your aerobic capacity, especially when you return to sea level. These adaptations include increases in erythropoietin (EPO), hemoglobin, myoglobin, and capillary and 2,3-diphosphoglycerate (2,3-DPG) concentrations, all of which are designed to increase delivery and utilization of oxygen at the working muscles. However, due to low PO_2 and a decreased ability to buffer lactic acid, you will not be able to train as hard or as long at altitude, possibly offsetting some or all of the benefits. Research has provided mixed results on training at altitude and racing at sea level. The reverse—living at altitude and training at sea level—on the other hand, appears to be a promising scenario, for which most research shows a significant increase in performance.

Although there is currently no research to support this theory, I think that living at altitude and a combination of training at sea level and at altitude elicits the best response. The reasoning is that training at sea level most of the time would allow you to work at a higher intensity to increase VO_2 max, threshold, and overall performance. (These terms are discussed in Chapter 10.) Then training at altitude just one or two days per week would create a hypoxic state that would increase oxygen absorption and transfer under the stress of exercise, whereas living there would keep you in a slightly hypoxic state for improved oxygen dynamics.

Much attention has been paid to the effects of altitude on performance, but many questions remain unanswered, and no one knows which of these scenarios is most beneficial: living at altitude and training at altitude, living at altitude and training at sea level, or living at sea level and training at altitude. Also unknown is the optimum dosage of each variable. Keep in mind that there are huge differences in how each individual responds. Does altitude training work? Maybe. Is the probably small payoff worth the time, money, and effort? That's up to you to decide.

safety

Cycling is a great sport, but it has its hazards. Public roads can be dangerous places; you must interact for better or for worse with traffic, pedestrians, other cyclists, and animals, and deal with adversities such as poor road conditions and weather. And as with any sport that involves hours of high-intensity training, cycling has the potential to lead to overuse injuries.

PREVENTING ACCIDENTS

When you ride on the road, you have the same rights as motor vehicles and must follow the same laws. There are two exceptions to this rule:

◘ You must stay to the far right of your lane unless making a left turn. This prevents cyclists from impeding the natural flow of traffic.
◘ You must use bike lanes when they are present.

Check local laws; they vary from place to place, and you can be ticketed for not following them. Running red lights and stop signs are two quick paths to the hospital or the morgue.

Select routes with wide lanes and as little traffic as possible. Consider the types of vehicles that use the road. Even in little-traveled rural areas, wide, heavy trucks carrying logs or ores can be a hazard.

Riding defensively requires an awareness of your surroundings at all times. If you are riding with music in your ears, you won't be able to hear a car coming up behind you, a dog coming at you from behind a bush, or cyclists yelling "on your left" as they pass. Cyclists have been hit and killed by trains while traveling through railroad crossings. If you have headphones on, you can't hear an oncoming train. Save the MP3 players and headphones for indoor use only.

Law of Gross Tonnage

The law of gross tonnage states that if another vehicle weighs more than yours, you better get out of its way. I have observed this scenario more times than I care to count: a cyclist gets to a four-way stop and stops, just before a car arrives on the intersecting street to the left. The car does a rolling stop and continues through the stop sign. The cyclist sees this and takes off anyway. The car slams on the brakes and the cyclist rides on.

I've approached and spoken to some of these cyclists, and they explain that they saw the car do a rolling stop but were asserting their right-of-way. But it doesn't matter who had the right-of-way if you are smashed flat as a pancake. Use your head, err on the side of safety, and remember the law of gross tonnage. If you can see a vehicle, assume it can hit you. There is a fine line between asserting your rights and recklessness.

Stay Calm and Quiet

Encountering inconsiderate motorists is inevitable. I have had insults and hard objects thrown at me while riding. In the past, I returned the insults as loudly as I received them. I changed my tactics after a local cyclist was run off the road by a motorist who had begun the altercation by yelling at him to get off the road, then reacted badly to the cyclist's middle-finger response.

With so many crazy people on the road, discretion is the better part of valor. A good friend handles the shouted insults in the ideal manner—by simply ignoring the driver's existence. Unfortunately there is no law against stupidity.

There are, however, laws against harming people. If someone throws an object at you or attempts to run you off the road, get as much information as possible and inform the police. Write down the license plate number, the make and model of the car, and a description of the driver. Events such as this usually happen quickly, but it pays to take the time to notice these details.

I once heard a story about Lance Armstrong, the truth of which I can't vouch for. Same old story: driver shouts an unprovoked insult; Lance shouts back; driver turns around and runs cyclist off the road. Then Lance picks himself up and hears a voice from the heavens: "Do you want his license plate?" Lance looks up and there's a telephone lineman, high on a pole. The police caught and prosecuted the motorist.

Cell Phone

You never know when a situation will occur that prevents you from making it back home on your own. You can crash, have a mechanical that can't be fixed in the field, or get hit by a storm that's not safe to ride through. The solution is to always carry a cell phone in a waterproof container. I usually put mine in a ziplock bag and slide it into a pocket.

Never answer your phone while riding; stop to answer calls. If you are paying attention to your phone, you are not paying attention to the road or the people around you. Unlike driving a car, you really do need both hands to ride. If you don't want to be bothered by calls while you ride, turn off the ringer. But leave the phone powered on so you can be located in an emergency.

Enter an emergency contact number under the name "ICE" (In Case of Emergency) in your phone's memory. In many areas emergency personnel are trained to look for this if you're incapacitated. Check with your local police or fire department or ambulance service to determine whether they follow this protocol.

Dogs

Man's best friend can turn into his biggest nuisance when you're riding. It doesn't matter whether it's a nice doggy who wants to play or Cujo's littermate wanting to bite off your foot: when a dog gets under a cyclist's wheels, the result is often an invigorating treatment of asphalt dermabrasion.

Leash laws usually don't apply on the country roads where cyclists do most of their riding. There are, however, three ways to protect yourself against dogs:

- Be aware of your surroundings. Assume that any dog you see will come at you, and ride defensively. On some routes you'll learn where the problem dogs live, and you can be ready for them.
- Carry pepper spray, which stops dogs in their tracks. Some spray cans are designed with a strap specifically for carrying on bikes. Avoid spraying fellow riders, and don't spray into the wind or you might spray yourself. If you spray other riders, the dog will probably be the least of your worries.
- Probably the most important thing you can do is report nuisance dogs. In most cases the owners will be given the choice of confining their dog to the yard or losing the animal.

Requiring dogs to be kept under control benefits dogs as well as cyclists. How many dogs have you seen dead on the side of the road? Reporting a nuisance dog will also leave a record of the dog's behavior in case there are future attacks.

Regardless of whether there are leash laws where you ride, owners are legally responsible for their dogs. If a dog causes a cyclist to crash, the owner may be liable for damages.

Protect Your Eyes

Wearing glasses protects your eyes from these types of hazards when riding:

- ultraviolet (UV) rays, which can damage your vision after lengthy, repeated exposures
- bugs, dust, and small debris
- larger objects such as rocks thrown up by passing vehicles
- wind, especially during fast descents and on windy days

Cycling glasses should be optically correct, provide 100 percent UV protection, and be vented to prevent fogging. Try them on before you buy them and check the field of vision. Most sunglasses block peripheral vision, which creates a potentially hazardous situation in which you don't see other cyclists or vehicles off to the side. Get into a tucked or aero cycling position and make sure the top of the glasses does not interfere with your vision looking down the road.

Many sports glasses come with interchangeable lenses. Use dark lenses on bright, sunny days, and rose-tinted or clear lenses on overcast days. I usually prefer rose-tinted lenses on overcast days because they make things look a little brighter. The downside is that you might not realize just how dark and ominous the clouds have become.

Sunblock

Cycling involves exposure to the sun for prolonged periods of time, so you may want to use sunblock to protect your skin from the sun's damaging rays. The higher the SPF, the better the sun protection. Purchase sunblock specifically designed for sports so it will stay on as you sweat.

Safety Inspection

A friend had just returned from a big race, one that he had trained for specifically all year. I asked him how he did, and he told me the race went well, right until his crank arm fell off; his race ended then and there. He had replaced his crankset a couple of weeks previously and had not checked it since then.

Over time, road vibrations can cause bolts to loosen, and the repeated stress applied to the frame caused by hard riding can cause it to fatigue and crack. Make sure your bike is safe to ride by routinely giving it a thorough exam. Start by regularly checking the following items for tightness:

- pedals
- crankset
- headset
- stem
- handlebars
- saddle and seat post

Check that your wheels are true, the quick releases are tight, and the spokes are properly tensioned. Examine the tires carefully for cuts or embedded debris that could work its way through and cause a flat.

Examine the bike frame regularly for stress cracks. If you are involved in an accident, check the bike thoroughly before your next ride.

HEALTH AND INJURY

It's said that there are two types of athletes: those who are injured and those who are about to be. This section is designed to give you general advice on health, disease, and injuries as they relate to cycling. But it should not be substituted for competent medical advice. Refer to the Appendix for additional resources if you want to read more on the subject.

Physical Exam

Many cyclists ride not only to increase fitness but also to improve their health. Exercise can extend and improve the quality of life and help prevent many disease states, such as the following:

- high blood pressure
- high cholesterol
- cardiovascular disease
- type 2 diabetes

Some research even indicates that exercise decreases the risk of developing certain types of cancers.

Exercise also entails risks, however, because it can worsen certain conditions. Many disease states are asymptomatic, having no outward signs. Cardiovascular disease can be asymptomatic right up to the point of a heart attack, which, although more common in older individuals, can occur at any age. Therefore, before starting an exercise program, you should have a physical examination. This is especially true if you are older, have been sedentary up to this point, and/or have not had an exam in a while.

If you have any known medical complications, talk to your doctor about your condition before you begin cycling. Having medical complications does not necessarily mean you will not be able to cycle. In fact, exercise is often recommended for rehabilitation and secondary prevention (preventing a reoccurrence) in many disease states. But only a physician is qualified to make these determinations and provide guidance on exercise limitations.

Choosing a Doctor

It is important that athletes choose a sports physician as their adviser. If you can find one with particular experience in cycling, so much the better. Sports doctors deal with athletes on a daily basis and are familiar with overuse injuries and acute injuries that you are likely to sustain. To the extent that they know cycling, they will be knowledgeable about the biomechanics that lead to cycling-related injuries.

Another important difference between sports doctors and other physicians is one of philosophy. If a cyclist goes to a regular doctor complaining of knee pain while riding, that doctor will probably tell him to stop riding until the pain goes away. From the medical perspective, this may be sound advice, but it is often unacceptable to athletes. Sports doctors understand that. In the same situation, a sports doctor will likely work with you and try to keep you on your bike, perhaps by suggesting changes to your riding position, your equipment, or your training regimen.

Training and Illness

Exercise increases the strength of the body's immune system, so athletes are usually less likely to "catch something" than the general populace. But there's a catch. Training is catabolic: it breaks tissue down inside your body and briefly reduces immune system function. (The strengthening occurs by repeatedly breaking down and rebuilding, getting stronger each time. This is discussed at length in Part III.) The harder you work out, the more susceptible you are to illness directly afterward. So following a hard workout, it's a good idea to avoid contact with individuals who may be infectious. (Endurance athletes with extremely high training volumes may have a poorer-functioning immune system than nonathletes. This is probably due to the excessive stress of a high-volume training plan, which may not allow for complete recovery.)

Should you train during an illness? It depends on the situation. On one hand, if your body is already fighting an illness, training hard will further lower your immune system, making matters worse. Let's say you contract an illness that with rest and recovery will last five days. By training through the illness, you might compromise your immune system so it takes ten days before you fully recover and can resume your normal training intensity.

On the other hand, if you stop training altogether during those five days, you may lose a lot of ground in your training.

A good guideline states that if an illness is above your shoulders (colds and sinus infections, for example), it is OK to train lightly provided that you have no fever, no headache, and no aches or pains associated with the congestion. If symptoms move into the chest, you should not train.

If you are taking decongestants for sinus or cold symptoms, be cautious when cycling. Decongestants increase the resting and submaximal heart rate, especially in individuals with a smaller body size. Decongestants can also lead to dehydration. Some make you drowsy and impair concentration, which could lead to an accident.

Never train with a fever. A fever is the body's way of fighting an infection. Bacteria and viruses can live only within a certain temperature range; because that is around 98.6° F, humans are ideal hosts. The body drives up the temperature to kill off the infection. Training will only lower your immune system and skew the advantage toward the infection. Another consideration is how you feel. If you feel too bad to ride, don't. It's better to be a little undertrained than to make your illness worse. If you feel bad, take a couple of days off to relax and recover. If in doubt, seek medical advice.

Psychological Stress

Some individuals thrive on challenge and perform better than others under stressful situations. But for every individual there comes a point where stress begins to have a negative impact on health. Psychological stress depresses the immune system and increases healing time, possibly compromising

the ability to recover from a hard training bout. The good news is that exercise reduces stress.

Preventing and Addressing Specific Injuries

Saddle Sores

Many cyclists refer to any pain on their bottom or groin area as a saddle sore or saddle soreness. Symptoms commonly associated with saddle sores include tenderness, open infections, ulcers, boils, and abrasions.

Tenderness is usually due to pressure from the saddle, which supports a large portion of your weight. "Hot spots" often occur where the saddle presses against the ischium, the portion of the pelvis known as the "sit bones." Proper saddle selection, as discussed in Chapter 1, can reduce or eliminate this pressure, numbness, and chafing (the latter two are discussed below), as can a good pair of cycling shorts with extra padding in the groin area.

Riding more can also help. Tenderness may first occur when you begin riding seriously or increase mileage significantly. As you ride more, your body may adapt to the added pressure and the tenderness may recede. You can also try standing out of the saddle periodically; even a brief release of pressure may relieve the overall feeling of tenderness.

Numbness in the groin area may occur due to pressure against the nerves located in that region, and men may experience penile numbness while riding. This usually fades quickly once you are off the saddle. If it persists, it can be cause for concern and you may wish to contact your doctor. If you experience frequent numbness, check that your saddle nose is level, not pointing upward. Riding in an aero position causes your pelvis to tilt forward; if that's when numbness occurs, you may need to point the nose of the saddle slightly downward. Tilting it down too much, however, will make you slide forward and sit on the nose of the saddle.

Any part of your leg that moves across the saddle repeatedly as you pedal is susceptible to chafing. This is especially true if the saddle is set too high because it causes the cyclist to shift side to side with every pedal stroke. If your saddle is pointed down, it will cause you to slide forward, then compensate by pushing back on the saddle, and this repeated fore and aft movement can also cause chafing. Rubbing chamois cream into the chamois of your shorts can help reduce the friction.

Bacteria are the main culprit in the development of saddle sores. Bacteria interacting with open skin lead to infection and saddle sores. Boils, which can range from small annoying pimples to debilitating cysts, develop when bacteria enter pores and cause infection. If left unchecked, a boil can increase in severity and require lancing.

Bacteria thrive in a wet, warm environment; wearing soiled cycling shorts on a long ride is bound to lead to saddle sores. Wash cycling shorts after every use. After a ride, take them off as soon as possible, wash and dry your groin area, and change into dry clothes, especially if you have a patch of chafed skin.

Numb Hands

Numbness in the fourth and fifth fingers is a common problem among cyclists. It's caused by a combination of road vibrations transmitted through the handlebars and the pressure of supporting your upper body with your hands. (It is the ulnar nerve, located in the palm of the hand, that is affected.) The longer the ride, the greater the chance of developing numbness. Symptoms usually subside shortly after finishing the ride.

Following these suggestions will minimize or alleviate the problem:

- Wear padded gloves.
- Wrap the handlebars with padded tape.
- Make sure your bike is set up correctly. A nose-down saddle forces you to place more weight on your hands.

Overuse Injuries

Overuse injuries occur over time due to repetitive movements. They are usually accompanied by chronic pain—pain that continues over time. If left untreated, chronic pain can turn into a severe overuse injury, and a problem that might have been resolved with minor changes in training could end up keeping you off your bike for a long time.

Cycling consists of a repetitive motion that occurs over a long period of time in a relatively fixed position—the perfect scenario for overuse injuries to develop. It is, therefore, extremely important to have your bike set up to your personal anatomical specifications so as not to subject your musculoskeletal system to undue stress.

Knee pain, the most common overuse injury, usually occurs for one of three reasons:

- Trying to accomplish too much too soon places a large amount of strain on the muscles, ligaments, and tendons before they are ready to handle the load.
- Riding in too high a gear (usually at too low a cadence) also places too much strain on the joint.
- A too-low saddle places a lot of torque on the knee at the top of the stroke, leading to anterior (front side) knee pain. A too-high saddle causes the knee joint to lock out at the bottom of the stroke, leading to posterior (back side) knee pain. Improper cleat position can also place undue torque on the knees as well as strain on the Achilles tendons.

Plantar fasciitis is pain at the base of the heel caused by damage and inflammation of the long plantar ligaments that help support the foot. It is usually worse after a workout or first thing in the morning. Plantar fasciitis can be caused by a cycling shoe with a flexible sole, a cleat that's placed too far forward on the shoe, riding in too high a gear, riding too hard too soon, or any combination of the four.

It is almost inevitable that you will develop some form of overuse injury at some point in your cycling career, but by avoiding the three main culprits (training too hard, pushing large gears, improper position), you'll significantly reduce their occurrence and severity.

Road Rash

Road rash, the skin abrasions that occur when you take a fall, is a common, almost inevitable occurrence in cycling. It can be superficial or serious, depending on a wide range of variables including the nature of the road surface, the speed and position at which you hit the ground, and the clothing you're wearing at the time.

It isn't good practice to put your hands out to break a fall, but most of us instinctively do it, so wearing gloves often helps keep some skin on your hands. Far better than sliding across the road surface is rolling with the fall.

Prompt, proper wound care helps avoid infection. Rocks, dirt, material from your cycling jersey, and other debris may be embedded in the wound; all should be removed. This is best accomplished with a clean brush designed for the purpose, sterile wipes, or a Water Pik. A washcloth from home may leave lint in the wound. Use antibacterial ointment to decrease the risk of infection. If you cannot remove the debris yourself, or if the wound appears to be severe, seek medical attention immediately.

Should you cover the wound or leave it open? Both methods seem to work, so rely on your doctor's recommendation and common sense. Left open, road rash has a tendency to stick to clothing and bedsheets, and separating the cloth from the wound can be painful and increase the risk of

Road rash must be properly cleaned, disinfected, and dressed to avoid infection. Knees are a common location for road rash.

infection (to say nothing of damaged clothing and bedding). Because of this I usually keep my road rash covered until it is beyond the oozing stage.

As the wound heals, watch for signs of infection. If you notice any of the following, contact your doctor immediately:

- red puffy skin around the edges of the wound
- red lines radiating from the wound
- oozing after the wound has scabbed
- odor

races and rides

I suspect that the majority of cyclists who are reading this book are into the sport for a little racing and for the health and fun of riding. Even cyclists who are not interested in racing may be interested in watching competitive cycling. All cyclists can benefit from an understanding of the different categories of racing. And noncompetitive as well as competitive cyclists may be interested in participating in group rides.

RACING

When people think of bicycle racing, what usually comes to mind is a road race with a mass start, a set distance, and a finish line. This is not always the case, though; there are other types of races with variations of these characteristics. The USCF rule book (see Appendix) gives detailed rules for all of the racing events discussed here. But for a general discussion, read on.

Road Races

The archetypical race with which most people are at least vaguely familiar is the road race. It is held on a public road, with distances usually ranging from 25 to 130 miles and courses of one of four different designs. A point-to-point race involves starting in one place and finishing in another. An out-and-back race involves racing to a turnaround point, then returning by the same route. Many road races are single-loop races, where cyclists race in one large loop, starting and finishing in the same place. A circuit race involves a smaller loop that cyclists cover a number of times. Circuit races are the most spectator-friendly because the crowd sees each rider more than one time. Another advantage of the circuit race from the organizer's point of view is that there is less road to close and patrol.

In many road races, different individuals race different distances based on their experience level as established by the USCF in the States, and other governing bodies elsewhere. (The USCF is the road racing division of USA Cycling, the sanctioning body for all types of bicycle competition in the United States.) Beginners start in Category 5 and move up through the categories as they improve.

Road racing is what typically comes to mind when you hear a reference to competitive cycling. (Barbara Dowd)

For example, in one given race event, Category 5 riders may race 30 miles, Category 4 riders 45 miles, Category 3 riders 65 miles, Category 2 riders 80 miles, and Category 1 riders 130 miles. Many times, two or more divisions are grouped together at the same distance.

Criteriums

Criteriums (called crits) are short, fast races involving a looped course that cyclists race around numerous times. These courses are usually 1 to 2 miles long, with turns that can make the race difficult and technical, especially at the speeds that the cyclists hold throughout the race. The courses used in these races are usually flat but can be hilly. The length of the race may be determined by a number of laps or by a time limit.

To keep the pace fast, prizes are offered on specific laps. These prizes, called primes, are awarded to the first cyclist past the line on a specific lap.

Other methods to keep the pace fast are pulling out the last man on each lap, or pulling out lapped riders.

Due to the fast pace and tight turns, crashes are likely. This has resulted in another unique aspect of the crit: the free lap rule. If you crash or have a technical (a problem with equipment), you are awarded a free lap.

The combination of a short looped course, technical corners, fast pace, and primes makes these races exciting for spectators.

Time Trials

Time trials allow individuals or teams to race against the clock without the interference or help of other riders or teams. Individual time trials are unique in that the outcome depends entirely on each cyclist's ability. Time trials usually range from 5 to 35 miles and may be over flat or hilly terrain. Because of the lack of drafting (riding in

Criteriums involve a short looped course, usually about one mile, that riders race around multiple times. The duration of the race may be a fixed number of laps or a set time limit.

Time trials require that cyclists ride on their own against the clock. (Bill Parsons)

another rider's slipstream, which is common in road races and crits), aerodynamics are extremely important in time trials. This has led to the development of special equipment and bikes designed to improve aerodynamics.

Stage Races

Stage races are a combination of two or more of the race types listed above; they range from two days to three weeks. (Most stage races in the United States last two days and consist of a road race, a time trial, and a crit.) Large stage races, known as grand tours, may include several iterations of each event. The most famous stage races are the Tour de France, Vuelta a España, Giro d'Italia, and, most recently, the Tour of Georgia and the Tour of California. The 2007 Tour de France consisted of three individual time trials and eighteen road races that varied from flat to mountain stages.

Track Racing

This book does not address track racing in detail, although it is briefly described to complete the picture of performance cycling (leaving aside off-road events as 100 percent valid but nonetheless a different sport altogether).

Track racing consists of racing short distances on a round track called a velodrome. Most tracks are 333 meters long but can range from 200 to 500 meters and are banked for cornering.

Races vary in distance and type. The most common distances are 200 and 500 meters and

The Tour de France is the world's best-known stage race. (Micah Rice)

Track races are conducted on a racetrack called a velodrome. These races are short and fast. (Barbara Dowd)

1, 3, and 4 kilometers. Some of the most common forms of track racing are individual and team pursuit, time trial, elimination, and keirin, in which the racers are paced by motorcycles.

Cyclists use special track bikes with a single-speed fixed gear and no brakes. It takes a little while to get used to riding a fixed-gear bike because you do not stop pedaling to slow down; you slow down by slowing your cadence. Fixed-gear bikes are relatively inexpensive but may not be cost-effective if you do not live near a velodrome.

Most velodromes offer track racing lessons, and some even require them before allowing you to race. Many velodromes also rent bikes so you can experience track racing before investing in a specialized track bike. There are about fifteen velodromes in the United States; they are listed on the website of the American Track Association (see Appendix).

NONCOMPETITIVE RIDING

Many cyclists who have no interest in racing are nonetheless serious, committed riders. They enjoy noncompetitive events, which test their abilities outside a race situation and provide opportunities to ride and interact socially with other cyclists.

Supported and Charitable Rides

Supported rides provide resources and assistance to cyclists throughout the ride. A well-supported ride has aid stations at regular intervals along the route that provide food, drinks, bathroom facilities, and shaded areas to rest. One pays an entry fee to participate. Organizers run SAG wagons (defined variously as support- or service-and-gear), vehicles equipped and staffed to provide mechanical assistance and medical and safety support and to pick up cyclists who cannot continue for any reason.

Some well-organized rides are run on closed or semiclosed routes. The fewer cars allowed on the route, the more pleasant the ride and the smaller the chance of an accident. Route maps are often provided, and turns along the route are well marked with paint or signs. In some cases, volunteers supervise the turns, to keep riders from getting lost and to assist in traffic control, especially at busy intersections.

Supported rides are frequently sponsored by charitable organizations, some of which do a fine job of raising funds through well-organized events. See the Appendix for three of the biggest supported rides (and their websites) that benefit charitable organizations; there are dozens, if not hundreds, more. Visit your favorite charity's website to see whether it has a supported ride in your area. If it doesn't, consider organizing one and get in touch with the charitable-giving coordinator.

Nonsupported Rides

"Nonsupported" means just that—the group must be self-sufficient. The course is completely open, and there is no SAG wagon and no aid stations along the way. Participants meet at a designated time and place to ride as a group. The majority of local group rides fall into this category. Your local bike shop should be able to tell you when and where local group rides occur.

If you are responsible for organizing a group ride, keep these factors in mind:

- Plan water stops, especially during periods of extreme heat. Churches, schools, and some businesses may provide good places to stop.
- Consider traffic patterns, and plan the safest route possible.
- Designate a sweeper to avoid leaving anyone behind.
- Require everyone to wear a helmet on all organized group rides.
- Develop route maps of the most common local rides.

If you are organizing structured group rides, you may want to have the participants sign an informed-consent release before their first ride. The more structured the ride, the greater chance that you could be held liable for injuries.

FINDING EVENTS

Once you start looking for races or rides in which to participate, you'll be surprised at the number and variety within a reasonable distance from your home.

The USCF lists all sanctioned events on their website (see Appendix). Use the "Road" drop-down menu and select "Find a Race," then click on the state of interest to obtain race locations, dates, and contacts for more information. Many listings include links to websites for specific races.

Probably the most comprehensive site for racing and noncompetitive cycling events is active.com (see Appendix), where you can register online (for a few extra dollars) for most events.

Small, local events may not be listed online, so visit local bike shops, most of which have an area for event announcements. The shop staff can often provide insights about local events, such as how popular, competitive, or well organized they are. Race and event information also appears in some enthusiast magazines such as *VeloNews* and *Bicycling*.

After you've collected the information, select the events you wish to participate in. Identify the key events that relate to your competition or fitness goals—where you want to be when you're at the top of your form (see Chapter 9 for details).

REGISTRATION

Many event organizers require registration prior to the day of the event. There are often two cutoff dates: an early one before which you can register for a reduced fee, and a second one that represents the actual deadline. Registration fees are not refundable, so don't register for all your planned events at the beginning of the season. If you become injured and cannot compete, you'll forfeit a large amount of money. Instead, mark the cutoff dates on your calendar and register for one at a time, preferably before the fees increase.

There are a couple of exceptions to this recommendation. Some events cap the number of entrants; if you wait too long, you won't get a spot. To avoid being locked out, contact the race director to determine how fast the event fills up. Also, registering early may motivate you to train harder because you've already paid for the event and you know there won't be a refund.

MONEY

Racing can be expensive: entry fees, travel, hotel, food, miscellaneous expenses, and the cost of an annual racing license. When you budget for the upcoming season, include the cost of transporting your bike. Most airlines charge about eighty dollars.

Any weekend event away from your hometown will easily cost several hundred dollars. Before you get in over your head, calculate the total cost of your season. Keep in mind that this does not include upkeep and maintenance on your bike and gear.

Funding

Once you see the breathtaking total, you'll have to figure out how to come up with the cash. Consider establishing an "events fund" and putting aside a set amount each payday.

Many bike clubs hold fund-raisers to support their race teams, and commercial sponsorships are not out of the question. Many companies are interested in supporting athletics in their local communities and have money budgeted specifically for this purpose.

To make an effective pitch for some of that money, you'll need a good presentation. It should include the following:

- Team profile, including riders, director, coach, and other staff members.
- Team's past achievements and long- and short-term goals.
- What the company will gain from its sponsorship. Estimate the number of "eyeballs" that will view the sponsor's name through the exposure that your team or club will provide. You can offer advertisements on the team's jerseys, T-shirts, banners, and website. Signage on the team vehicle can range from large sign magnets to full-coverage graphics. Include images or examples of what you're offering.
- Altruistic benefits of the company's sponsorship: for example, raising funds for charity, or to promote fitness or athletic competitions.
- Outline of detailed operating expenses for one year of training and racing, to justify the need for sponsorship.

LOGISTICS

Do your planning well in advance to avoid stress over logistics as the event nears. Know where your accommodations are and how to get there. The race director can give you information about nearby hotels and campgrounds. Hotels near major races fill up quickly, so make your reservations early.

Whether you spend the night in the area before the race or drive to the area early in the morning, give yourself plenty of time and know exactly how to get there. The start of a race is stressful enough without having to worry about being on time, finding parking, checking in, and so forth. Assume that everything will take longer than planned and include a margin of error.

If possible, travel a day or two in advance and stay the night, especially for an important race. This will allow you to sleep later on race day and give you time to familiarize yourself with the course. Taking a "pre-ride" allows you to determine which sections of the course are easy or difficult so you can plan your race strategically.

The importance of a pre-ride is made clear by the experience of a friend who was unable to pre-ride the course and was unfamiliar with the territory. He did know that there was a long, hard climb near the end of the race, so, as a strong climber, he decided to *sit in* (staying in the slipstream and off the front) through most of the race, then attack on the climb. Following this strategy during the race, he waited until he saw the crest of the hill in the distance, then he turned on the juice. No one came with him, and the gap just grew and grew. Although he was beginning to fade as he reached the top, he still thought that his success was assured. When the road flattened out, he breathed a sigh of relief. Then the road curved to the right. As he came around the bend, his jaw dropped as he looked at the remainder of the climb. He estimated that he still had a mile to go before the true summit. The peloton caught him on the last section of the climb and dropped him out the back. His misjudgment on the length of the climb cost him the race.

Find out from the race director whether there is *neutral support*—mechanical support provided to all riders in the race. At some races neutral support provides wheels for flat changes, but most of the time you have to supply your own wheels, which are carried in the neutral support vehicle. Many smaller races do not have neutral support. At most criteriums there is a pit area where you

At larger races, neutral support provides wheel changes for all teams. (Kathleen Poulos, Toyota-United)

It's advisable to lay out your equipment and check it off a list before packing it for a cycling event.

can place your spare wheels. You also need to determine the location of feed zones (specified zones where water and food can be passed off to riders), so you can plan accordingly.

EQUIPMENT CHECK

Can you imagine showing up at a race without some critical piece of equipment? It happens all the time. One of my cyclists arrived at a mountain-bike race without his front wheel, and a friend rode the bicycle portion of a triathlon wearing running shoes because he had forgotten his bike shoes.

We all run through a mental checklist before we leave for a race, but that's how we forget things. It's essential to have a physical list, such as the one below, on which you check things off in pen as you collect and pack your gear. (Photocopy this list for reuse, or write your own with your personal preferences.) Lay out your gear, and check off each item as you pack it. Do this the night before you leave.

Equipment Checklist

- ◘ bike (tuned and in working order)
- ◘ race wheels
- ◘ spare wheels for support
- ◘ helmet
- ◘ shoes
- ◘ jersey
- ◘ shorts
- ◘ socks
- ◘ gloves
- ◘ tire pump
- ◘ toolbox, spares, and supplies
- ◘ water bottles
- ◘ nutrition
- ◘ stationary bike trainer (for warm-up)
- ◘ proper rear cassette (you may need more than one depending on terrain)
- ◘ sunglasses
- ◘ sunblock
- ◘ medications (if needed)

Make sure your bike is in working order before you leave for the race. Check all bolts with a torque wrench. Check that your wheels are true and the spokes are properly tensioned. Check that the derailleurs shift properly and the brakes work well. Examine your tires; remove any foreign objects embedded in the tread.

Pre-Race Maintenance Checklist

- ◨ all bolts, but especially on the seat post, stem, and crankset
- ◨ pedals
- ◨ brakes
- ◨ shifters and derailleurs
- ◨ cleats on shoes
- ◨ wheel sets (trueness, spoke tightness, tires; check quick-release tightness on race day)
- ◨ headset
- ◨ frame and handlebars (check for cracks)
- ◨ chain (check for wear and lubricant)

Side placement for a race number.

It is also a good idea to outfit a dedicated toolbox to carry to races; it should contain all the bike tools and spare parts you may require. Many events have mechanics to help those in need before the race starts, but it is unwise to count on the availability of that support.

RACE DAY

You will need to awaken early on the morning of the big event. Bring a battery-powered alarm clock for insurance against a faulty hotel clock or a forgotten wakeup call. Get up early enough so you can eat breakfast two hours prior to the start of the race. Arrive at the race grounds early so you have time to park, check in, confirm start time, get organized, and warm up.

Sign in and pick up your race packet and race number at the registration/check-in table. Ask the race officials how your number should be pinned: along your side or across your back. Attach numbers so they catch as little wind as possible. Check for your start time. If you are racing a time trial, you need to determine your own exact start time. A race may start at 7 A.M., but your individual start may not be until 8:30 A.M. This knowledge will allow you to better plan your warm-up so you can come out of the start gate primed to go.

Back placement for a race number.

It is inevitable that there will be too many riders and too few portable restrooms (with hyped nerves, there's always an increased demand for the facilities). This leads to long lines, so don't wait until right before the start. Use the facilities before your warm-up.

Spend 20 to 40 minutes warming up before the start of your event. Time it so you arrive at

A stationary trainer allows a cyclist to warm up while remaining close to the start and avoiding road traffic.

the start line at the same time as most other riders—usually 5 to 10 minutes prior to the start of the race. Warming up on a trainer allows you to remain close to the start line and away from the chaos on the roads. Besides, it may be difficult or impossible to warm up by riding on the road prior to a race. If feasible, use a nonrace rear wheel on the trainer, and switch to your race wheel after warming up. This will prevent you from prematurely wearing the tread on your race wheel.

racing skills, strategy, and tactics

Success in racing depends on a combination of four elements: physical fitness, bike-handling skills, strategy, and tactics. In addition, there is the bike itself (see Part I). There is also psychological motivation, but that's beyond the scope of this book. Bike-handling skills, strategy, and tactics are addressed here; fitness is addressed in Part III.

Riding in a tight group, or peloton, is an integral part of racing. The peloton sets the pace for a race and provides protection from the wind for most of its riders most of the time. Although there are times when you must break away from the peloton if you hope to win a race, it's essential that you learn to ride effectively within the group.

MAKING CONTACT

When riding in a peloton, you literally rub shoulders and bikes with other riders, so it is important that you learn how to maintain control in these situations. The best way to learn is to practice with a partner and an old bike in a grassy field. If you fall, the grass is a lot more forgiving than asphalt.

Start by gently touching shoulders as you ride. Then work your way up to leaning into each other and pushing off. Keep both hands on the handlebars and use your shoulders, elbows, even your head to push off. Don't allow the bikes to touch because you'll probably go down. And as tempting

Physical contact with other cyclists is inevitable when riding in a group. (Charles Herskowitz, Toyota-United)

as it may be, don't try to knock your partner over; this is not a king-of-the-hill contest. Even on grass at slow speeds, you can become seriously injured.

When you're comfortable pushing off, work on touching tires, again using old bikes on grass. While riding slowly, approach from behind and gently touch the side of your front wheel to the opposite side of your partner's rear wheel. (Keep

Practice making contact in a controlled situation before it happens on the road.

the point of contact behind your partner's rear axle.) When the wheels touch, instinct tells you to pull away immediately. Resist doing that; it often results in a crash. Hold your bike straight, maintain control, then gently pull away. Don't attempt this drill with a nice set of wheels.

When racing, you'll often need to move up through the peloton toward the front, where you can react to situations that occur there or create some of those situations yourself. Most of the time, riders will give way when they realize that you're intent on coming through. But they won't always do that, so you must learn to "push" your way through. This is another skill to practice in a grassy field.

You'll need at least two other riders to conduct this drill. While your friends ride next to each other at a slow pace, you come up from behind and work your wheel into the gap between them. Verbally let them know you're there, then push through. You may make some contact with one or both of the

riders. Stay calm and work on maintaining control using the skills just discussed. Keep in mind that you are not physically pushing your way through. Because you've let the riders know verbally and physically that you're coming through, they will make way. This drill is designed to give you confidence when moving up through the pack. Concerning the "verbal" part of this procedure, be as loud as possible without being rude. You want to leave no doubt that you're coming through, but you don't want to start an argument.

All of these drills contain the potential for crashes and injury. Wear a helmet, keep things slow and controlled, and use common sense. Ride an old bike so you won't care if it becomes damaged, or a mountain bike, which is more rugged and stable than a road bike.

PACE LINE

Conserving energy is among the most fundamental of race strategies, so cyclists form pace lines to save energy while maintaining a faster pace than they could do by themselves. Pace lines are single- or double-file columns of cyclists in which the rider at the front blocks the wind for those behind. There are a few conditions that determine whether it will be a double or single pace line. High speeds tend to lengthen the peloton into one long line. During group rides it is difficult to be social when riding in a single pace line, so most social rides are usually ridden in a double pace line. Safety also determines whether to ride in a single or a double pace line. On narrow roads or in areas of high traffic, cyclists should ride in a single line.

In a pace line the lead rider rotates frequently off the front and is replaced by the rider behind him. Thus everyone shares the hard work in small bits, and everyone benefits aerodynamically. There is an estimated work reduction of 30 to 40 percent when riding this way compared to cycling alone.

To obtain the optimal effect, riders must keep their front wheel 4 to 12 inches from the rear tire

Pace lines can be conducted in a single line (top) or a double line (bottom). (bottom photo by Charles Herskowitz, Toyota-United)

in front of them. Any more than that and they will have to ride just as hard as the individual on the front of the line but receive no benefit.

It takes good bike-handling skills and a lot of practice to ride comfortably in a pace line. It is your responsibility to stay off the wheel of the rider in front of you. You must hold a steady, predictable line, guiding your bike smoothly and without

extreme steering deviations. A cyclist who swerves back and forth is impossible to draft and creates a precarious situation. Practice while riding alone: hold a line by riding along the white line at the side of the road. Once you can do this without extreme concentration, you're ready to start working with a group.

Keep your hands near the brake levers, and pay attention to the riders in front of you as well as the road itself. (If your bike has aero bars, don't use them in a group or pace line. They place your hands away from the brake levers, thus slowing your stopping time. The one exception to this rule occurs in training for team time trials.) Do not overlap the tire of the rider in front of you; that's just asking for a crash, which will likely cause a chain reaction involving everyone behind you.

When you, as the lead rider, are ready to drop off the front, pull to the side and drop to the back of the line by moving to the right or the left. Both sides have advantages and disadvantages. Dropping back to the left (outside) gives you more room to maneuver but puts you in the path of traffic. Dropping back to the right (inside) keeps you out of traffic but provides only a narrow path to the back of the pack. It also puts the group a little farther into the road. You should not randomly decide to drop back to the inside or outside. Instead, the group should determine ahead of time which side the lead rider will use, then maintain that side throughout the ride, so everyone's movements are predictable.

Before pulling to the side off the front, you should look to ensure that your path is clear to the back. Pull off and slow slightly. When you are within two or three riders of the back, begin to pick up speed again, then slip onto the back. If you wait until the last person passes you before you accelerate, you'll have to do more work to get back on.

How long a rider stays on the front varies with the individual and the goal of the pace line. During races, riders spend only a short time on the front, allowing a faster pace to be maintained without wearing down any individual cyclist. During easy training rides where the pace is slower, cyclists spend longer pulling on the front.

Individual fitness and race tactics also influence the time spent on the front. If you're on a breakaway with individuals who are stronger than you are, you may need to spend less time on the front and more time recovering by sitting in (staying in the slipstream and off the front). You may even need to sit out a few turns every so often to recover, or stay off the front completely. To stay off the front, stay on the back; when the rider at the front pulls off, create a gap between yourself and the rider in front of you, allowing the rider coming back to enter the line in front of you. Although this will not win you friends, it will enable you to stay with the group when you might not be able to otherwise.

One of the most common mistakes that new riders make is staying too long on the front and slowing down the pace. If someone is yelling for you to get off the front, oblige him or her. If you are not slowing the pace, other cyclists will happily allow you to stay on the front as long as you want, wasting your energy while they conserve theirs. Do not stay on the front until your legs are screaming, though. In either case, rotate back, recover, and await your next turn.

Do your best to maintain contact with the group. Avoid being dropped off the back of the peloton; if you are alone, it is extremely difficult to get back on. If you are not the only cyclist dropped, you may be able to work together to close the gap. But if you are having difficulty keeping contact with a small breakaway, you may want to drop back to the main group and hope they catch the break before the line.

Rotating Pace Lines and Echelon

Riders in a rotating pace line and echelon (explained later) continually rotate in a circle to keep

the group moving at a fast pace. No rider spends more than a few seconds in the front. It takes more coordination to ride in these formations than in a regular pace line.

A rotating pace line is used in a headwind, a tailwind, or when there is little or no wind. Two columns of cyclists ride side by side. The inside column moves up and the outside column moves back. The lead rider on the inside moves over to the front of the outside column at the same time that the last rider in the outside column drops back and moves to the end of the inside column, immediately resuming the pace of the rider in front. Riders continually rotate, spending little time on the front, in order to keep the pace of the

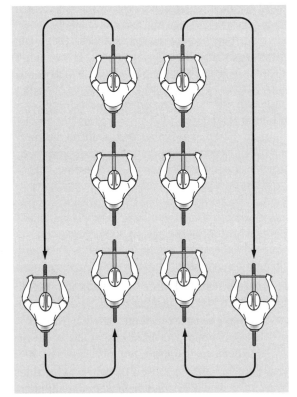

In a double pace line, the cyclist in front will pull off and drop to the back of the line on their respective side.

entire group high. The inside lane is usually referred to as the fast lane, and the outside lane as the slow lane.

An echelon is used in strong crosswinds; the line slants in the direction of the wind to shield the greatest number of riders. A slanted echelon rotates across the lane instead of straight back, so it's important that it not cross the center line into oncoming traffic on an open course.

Think of a slanted echelon as having front and back rows. The front row circulates into the wind. The most exposed rider in the front row drops back to the second row and begins circulating away from the wind. The angle of the echelon tends to adjust itself automatically as riders feel themselves in the most sheltered position from the wind.

Slanted echelons have only about six to eight riders, depending on the width of the road. When more riders want to keep the same pace, more than one group forms, one behind the other.

A slanted echelon is much harder to maintain than a straight one and takes longer to learn. When moving through rotation, you must pay close attention to the riders around you to ensure that you do not cross wheels.

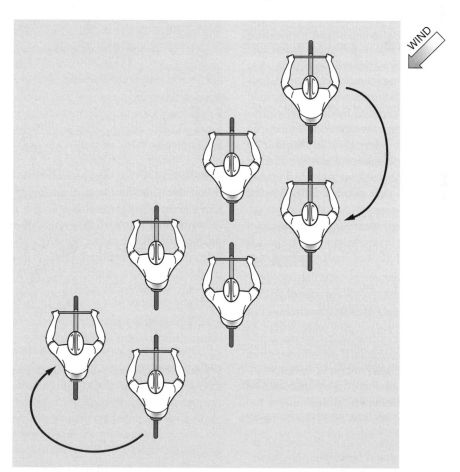

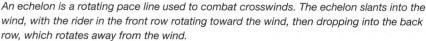
An echelon is a rotating pace line used to combat crosswinds. The echelon slants into the wind, with the rider in the front row rotating toward the wind, then dropping into the back row, which rotates away from the wind.

STRATEGY

On the surface, a cycling race appears to be nothing more than many riders trying to beat one another to the finish line, and the fastest rider wins. In reality it is as complex as any chess game, and often it is the smartest rider, not the strongest, who wins. Strategy consists of an overall game plan for the race, and a choice of tactics at the appropriate times.

Pacing

Athletes learn early to pace themselves. If you go too hard too soon, you will "blow up" and have to drastically reduce your workload just to complete the distance. If you go too slow and lose contact with the peloton, you forfeit the benefits of drafting and will probably never catch up. An optimal race pace is the highest one you can maintain without blowing up, right up to the finish line. Nevertheless, there are times when pacing goes out the window.

The best example of pacing in cycling is the time trial, where each cyclist rides against the clock. If you ride too hard, you blow up before the finish; if you don't ride hard enough, you still lose. It's a fine balancing act.

Each cyclist's pacing strategies are based on previous experiences racing similar distances. The more experience you have, the better you can pace yourself through a time trial. Most experienced riders start with a slightly elevated pace, quickly level off into a maintainable rhythm, and pick up the pace near the end, usually 1 to 2 km from the finish. Beginners often go too hard in the beginning. All cyclists tend to make small adjustments throughout a race based on how they feel and how many miles remain.

Pacing in a road race or a criterium is usually set by the riders on the front. Due to the benefit of drafting, the group is able to maintain much higher speeds than individual cyclists can on their own. Staying with the main group during most of the race is necessary; however, there are times when

Pacing is the key to riding a time trial. Cyclists must adopt a pacing strategy that allows them to push as hard as possible without prematurely fatiguing. (Kathleen Poulos, Toyota-United)

you should set your own pace. During long climbs, if you can't handle the pace of the group without blowing up, drop off the back and try to get back on during the descent. Attacking also requires individual pacing. Once free from the group, you will need to hold your individual time-trial pace. In a small group that has broken away, pace is determined by the fitness of the riders in the break.

Racing as a Team

Although cycling is very much a team sport, it is perhaps unique in that individuals and teams compete simultaneously, and individuals, not teams, are the victors. A cycling team works together so that one of its members will win the race.

Professional cycling teams hire riders with specific skills to fill specific positions. They hire climbers to climb, sprinters to sprint, and *domestiques* to work for the lead riders on the team. During flat stages, teams work to ensure that their

Although cycling appears to be an individual sport, it's very much a team sport. (Barbara Dowd)

sprinter is in position to sprint for the line at the end of the race. When racing through the mountains, the team works to protect their climber so they can exploit their strengths while climbing the mountain and win the race. The goal of a cycling team is to use the strengths of their team members to place their lead rider in an optimal position to cross the finish line first.

Racing clubs usually need to be more egalitarian, but it's sometimes hard to convince an individual to throw away his chance at victory in order to assist someone else's. A club must try to persuade its riders that they are all working for a common goal and should perform their assigned tasks to the best of their ability to secure a win for the team.

Racing as an Individual

For many cyclists—especially beginners—there are few opportunities to race on a team. Racing as an individual can be difficult, especially at races where teams dominate.

Individuals constantly form ad hoc agreements with other riders to cooperate on tactics—for example, cooperating on a breakaway or a chase. These agreements may be explicit or implicit, symbiotic or one-sided, but they are fragile and transitory, and ultimately you are competing against these temporary partners.

As an individual rider, you cannot depend on anyone to blunt the wind for your benefit exclusively or assist you in pushing up through a group, so you must use smart tactics. Try to stay near the front, ready to respond to moves from other individuals and teams.

One advantage to racing as an individual is that you can conserve energy by staying off the front of a pace line because you don't have to blunt the wind for anyone.

TACTICS

The methods by which you implement strategy are called tactics. Doing the right thing at the right time involves understanding what's happening around you, knowing where you should be in the peloton at any given moment, knowing how to create desirable tactical situations, and deciding whether to instigate, join, or hinder an attack.

Several terms need to be understood before reading this section on tactics:

- **Attack.** A swift acceleration designed to separate a rider from the pack.
- **Breakaway.** An individual rider or a group of riders who have created a significant gap between themselves and the main pcloton or smaller group of riders.
- **Bridge.** The act of closing the distance to a rider or group of riders when they have created a gap.
- **Chase.** When the peloton or small group of riders is working to close the distance to a rider or group of riders who are out ahead of the group.
- **Counterattack.** The act of attacking from within the chase group immediately after the group has caught the rider or riders whom they were chasing down.
- **Lead out.** The act of riding hard and fast at the front to provide shelter for a teammate and set him up for a sprint to the finish.

Stay Near the Front, Not on the Front

I have seen this situation occur innumerable times. A rider trains hard and well all year for the first race of the season. The race starts out a little slow, so this rider goes to the front and picks up the pace. He's feeling strong, and for miles no one escapes off the front, although several drop off the back. Finally, less than three kilometers from the finish, the attacks begin. The rider finds that he can't respond, his lead disappears, dozens of "weaker" cyclists blow by him, and he finishes near the back of the pack.

Although many tactics are employed in cycling, beginning cyclists frequently ignore the most important one: do not work harder than you have to. Stay in the group and enjoy the benefit of drafting. This is especially true for individual cyclists and weak teams. (Strong teams can afford to have cyclists on the front pushing the pace for their main riders.)

By staying near the front, rather than on the front, you'll be in a position to respond to attacks or make a move of your own. (You'll also minimize the risk of being involved in a crash.)

This does not mean you should never be on the front. If you are a strong cyclist and the pace is too slow, go to the front and attack aggressively, as discussed below. Once the pace has picked up, drop back and allow someone else to do the work, and get yourself ready for the last few kilometers.

Breaking Away

A breakaway occurs when one rider or a small group of riders attacks and breaks from the main group. This is designed to get the cyclists near the finish line with as few competitors as possible during the final sprint. A breakaway is therefore a good idea for strong riders, but not for strong sprinters who expect to come on strong at the end.

Initiating a break is always a gamble. If you never risk anything, you can never win, but breaking

When initiating a break, attack hard so other cyclists are not able to go with you.

away isn't like bluffing at poker, so don't attempt it if you don't have the fitness level to pull it off. However, if you feel strong and the situation is right, attack like there's no tomorrow.

To initiate a successful break, you must surprise your competitors. Wait for a moment of inattentiveness and be careful not to advertise your intentions. Avoid attacking from the front. Instead attack from the side and behind the lead riders. The leaders won't see it coming, and those bunched elsewhere in the group will have trouble getting around the leaders to respond. Because everything happens so fast, you'll be off the front before anyone can respond.

A successful break always begins with swift acceleration. If you slowly ramp up to speed, you'll find a large group of grateful riders sitting in behind you. If you intend to initiate a break, attack and attack hard, creating a gap between you and everyone else.

Once you have been off the front for about 400 meters, look back to make sure you're not giving the peloton a free ride. If you are, ease up and try again later. If you're alone, keep up the speed a little longer, then work into a time-trial pace. If you brought along a small group that broke away from the peloton, immediately begin working together in a pace line.

Certain times are particularly opportune to initiate a break:

- When there is a lull in the race, or the peloton is inattentive, is a good time to initiate a break.
- Immediately after a breakaway has been caught is an ideal time to *counterattack*. The riders from the first break will be tired, as will those driving the initial chase, and there will be confusion as to who will lead the next chase.
- If you can accelerate on hills, attacking near the top of the climb is a good idea. Do not attack too early on the climb, or you will pay for it before the top.
- Winding roads with tight turns are another good place; it's easier for an individual or a small group to maneuver through turns than it is for a large peloton. Pulling out of the peloton's line of sight around a corner deprives chasers of a visual carrot.

Attempting a solo breakaway in a strong head- or crosswind is a bad idea, but a small group may excel under these circumstances. No one will want to get on the front and do the work necessary to bring the group back.

Joining a Breakaway

It's a gamble to join a breakaway because you don't know whether it will succeed. Familiarity with the other riders and teams in a race makes it easier to gauge a break's chances, but this comes only with experience. As a coach, I usually prefer aggressive mistakes to passive ones; I would rather see a cyclist go with a break that fails than have him sit in and miss the winning break. (Having said this, I would not want to see one of my cyclists make a break 10 miles into a 50-plus-mile race.) Don't be afraid to take a chance. You can learn as much from your mistakes as from your successes.

If you think a break will succeed, jump on quickly. If you did not initially make the break and it appears that the peloton will not respond, you must make a realistic judgment as to whether you can close, or bridge, the gap. If you decide to go for it, use the same methods as for initiating a breakaway.

If you join a breakaway, work with the other riders to ensure that the break will hold until the finish line. Even at the professional level, breaks sometimes fail at the finish because riders refuse to cooperate over the last kilometers: no one wants to work on the front, and the pace drops while the peloton picks up the pace and closes the gap. Save the tactics for the sprint to the finish. It's better to have a top-five finish than to be caught and spit out the back by the peloton right at the finish line. On the other hand, try not to lead out your rivals in a sprint for the finish line by allowing them to sit in your slipstream until the end.

As you approach the finish line, there may come a time to drop the rest of the breakaway. When you decide to go solo, attack from the rear. After your turn on the front, drop to the back and fall a few bike lengths behind the last rider so you can build up speed and attack. Your momentum will carry you past the riders before they can respond. If you are strong enough or lucky enough, they will not close the gap.

If you have a teammate in the break, attempt to wear down the rest of the riders with a series of attacks. Rider A attacks while Rider B, usually the stronger of the two, sits in on the chase. The moment the group catches Rider A, Rider B comes over the top and attacks. If it works correctly, Rider B will be off the front. If not, Rider A sits in on the chase and waits to attack when Rider B is caught.

If your break is not close to the finish line and is being reeled in quickly, you have a decision to make. Can you and your group pick up the pace and maintain the gap? If not, don't blow yourself up. Drop back to the main group, stay near the front, conserve energy, and wait for the next attack.

Help or Hinder?

When riding as an individual, you should always help in the breakaway because you want to reach the finish line with as few people around you as possible. But if you know that the catch is imminent, shut it down and wait to be caught. Team riders may also choose to hinder the break if their main hope for a podium finish is back in the peloton.

There are two main strategies for slowing the break:

- sit in, and do no work that benefits the break
- actively slow the breakaway

Be subtle when attempting to slow a breakaway. Pull through when it is your turn, then slightly lower the pace and stay on the front a little longer than normal. Do not drastically slow, or the others will just pull around and pick up speed. Split the break by allowing a gap in the middle of the pace line. If you're lucky, the riders behind will not notice until the gap is significant. You will not make friends with this last tactic, and it will rarely succeed more than once during a break.

Chases

If a break goes off the front and gains ground, the peloton must decide whether to bring it back

When a breakaway occurs, the peloton needs to chase it down.

immediately or gradually, but it must be brought back. If it's early in the race, stay calm and work the break back slowly. If it's near the end or the group contains strong riders, bring the break back immediately.

How to Chase

The main group must work to bring a break back, but who will do it? Be patient; wait and see who will take up the chase. Many times, a team will come to the front and pick up the pace. If a team is willing to do the work, great. Sit in and conserve your energy. If a team has a rider in the break, however, the team may not be interested in bringing it back, especially if it's one of their strong riders.

If no one takes the initiative, you can attempt to lead out a chase. Go to the front and ramp up the speed. Stay on the front for a brief period, then pull off. Hopefully the group will maintain speed and you can sit in. Unless you're working for a team, don't stay on the front when chasing down the break. If you're able to put in that kind of effort, attack and attempt to bridge instead, making your own break from the peloton to join the leading group.

How to Stop or Slow a Chase

Individual riders should never stop or slow a chase: it is always in their interest that the break be run down. However, if you are part of a team and have a strong rider in the break, here are a few strategies you can use to hinder the chase:

- If no one has initiated a chase, move close to the front and just sit there.
- Once a chase has started, go to the front and slightly increase speed to give riders the impression that you're working on the chase, then gradually decrease speed to set a false pace. Eventually someone will catch on and pull through to set a real pace to bring the group back, but you'll have at least delayed the chase, which might be enough.

- Place riders strategically near the front, having them slow and create gaps between the lead chasers and the peloton. This will force riders to come around you and interfere with the chase.

Hills

If you are a good climber, hills are the ideal place to break away or keep the pace high and hurt the other riders. Watch for weaker climbers and try to stay in front of them. If they allow a gap to form between themselves and the riders in front of them, you may not be able to come around and close the gap; even if you can, you will expend extra energy doing so.

If you are a poor climber, you may want to move to the front before the climb begins. If you're lucky, the group will allow you to set the pace for a while. Immediately or eventually they will pass and you will begin to drift back through the group, but if things work in your favor you will still be close to the group when it crests the hill. If instead you start the climb in the back, then the gap will only get larger. Do not blow yourself up on the climb. Instead ride at a pace you can handle, and attempt to close the gap after the climb.

If the climb is long and hard and the main group is keeping a pace you cannot handle, drop from the group and ride your own pace. In most cases you won't be the only one off the back and you'll have other riders to work with.

Beware of pushing too high a gear up hills, or you'll tire quickly. Do not allow your cadence to drop below 70 rpm unless you're standing. When climbing out of the saddle, cadence is determined

Climbs are ideal places for strong climbers to make a move. Weaker climbers must make tactical decisions on how best to proceed. (Barbara Dowd)

by the gradient and personal preference. Through trial and error you will be able to determine what cadence works best for you when climbing out of the saddle. This is usually determined by the steepness of the climb.

Descending

Descending hills offers an excellent opportunity to gain time on your rivals. This requires a lot of confidence, which comes only through practice and trial and error.

Get in an aerodynamic position that still allows complete control. Keep your head up and look as far down the road as possible. When you are going so fast that pedaling is useless, get low on the bike and bring your elbows in. Position your cranks parallel to the ground and bring your thighs in against the top tube. If your bike begins to shake, stay calm and gently slow until the wobble subsides. Most high-speed wobbles are caused by the rider

being too tense. Trying to compensate instead of relaxing usually makes the wobble worse. Some wobbles, however, are caused by the bike. Check for a loose headset, spokes, or wheels.

Sprints

There's more to sprinting than just pedaling as hard as you can for the finish line. You must make decisive tactical decisions from the approach to the sprint all the way through the finish.

Your sprint strategy begins even before the race. Scout the approach to the finish line. If there are turns on the approach, determine your best route through them so you can position yourself optimally in the peloton before reaching that point. Note potholes and other obstacles, and look for prominent landmarks that will help you gauge your distance from the finish line.

You cannot sprint timidly and expect to win. You have to be right up near the front, and when

Being able to descend hills in a fast, controlled manner gives you an advantage over many competitors.

Sprints are controlled chaos, with every cyclist contending for the best line to the finish. (Kathleen Poulos, Toyota-United)

you decide to go, do it decisively and own your path; it should be the straightest route possible from your current position. Avoid getting trapped between the group and the roadside barriers, which will seriously limit your options and create a potentially hazardous situation.

Do not initiate your sprint until you're sure you can hold it to the finish line. Instead, sit on the riders that begin their sprint too early, and come around when you're ready to sprint for the line. Initiate the sprint in the same manner as a break. If there is a crosswind, attempt to attack from the downwind side so your competitors are blocking the wind. Focus solely on your path and the finish line, give it your all, and ignore the other riders. As you approach the finish, focus your sprint about ten meters past the line to avoid slowing prematurely. Finally, "throw" your bike forward at the line by rapidly straightening your arms. The minute fraction of a second gained is often the difference between winning and second place.

"Throwing" your bike forward at the finish line can mean the difference between first and second place. (Charles Herskowitz, Toyota-United)

PART III

training and fitness

training programs

Many cyclists train without any specific structure or plan. This haphazard approach severely limits their potential for optimal performance and in many cases leads to overtraining. Too many cyclists train at threshold every time they train, always ride the same distance, or train randomly. To gain your desired level of performance, it is important to have a structured and well-developed training plan.

A large number of "boxed," or standardized, training plans are available. If followed, they will likely increase your performance, but because they are one size fits all, they do not allow the majority of cyclists to reach their full potential. The best training plans take into account the individual's goals and physiology. Some cyclists recover more quickly than others; some can handle higher volume, and some higher intensity.

Although more expensive than boxed plans, a good trainer or coach is probably the best source of a well-crafted training plan. A coach monitors how your body is adapting to training, decides when you have built a strong enough base to start interval training, helps you peak for specific events, gives advice on equipment, and recognizes overtraining. A coach also provides feedback on your performance, advice on bike handling, and tactics that you might not get anywhere else.

DEVELOPING YOUR OWN TRAINING PROGRAM

Using a set of general guidelines, cyclists can also develop their own structured training program, or customize a boxed program to their own goals and abilities. This procedure is similar to how coaches approach the task.

Set Goals

First you must determine your long-term goals. Then you will break those down into short-term goals that are more readily achievable.

Long-term goals define the big picture of what you want to do with your cycling. Do you want to race? Participate in a charity ride? Complete your first century? Perhaps you want to ride for fitness, in which case you should define a specific fitness goal. Or maybe you ride purely for enjoyment but feel that riding faster would be more fun; in that case, how fast do you want to get? These questions will help you focus your training and make the selection of short-term goals logical.

Let's say your long-term goal is to complete your first century, and your longest ride to date has been 30 miles. That's a huge jump to handle all at once, but if you extend your range in 10-mile increments—so your short-term goals are to reach 40 miles, then 50 miles, and so on—no single step will be terribly daunting.

What if you want to drop your 10-mile time-trial time by 2 minutes? Again, this is a big challenge, so break it down into short-term goals of 10-, 15-, or 30-second increments.

Goals must be realistic and achievable. If your longest ride has been 30 miles, it would be unrealistic to target a century ride scheduled less than a month away; the chances of failure and disappointment are too great. A better goal would be a century later in the year or the following year. This would allow you to finish the ride without hurting yourself, and to enjoy it.

On the other hand, your goals should be challenging or you will never reach your full potential. The trick is to shoot for the stars with a well-developed plan.

Don't be afraid to change both short- and long-term goals. You may find that your short-term goals are too easy to achieve and feel that you can progress more quickly, or that they are too hard and need to be broken into smaller pieces. If your long-term goal changes, change your short-term strategy to suit.

Determine Current Fitness Level

To develop a sound training plan, it is important to determine your current fitness level. If your goal is to increase your fitness level or become a faster rider during the course of the year, it is important to know where you stand currently. Otherwise, how will you know if you have improved?

One of the most effective ways to determine cycling fitness is to measure your VO2 max. It is the maximum volume of oxygen that can be transported to and utilized by the working muscles. It is commonly used by elite athletes to monitor progress throughout the season, but the test requires expensive gear and trained technicians and is therefore impractical for most cyclists. (See Chapter 10 for details.)

Another method used by professionals is marker sets—a measurement of time over a known distance. Many cyclists use this method without even realizing it.

Select a fixed distance that is close to the length you plan to race. Common choices are 10, 20, and 40 km, but choose a longer one if you wish. Select a course that is flat and relatively free of traffic and has as few intersections as possible. Choose a day that is not too windy or too hot and not plagued with other adverse conditions. Make sure you are well rested and well hydrated and have not had anything to eat for at least two hours before you begin.

Warm up for 10 to 20 minutes, then ride the course as fast as you can and record the time. As you train during the season, complete this marker set periodically, keeping conditions as similar as possible to accurately measure your progress. Compare your current times to your previous times to determine improvement.

If your main concern is distance rather than speed, use distance to determine fitness level. Simply keep track of your long ride for the week and attempt to go a little farther each week.

Keep a Training Log

A training log is one of the most valuable training tools you can have; it enables you to keep track of your training, your marker sets, and any accomplishments or setbacks. Because adaptations occur gradually, they may be hard to recognize unless you keep a log to track changes. A log acts as a training assistant, helping ensure that you follow your training program as prescribed, and it allows you to look back over the season and identify what did and did not work.

The log should record the following:

- Date and day of week.
- Body weight. This will allow you to monitor changes that occur with training, especially if one of your goals is to lose weight. If you have a sudden weight loss, you may be dehydrated. If you have an unexplained, continuous loss, you may be overtraining.

- Resting heart rate. With endurance training your resting heart rate should drop. A resting heart rate that becomes elevated and stays there may indicate overtraining. See "Monitoring Training" for details on measuring resting heart rate.
- Sleep. Record the amount you sleep as well as its quality. Record any naps. This will help you ensure that you're getting the quality of rest an athlete needs. Sleep disturbances can be a sign of overtraining.
- Type of training. Record whether your workout was long slow distance (LSD), interval, tempo, hill, or recovery. (These terms are discussed in Chapter 11.)
- Distance. Keep track of the distance you ride each day, and summarize for the week and the month.
- Ride time. Record the time spent riding. A 50-mile ride in the mountains will take longer than a 50-mile ride on flat ground.
- Course details. Was the course hilly or flat, familiar or new?
- Weather conditions. Record whether it was hot, cold, windy, rainy, or sunny.
- How you felt on the ride. Were you tired or did you feel strong? Did you have any particular aches or pains?
- General comments. Write down anything else of importance. Did you ride in a group or alone? Did you have a mechanical? Take a wrong turn? Beat a previous time on a marker set?

You can work these categories into a program on your computer and print them as you need them. Making your own log allows you to adapt it to your specific needs. If you don't want to make your own log, look for commercially available training logs for cyclists; a few companies make them. Or make copies of the log provided at the end of this chapter.

Determine Frequency

Professional cyclists spend from three to seven hours on their bike every day of the week. Cycling is their full-time job and, other than family, their main obligation. The rest of us have to work around our job and family obligations. You should train a minimum of three days a week and up to seven, depending on your abilities and goals. The more days you train, the stronger your cycling will be, as long as you do not overtrain.

You may have to train early in the morning, before work or school, and schedule your long rides on weekends. Consistency is important, so develop a weekly schedule and maintain it. Increase frequency gradually, and don't try to do too much at once. Keep in mind that your body needs time to recover from training and you cannot train hard seven days a week.

Determine Duration

The "25 percent rule" for determining duration states that your longest training rides should be at least 25 percent longer than your longest race. (See Chapter 11 for details.) Your long rides will be on your LSD days; your hard days and recovery days will be shorter. For example, if your longest race is 50 miles, your longest ride should be at least 65 miles. Your threshold day when you are riding tempo should be 30 to 50 miles; your interval training may cover only 20 to 26 miles; and a recovery ride may be 20 to 30 miles of easy spinning.

Determine Intensity

Next you want to establish the intensity for each training ride. Here are a few terms you should be familiar with before proceeding:

- Base. This is considered your basic fitness foundation and is built through long, slow distance.
- Intensity. This is the "how hard" of your training. You can train only at three intensity levels: below threshold (recovery and long slow distance), at threshold (race pace), and above threshold (interval).
- Interval. This consists of a warm-up, followed by a series of hard pedaling above

threshold followed by soft pedaling for recovery, and ending with a cooldown.

- Long slow distance (LSD). This is how you establish your base miles. You will ride long distances below threshold. The "long" varies from individual to individual.
- Recovery ride. This short ride is designed for active recovery. You pedal at a slow easy pace that does not tax the body.
- Tempo. Riding at tempo requires that you ride at your race pace for a given distance.
- Threshold. Also known as anaerobic threshold, this is the level of exercise intensity at which the production of lactic acid exceeds your ability to remove it. (This is discussed further in Chapter 10.)

If you are just starting out, don't worry about "hard days" where intensity is at or above threshold. Instead, work on building a base by increasing your distance. Distance should be increased by no more than 10 percent of total volume each week. Once the base is established, throw in one day a week of tempo training to increase your speed. The next step is to incorporate interval training, but the speed will do you no good until you can complete the desired distance.

If you have a strong base already, you want to start working on your speed by increasing intensity. Unless you are on a specific periodization plan, don't do more than two hard days a week. The rest should be long slow distance and recovery. Here's an example:

Sample Weekly Training Plan
  DAY 1. LSD
  DAY 2. Intervals
  DAY 3. LSD
  DAY 4. Recovery ride or day off
  DAY 5. Tempo
  DAY 6. LSD
  DAY 7. Recovery ride or day off

Once you've designed your program, stick to it, keeping your intensity at the desired level every day. Riding with a group can be hazardous to your training because rides that are supposed to be easy often turn into impromptu races. If it's your easy day, swallow your pride and let the group go. Your body needs time to recover.

Peaking

You cannot perform optimally at every race during a season, so before the season begins, choose the races where you want to be at your best, then tailor your training to suit. You'll have to sacrifice performance at other races, but in the end you'll be better off.

You will probably be able to peak only two or three times in a season. This does not necessarily mean just two or three races, however. If there is a series of races two or three weeks in a row, you can develop your program to peak for that period.

The type of event will also determine how often you peak. Track cyclists can peak more than three times a year because of the short distances involved. The Tour de France represents the opposite extreme, and any cyclist who hopes to be a true contender in le Tour will plan to peak just that once in the year.

Choosing just a few races for your peak performance does not mean that you should not compete in other races. You should, but with the understanding that you may not be in top form. Competition is a good way to increase performance, and only a race can give you practice in true racing conditions. You must also be careful not to race too often because this will keep you from peaking properly. To accomplish this goal, you will need to use periodization when developing your program.

Periodization

Once you've decided when to peak, you can develop your training plan for the year. You will do this on three time scales, known as the macrocycle (covering the full year), the mesocycle (covering a few weeks or months at a time), and the microcycle (the details of the weekly schedule and the daily workout). Known collectively as periodization, this process requires careful consideration to maximize your fitness and to peak at the right times, especially if qualifying races and championships are close together. You need about eight weeks between peaks if you wish to peak more than once in a season.

Macrocycle

The macrocycle, which defines your training plan for the year, consists of four phases:

- Off-season. You cannot train at full throttle year-round. The off-season promotes mental and physical recovery from the grueling race season and provides a chance to build leg strength.
- Preparation. This phase builds a base for the upcoming race season—a necessity before you can work on developing speed over the distances that you will race.
- Competition. Individuals who train hard year-round often finish near the top in early races, but their performance does not improve as the season progresses. Those who practice sound periodization, on the other hand, improve throughout the season. Use early races as training events, and keep your sights on the races at which you want to excel. As the season progresses, this becomes a maintenance phase.
- Transition. As the hard racing season winds down, this phase allows you to recover and get ready for off-season training.

Mesocycle

During the mesocycle period of a few months or several weeks, you will prepare for and peak at specific races or events as follows:

- Preparation. To build a strong base, concentrate on increasing mileage and don't worry much about intensity.

- Building. Work on increasing speed by increasing intensity. Spend at least a month building for the next race.
- Tapering. For one to two weeks prior to the race in which you want to excel, allow your body to recover by refraining from hard training sessions. Training hard right up to a race will not improve your performance and in many cases will actually hurt it.
- Race. Now you are ready to race. There may be more than one race before you move into the recovery stage, but don't try to peak for more than two to three weeks at a time before moving to recovery.
- Recovery. Begin active recovery after your peak period. This will last one to two weeks before you begin to prepare for your next peak.

This process can usually be repeated two or three times during the race season, depending on the distance of the races and your own ability to recover.

Microcycle

The microcycle is the details of your daily and weekly training, targeted at your specific short-term goals. A common saying is "Train your weaknesses and race your strengths." In other words, spend your training time improving your weakest areas. You may spend a week on hill training or a day on tactics—whatever you need to turn your weak points into strengths.

Developing a comprehensive periodization plan can be difficult, but the results are rewarding, and it is far better to have a merely acceptable plan than none at all. No matter how well structured your plan, you need to remain flexible to accommodate unpredictable family or work obligations and your own injuries and sickness. Don't let these throw you off your training entirely; just make the necessary changes to your program and continue on. And avoid falling into the trap of rationalizing every outside event into continuous changes to your program. Stick to it to the greatest extent practical.

Put Your Plan in Writing

One of the most important things you can do while developing your training plan is to put it in writing. Research has shown that people are more likely to follow through and succeed if their goals and their plans for how to achieve them are written down. Putting your training plan in writing is making a contract with yourself.

Designate a specific calendar for your training and race schedule. To break your upcoming year into the phases of the macrocycle, start by identifying the competition phase—when your season begins and ends. Then you can determine the preparation, transition, and off-season phases. Mark these on your calendar.

Next, identify your key races, and develop your mesocycles to allow yourself to peak for them. Keep in mind that you can peak only two or three times per season.

Now work on your microcycles, establishing your weekly goals and choosing your daily workouts. Have your daily workouts planned at least a month in advance. You don't have to determine the daily plan for the entire year as long as you have your monthly and weekly goals planned. On the other hand, don't make them up day by day.

MONITORING TRAINING

It is important to monitor your training to determine what does and doesn't work for you. Your training log is an important tool here. Your log records time, speed, and heart rate for each workout (and power production if you have a power meter; see page 149). By comparing data from one marker set to another, you'll be able to determine whether your performance and fitness are improving.

Monitoring resting heart rate is the most practical method for most people to track improvements in cardiovascular endurance. (Monitoring changes in VO₂ max, as discussed in Chapter 10, is another excellent method, but testing on a regular basis can be problematic.) Reductions in the resting heart rate and the submaximal heart rate (any heart rate that is below the maximum heart rate) are good markers for improved cardiovascular fitness.

The best time to monitor your resting heart rate is in the morning before you get out of bed. When the alarm goes off, it startles you, so hit the snooze button and lie back down. Once you're completely relaxed and on the verge of falling asleep again, measure your heart rate by counting your pulse or using a heart-rate monitor. As your training progresses and your fitness increases, your resting heart rate will gradually drop.

It is not uncommon to see a two- to three-beat-per-minute (bpm) variation in resting heart rate from day to day, but an excessive or prolonged increase is a sign that something is not right. Just one or two days of increased heart rate may mean that you're not fully recovered from previous training. A prolonged increase may be an indication of overtraining or illness. Resting heart rate is a better tool for determining recovery than it is for assessing your current fitness level. If you're not fully recovered, your resting heart rate will remain elevated over a few days.

Bradycardia is a clinical condition characterized by a slow heart rate, usually defined as a resting heart rate less than 60 bpm. This can be a sign of serious cardiovascular disease, or the result of successful adaptation to a training program aimed at improving cardiovascular fitness. Many trained endurance athletes have a resting heart rate below 60 bpm, and some elite ones measure in the thirties and forties. If in doubt about your situation, contact your physician.

With improvements in fitness, you will have a lower heart rate at any given speed or level of power output, as long as it's below your maximum level of effort. For example, a cyclist who rides a 30-mile flat route on a regular basis averages 17 mph with an average heart rate of 160 bpm on a calm day. Three months after starting a structured training program, he rides the same route at 17 mph, but his average heart rate is now 145 bpm. He is doing less work to maintain the same speed. If the rider rode the same route the following day and maintained an average heart rate of 160 bpm, his average speed would increase to 18 to 19 mph. Now he is traveling faster for the same amount of effort as before training began. Both scenarios demonstrate that the program is working.

When measuring heart rate versus speed, the same conditions must exist between rides for accurate comparisons; differences in wind speed and direction and traffic can create erroneous measurements. Measuring heart rate versus power is more reliable. If your goal is to complete 30 miles at an average power output of 160 watts, speed is irrelevant. Traveling into a headwind at 160 watts will be slower than traveling with a tailwind at 160 watts, but you'll be doing the same amount of work in both situations, so a comparison of heart rates between the two is valid.

For example, a cyclist rides a 30-mile flat route averaging 160 watts at a heart rate of 155 bpm. Three months after starting a structured training program, he rides the same route, again averaging 160 watts but with an average heart rate of 140 bpm. This demonstrates that his fitness has improved and his training program is working. Keep in mind that heart rate fluctuates slightly from day to day.

Marker sets are useful for determining how well your performance is improving in relation to training. If your times are becoming faster, you're seeing benefits from your training program. If they' reunchanged or slower, you need to take a close look at your training. You may be doing too little to stimulate a response, or too much and overtraining.

COACHING

Although it's possible to advance on your own, few cyclists possess the knowledge necessary to fine-tune a boxed or self-developed training program for optimal gains. If you want to reach your full potential, you need a good coach.

Coaches offer more than just a training program. A coach assesses your current fitness level and abilities to determine where to start your program and gear it to help you achieve your goals. He or she continually evaluates your performance throughout training and racing, determining what does and doesn't work and adjusting your training accordingly. The coach identifies weaknesses in race strategy, tactics, and riding skills and offers suggestions for improvements. And a good coach motivates you in your training and racing with a pat on the back, a pep talk, or a kick in the rump when necessary.

Anyone can claim to be a coach, so you have to look into their qualifications. Here are the most important ones:

- Education. A degree in the field of exercise science indicates fairly thorough knowledge of human performance.
- Certification. Not all coaches are certified. The most respected certifying bodies are the United States Cycling Federation (USCF) and the Carmichael Training Systems (CTS).
- Racing experience. Giving advice from book learning without experience in the peloton is highly suspect. But racing success doesn't necessarily make a good coach either.
- Coaching experience. How long and who have they been coaching? Get a reference list of clients and contact them all, probing for how much the coach has helped them improve. You're looking for a coach who gets results consistently.

Your local bike shop and bike club can probably recommend local coaches. Many larger clubs have their own coach to whom you gain access with membership. The USCF website lists coaches by state and certification level (see Appendix). Some coaches require a year's contract, which can amount to a lot of money if you choose the wrong coach. Avoid signing a long contract until you've had a chance to determine whether the coach is right for you.

Several companies offer coaching over the Internet; the quality and level of service can equal or even exceed what might be available to you locally (although face-to-face contact with a local coach can be invaluable). Two companies I recommend looking into are CTS and Peaksware LLC; see the Appendix for their websites.

cycling physiology

Some readers will be tempted to skip this "boring science chapter." I urge you to persevere because knowledge of the basic principles of exercise physiology will help you understand how your body responds to exercise. You'll learn why you can't train at race pace every day, why interval training is necessary, why recovery is an essential part of training, and why the training methods recommended in this book will lead to improvements in performance. This knowledge will help you understand key concepts throughout this book.

THE CARDIORESPIRATORY SYSTEM

The cardiorespiratory system—the key system in all endurance activities, including cycling—consists of the heart, blood vessels, blood, air passages, and lungs. The cardiorespiratory system provides a pathway to extract oxygen from the air and transport it throughout the body to where it is needed, and transports carbon dioxide from the working tissues to the lungs for release into the atmosphere. The cardiorespiratory system plays an important role in transporting glycogen (the storage form of blood glucose, a sugar) from the liver to the working muscles to produce energy. And it provides a pathway to move by-products of energy production, such as lactic acid, away from the muscles. Most endurance training is designed to create adaptations that increase the transport and utilization of oxygen, which in turn increases performance.

The Heart

The heart is a specialized muscle (myocardium) made up of four chambers: the right atrium, the right ventricle, the left atrium, and the left ventricle. The right half of the heart pumps oxygen-poor blood to the lungs, a process known as pulmonary circulation. The left side of the heart pumps oxygen-rich blood from the heart to the other organs and the muscles; this is known as systemic circulation.

The cycle starts when oxygen-poor blood enters the right atrium. From there, the blood travels to the right ventricle, then to the lungs. At the lungs, carbon dioxide (CO_2) is released from the blood into the lungs and exhaled. When you inhale, oxygen (O_2) is absorbed from the air through the lungs and into the blood. The blood then travels to the left atrium and from there to the left ventricle. The blood leaves the left ventricle through a huge artery called the aorta, which divides into smaller arteries leading to the rest of the body. The arteries subdivide into smaller and smaller vessels until they become capillaries, the tiniest blood vessels, which run through all the body's tissues. Capillaries are where gases (particularly O_2 and CO_2) and nutrients are exchanged between

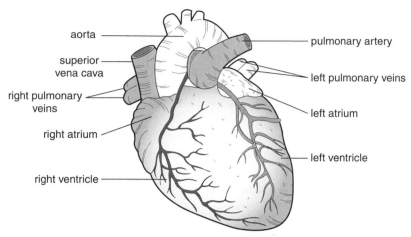

aorta

superior vena cava

right pulmonary veins

right atrium

right ventricle

pulmonary artery

left pulmonary veins

left atrium

left ventricle

The heart is a muscle that pumps oxygen-rich blood throughout the body.

the blood and the tissues. The blood then leaves the tissues as the capillaries form venules (small veins), then into larger and larger veins and back to the left atrium.

The heart is a strong muscle, but it is not strong enough to pump blood throughout the entire body unassisted. For the blood to return to the heart, it must overcome gravity. This is effected by a mechanism known as the "muscle pump." One-way valves, located at close intervals in all the veins, prevent blood from flowing backward through these vessels. As muscles in the legs contract, the veins are "squeezed," causing blood in the veins to be pumped toward the heart. It is theorized that because of the muscle pump, pedaling at a cadence of 90 rpm or greater increases blood return to the heart due to an increased number of contractions. This phenomenon also occurs in the thoracic (chest) region due to changes in pressure that occur while breathing.

Autoregulation of Blood Flow

The human body has the ability to direct blood flow to where it is most needed. This process is known as autoregulation. Blood flow is directed by means of vasoconstriction (narrowing of the blood vessels)

and vasodilatation (widening of the blood vessels). When the body is at rest, the skeletal muscles, kidneys, and liver receive about the same amount of blood, which totals about 65 to 70 percent of all the blood flow in the body. When we do anything that takes the body out of a resting state and increases metabolism in any area, blood flow is redistributed to supply the increased need in that area.

During exercise, metabolism is greatly increased at the working muscles. As muscles become active, they require more oxygen to work effectively, so blood flow is increased to the muscles doing the work. During vigorous endurance activities, approximately 80 percent of blood flow is redirected to the working muscles. There is also a large increase in blood flow to the myocardium to support the increased workload of the heart. Blood flow also increases to the skin—to help cool the body—and to the brain. To compensate for the large increase in blood delivery to the working muscles, blood flow to other areas, such as the liver and kidneys, is reduced.

Autoregulation takes some time to occur. By warming up before training or a race, you redirect blood flow to the muscles before it's needed, and therefore increase performance.

Consuming a meal greatly increases the amount of energy required by the digestive system, so, after eating, blood flow is redirected to the digestive organs. To prevent the digestive system from competing with the working muscles for available blood, it is important for athletes to time their meals in context with training or racing. If your muscles are demanding extra blood at the same time that your digestive system is trying to do its job, neither may get what it needs, and the result can be gastrointestinal distress and suboptimal performance. Athletes vary in the amount of time needed between eating and exercise. (See Chapter 13 for details.)

Blood

Blood is composed of plasma (the liquid part of blood), hemoglobin (red blood cells), and white blood cells.

Plasma, which accounts for about 55 percent of the blood, is the mechanism by which the other constituents are delivered to the body's tissues. Being about 90 percent water, plasma is a good heat conductor and plays an important role in cooling the body. Plasma also plays a role in decreasing blood acidity, through the process of bicarbonate buffering, and in transporting CO_2 to the lungs. Plasma is responsible for transporting about 2 percent of the body's oxygen needs.

The other 98 percent of the body's oxygen requirements are delivered by the red blood cells. Red blood cells contain hemoglobin that are constructed from a globin protein and a heme ring containing four iron molecules. When oxygen binds with the iron molecules, each heme ring carries four oxygen molecules. Hemoglobin normally has a life span of about three to four months; this is shortened by increased physical activity. The body continually produces hemoglobin to replace what is lost. Hemoglobin is thick and requires plasma for transport through the body.

The percentage of hemoglobin in relation to whole blood is known as the hematocrit. Hematocrit is determined by spinning blood in a centrifuge. The heavier hemoglobin and white blood cells settle to the bottom, and the plasma floats to the top. The average individual's hematocrit is approximately 45 percent.

If you follow cycling, you have probably come across the term *hematocrit* in relation to blood doping, in which additional hemoglobin is added to the blood to increase oxygen transport. At a hematocrit above 50 percent, however, blood starts to become too viscous to flow properly. This can and often does lead to cardiovascular "incidents." Exercise physiology textbooks often cite cyclists as examples of deaths related to blood doping. (See Chapter 11 for more details.)

Within the context of exercise physiology, white blood cells, which make up less than 1 percent of the blood's volume and play a key role in fighting illness, are not of great concern. But three important jobs that blood performs *are* of great concern in this context, gas exchange, nutrient delivery, and thermoregulation.

Gas Exchange

Oxygen and carbon dioxide move from areas of high concentration to areas of low concentration until equilibrium is established. The greater the difference in concentrations between adjacent areas (such as body tissues), the faster the rate of diffusion.

During exercise the working muscles use oxygen to produce energy, which causes a decrease in oxygen concentrations in the muscle. Oxygen therefore moves from the oxygen-rich blood in the capillaries to the oxygen-depleted cells in the adjacent muscles. The now-oxygen-poor blood returns to the heart and thence to the lungs. Here, oxygen is in high concentration, so it enters the blood, replenishing its oxygen level.

Carbon dioxide moves in a similar manner. As the muscles work, carbon dioxide builds up, creating a pressure differential between the tissues and the blood. Carbon dioxide therefore diffuses into the blood. When the CO_2-rich blood reaches the lungs, the CO_2 diffuses into the CO_2-poor air in the lungs, to be exhaled from the body.

Blood Glucose

Commonly known as "blood sugar," blood glucose is an important source of energy used by the muscles during endurance activities. Glycogen (a form of glucose) is stored in the muscles for energy production, and in the liver for future use. During exercise, muscles use up the glycogen stored there, so glucose moves from the blood into the muscles to replenish the supply. This in turn lowers blood glucose, so glycogen in the liver is mobilized into the blood to restore blood glucose to normal levels. This process is regulated closely by insulin and glucagon to keep blood glucose fluctuations to a minimum.

ENERGY SYSTEMS

The body requires energy to perform any type of movement. Energy systems may be aerobic (chemical processes requiring oxygen) or anaerobic (chemical processes that do not require oxygen). Both systems come into use when cycling. The chemical processes discussed here occur within tissue cells—for our purposes, muscle cells.

Carbohydrates, fats, and proteins are three sources that, once broken down, provide energy in the body. Through digestion, carbohydrates are converted to glucose, which enters the blood and is stored as glycogen in the muscles and liver. Glycogen can provide energy relatively quickly.

Fats, when broken down, provide more energy per gram than glycogen, but they require a longer period of time to provide energy, and they require that more oxygen be present.

The body breaks down protein for use as a main source of energy only when carbohydrates and fats are not available—in other words, in a starvation situation. If your body is using protein for a main energy source, you are in trouble.

The body cannot directly use carbohydrates, fats, or protein for energy. All of them must first be converted to an energy source known as adenosine triphosphate (ATP). The body breaks ATP into adenosine diphosphate (ADP) and a phosphate (P). It is only by breaking that chemical bond that energy is released in a form that muscles and organs can use.

There are four basic "energy systems," or pathways, through which ATP is made available for use. The first is the small amount of ATP that is stored within the muscles. This energy is immediately available and requires no oxygen to use, but stored ATP is good for only about two to three seconds, after which it is depleted and must be re-formed.

The second energy system is known as the ATP-PC_r system. In this system, phosphocreatine (PC_r) donates a P to ADP to re-form ATP, which can then be broken down again for more energy. This system does not require oxygen and is good for about three to fifteen seconds. The limiting factor in this process is the minute supply of immediate ATP (which provides the necessary ADP) and the stored PC_r.

The third energy system is anaerobic glycolysis, in which glucose and glycogen are broken down to form ATP. This system, which is good for about fifteen seconds to two minutes, provides a lot of energy relatively quickly and does not require oxygen. Anaerobic glycolysis ends with the formation of lactic acid. This occurs due to the high speed of glycolysis, lack of sufficient oxygen, and the inability of the body to transport excess hydrogen (a product of glycolysis) at high speeds. The excess hydrogen combines with pyruvic acid to become lactic acid. The intensity, speed of glycolysis, and presence of oxygen determine lactic acid production. At high intensities the body continues to build up lactic acid in this manner. Whereas the ATP-PC_r system alone is good only for about fifteen seconds of energy production, PC_r continues working during glycolysis to assist in ATP production.

These first three energy systems—good for producing short bursts of speed or power—come into play when you accelerate for a breakaway or a sprint to the finish. Because these systems function without oxygen, they can provide energy only for brief periods. For any activity lasting more than two minutes (that is, the majority of your riding), the body must use oxidative processes.

The fourth energy system is oxidative phosphorylation, which requires oxygen and, although it does not supply energy as quickly as the other systems, provides larger amounts of energy over a longer period. Oxidative phosphorylation proceeds by two chemical pathways: aerobic glycolysis and beta-oxidation.

Aerobic glycolysis uses glucose and glycogen as fuel. In this pathway the chemical steps of glycolysis occur in the same manner as in anaerobic glycolysis with two exceptions: glycolysis requires oxygen and requires more steps and time. During aerobic activities, you are working at a much lower intensity level in comparison to anaerobic activities. Due to this, aerobic glycolysis runs more slowly than anaerobic glycolysis, and the hydrogen ions do not bind with pyruvic acid and are not converted to lactic acid. Instead, hydrogen is transported to the electron transport chain (a chemical process that produces ATP), and pyruvic acid can be converted and transported to the Krebs cycle (citric acid cycle). The Krebs cycle in turn sends more hydrogen to the electron transport chain for a much larger energy gain. Due to the hydrogen being transported to the electron transport chain, there is no excessive buildup of lactic acid. To say it simply, these chemical processes provide energy through oxidative processes by creating ATP. You will get 39 ATP per molecule of glycogen.

Aerobic glycolysis provides a lot of energy relatively quickly, but the body stores only a limited amount of glucose. Trained cyclists have about 2,000 kilocalories (Kcal) of stored glycogen. Once these stores are depleted, you will "bonk," or "hit the wall." If you have been riding any length of time, you have probably experienced this feeling of having no energy and wishing you were home on the couch. This is why it's important to replenish glycogen stores during long rides. (See Chapter 13 for details.)

Beta-oxidation, the second pathway, oxidizes fat for energy. This process takes longer than aerobic glycolysis but provides about ten times more energy (about 460 ATP per molecule of fat, compared to 39 ATP per molecule of glycogen). Beta-oxidation requires a much larger amount of oxygen to be present to form ATP. The body stores considerably more fat than glycogen, so fat constitutes a virtually unlimited fuel source within the context of a race. Glycogen, however, is required to drive the process of beta-oxidation, and when glycogen stores are completely depleted, the body cannot effectively convert fat to energy.

How does this apply to cycling? The energy systems work on a continuum. For example, when you begin pedaling on a nice easy recovery ride, your body almost instantly uses up its stored ATP and quickly shifts to ATP-PC$_r$, then to glycolysis. As the ride continues, your body switches to using fat in order to spare glycogen. For the rest of the ride, oxidative phosphorylation is the main source of energy. Intensity also determines whether the body is using glycogen or fat as a primary energy source. The higher the intensity, the more the body relies on glycogen; the lower the intensity, the more the body relies on fat. This is why the majority of your training should focus on developing oxidative systems for endurance performance.

Anaerobic sources of energy, however, should not be overlooked. Let's say that you're 500 meters from the end of a race when the sprint starts. You stand out of the saddle and start sprinting. During the first second or two, your body uses stored ATP, after which it switches to the ATP-PC$_r$ system for the next three to five seconds, then to anaerobic glycolysis for up to two minutes. That should see you to the end of the race. But what if you miscalculated the distance to the finish line? After about two minutes of anaerobic glycolysis, your sources of instant energy are depleted, and large amounts of lactic acid have built up in your legs. Your muscles hurt and you have no option but to slow down, hopefully right at the finish line. Anaerobic energy systems are improved through conducting interval training.

MUSCLE FIBERS

Each muscle is composed of thousands of muscle fibers of three basic types: slow-twitch (ST) fibers (also known as slow oxidative, or type I fibers), intermediate fibers (fast oxidative glycolytic, or type IIA), and fast-twitch (FT) fibers (fast glycolytic, or type IIB). Slow-twitch fibers are more useful for endurance events due to their high oxidative (aerobic) capacity; fast-twitch fibers are better for power due to their high glycolytic (anaerobic) capacity. Intermediate fibers fall somewhere in between.

Muscle composition is determined genetically and cannot be altered. Most people are born with about 50 percent ST and 50 percent FT, but some people have a higher percentage of one or the other. (The percentage of FT includes fast-twitch and intermediate muscle fibers. Typically half of the FT percentage consists of intermediate fibers.) Elite endurance athletes, such as pro cyclists, may have up to 90 percent ST fibers, whereas a world-class power lifter may have up to about 70 percent FT fibers. Although these individuals were born genetically predisposed to their sports, they had to develop that gift in order to excel. This does not mean that you cannot compete well as a cyclist if you don't have a high percentage of ST fibers, but it does decrease your chance of becoming a professional rider.

Fast-twitch fibers are larger and have a higher glycolytic capacity than ST fibers, enabling them to produce power quickly, and without oxygen. The downside is that they fatigue quickly as well. FT fibers are important for track cyclists, who must generate large amounts of power over short distances. Even for endurance cyclists, though, FT fibers cannot be overlooked because they are critical in sprinting. (You may notice that strong sprinters usually have larger legs than the pure climbers.)

Slow-twitch fibers are smaller in size and therefore do not produce as much power; but they have a high oxidative capacity, so they tire more slowly than FT fibers. ST fibers have a higher capillary density, which allows more oxygen to be delivered to the muscle cells. ST fibers also have more mitochondria, the organelles within the cells where energy is produced using the oxidative system. The more oxygen that can be brought into a muscle and the more mitochondria that are available to produce energy, the better the muscle can perform in an endurance event.

Intermediate fibers can be recruited to either end of the spectrum by specificity of training. If an athlete trains for power, the intermediate fibers will lean more toward power production. If an athlete trains for endurance, the intermediate fibers will lean that way. Intermediate fibers will not perform as well as FT or ST fibers and cannot change their characteristics, but they provide valuable assistance to FT or ST fibers.

The most accurate way to determine an individual's muscle fiber composition is through a biopsy, usually in the gastrocnemius (one of the calf muscles). This is performed by inserting a special needle and removing a plug of that muscle. The sample is then sliced, stained, and examined under a microscope. The extraction process, which is painful and usually expensive, is not recommended for the recreational athlete. You might be able to reduce or eliminate the cost, however, if you can find a university that's looking for research volunteers. Universities that have the capability to conduct muscle biopsies are always conducting research of some form or another.

A simpler way to make a general assessment of your muscle fiber composition is by determining where you excel. If you perform better at longer distances, you probably lean more toward ST fibers. If you perform better at sprints and short, steep climbs, you probably have a lower percentage of ST fibers. You can also determine this by lean body size. If you have a tendency to bulk up when training, you may be more FT, due to the fact that FT fibers are larger in diameter than ST fibers. If you cannot increase muscle size to save your life, you are probably ST predominant.

Recruitment of Muscle Fibers

Muscle fibers are grouped in arrangements called motor units. Muscles are bundles of one hundred to six hundred motor units. For a muscle to function, of course, it must receive a signal via the body's nervous system. Nerves begin at the brain and spinal cord (the central nervous system) and branch into smaller and smaller units until they reach special nerve cells called neurons. Each motor unit consists of a single motor neuron and all the muscle fibers attached to it. Fast-twitch and intermediate motor units have many more muscle fibers per motor unit than slow-twitch motor units.

The body recruits the type of motor units needed to get the job done. For the majority of a race, you will hold a pace that you can maintain aerobically, which will use primarily slow-twitch motor units. As you approach the finish line and your pace begins to exceed the aerobic threshold (more on this below), the body will use more intermediate and fast motor units. When sprinting for the finish line, the body will recruit primarily FT motor units to apply maximum power for a brief period.

Your body also recruits only the number of motor units needed to do the job. When a signal is sent through a motor neuron to the motor unit, every muscle fiber within that motor unit contracts completely. There's no dimmer switch here—it's either on or off. But not every motor unit in a muscle receives a signal to contract.

Through experience, your body knows how many motor units to recruit to complete a task. Lifting a coffee cup to take a sip uses the same muscles as curling a 30-pound dumbbell, but your body has learned to recruit the right number of motor units so you don't slam the cup into your face. Likewise in cycling, your body automatically and unconsciously recruits the type and number of motor units necessary. As you begin a steep climb, you usually slow your cadence and put more power into each stroke to overcome gravity. Your legs become fatigued faster than when you're riding on the flat because your body is recruiting more intermediate and FT fibers, and more motor units overall. With training, your body learns to save energy by recruiting the fewest motor units necessary to accomplish the task.

VO$_2$ MAX

Much training is focused on improving the capacity to transport and utilize oxygen, which has a direct relationship to endurance capacity. The most accurate way to measure progress in this area is by testing VO$_2$ max (pronounced *vee-oh-two max*). VO$_2$ represents the volume of oxygen utilized by the body.

VO$_2$ max is the body's maximal ability to deliver oxygen to the working muscles, and the muscles' ability to use that oxygen to produce energy for movement. VO$_2$ max is commonly expressed as milliliters of oxygen consumed per kilogram of body weight per minute (ml/kg/min). A higher VO$_2$ max indicates a greater capacity to transport and utilize oxygen and is considered the single best predictor of endurance performance.

VO$_2$ max is "trainable"—that is, anyone can increase their VO$_2$ max with training—although the amount and speed of improvement varies from individual to individual. A sedentary individual will have a lower VO$_2$ max than a recreational cyclist, and a recreational cyclist will have a lower VO$_2$ max than a professional cyclist.

TYPICAL RANGES FOR VO₂ MAX IN ADULTS			
	Sedentary	**Trained**	**Elite Athlete**
Male	45–50 ml/kg/min	55–65 ml/kg/min	≥70 ml/kg/min
Female	35–40 ml/kg/min	45–55 ml/kg/min	≥60 ml/kg/min

Although training increases VO_2 max, each individual has a predetermined genetic ceiling, which cannot be broken no matter how hard an individual trains. There is also a gender component: women tend to be about 10 ml/kg/min lower than men at any given level, as shown in the table above.

Determining your VO_2 max periodically will provide insight into the success of your training program. Various methods used to estimate VO_2 max apply formulas that assume a linear relationship between heart rate and VO_2 max. Although these methods may give you a ballpark figure for your VO_2 max, they are not accurate enough for monitoring your training. Most fitness facilities can run these simple estimations.

The more accurate way to determine VO_2 max involves the use of a computerized test instrument (known as a metabolic cart) and a graded exercise test. The cyclist wears a mask covering the nose and mouth, with valves that allow breathing in room air and exhaling through a tube leading to the metabolic cart. The instrument measures the amounts of O_2 and CO_2 in the exhaled air and compares these measurements to the amounts in the room air, thus determining the volume of O_2 being used by the body.

The cyclist undergoes a graded exercise test on a cycle ergometer—similar to a stationary bicycle with mechanically regulated resistance. (Other test devices are used for other sports.) The test starts off at an easy pace and gets progressively harder as more resistance is added every two to three minutes (depending on protocol) until the cyclist can no longer continue. The highest recorded VO_2 figure is considered the VO_2 max. The cyclist must give a 100 percent effort and not quit early. If the cyclist doesn't push to the limit, the VO_2 max is not considered max, but rather peak VO_2.

The problem with this method is that it requires specialized equipment and trained personnel and is therefore expensive to administer. One of the most cost-effective ways of having this procedure conducted is through a university with an exercise physiology department that is currently conducting research. You may be able to get tested at no cost; some studies even pay for qualified subjects. Some sports training facilities will test for a fee.

Let's say that you've participated in a VO_2 max test and you learn that your VO_2 max is 65 ml/kg/min. According to the table above, you fall into the trained category bordering on elite. There's a strong possibility that you already know that, based on your race performance. If I had to put together a cycling team and could know only one thing about the cyclists, however, I would not

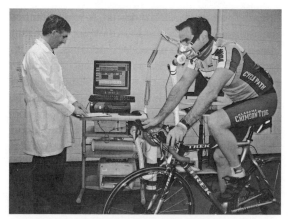

Laboratory tests with an automated metabolic cart are the most accurate way to determine VO_2 max.

choose VO₂ max as the deciding criterion. Instead, I would choose to know how well the cyclists performed during the past season. Performance is what it's all about. You do not train just to see your VO₂ max increase; you train to improve your cycling performance. Several factors besides VO₂ max play a role in determining who wins a race, such as the rider's pain threshold, bike-handling skills, and use of tactics.

That said, VO₂ max remains the best way to measure a cyclist's endurance capacity, and this is certainly one of the keys, if not the most important one, to cycling success. A gradual increase in VO₂ max in the span of a year is a strong indication that your training program is effective. If you're overtraining, you may see a decrease.

VO₂ max can also be a good predictor of hidden potential. If you are just beginning to train or have been training only haphazardly or sporadically and still score high on a VO₂ max test, it could be an indication of future performance.

ANAEROBIC AND LACTATE THRESHOLDS

Lactic acid is always being produced in the body. At rest and at low levels of intensity, the body is able to remove lactic acid before it's noticed and causes any adverse effects. At higher intensities of work, the body is unable to supply adequate O_2 due to the high speed of glycolysis. This causes the production of more hydrogen than the system can handle; this excess hydrogen bonds to pyruvic acid to become lactic acid. The point at which the body's production of lactic acid exceeds its ability to remove it is called the anaerobic threshold.

At high levels of concentration, lactic acid interferes with muscle contraction and can lead to cramping and a burning sensation in the legs. This pain can become unbearable, forcing a rider to slow or come to a complete stop until the excess lactic acid is removed. This occurs through various mechanisms in the body: lactate buffering,

conversion back to pyruvate, use of the lactate shuttle system, and the Cori Cycle.

There are three ways to define anaerobic threshold, all of which occur at the same point but differ in their specific markers. The first is characterized by an increase in blood lactate levels just above those normally found at rest in the individual being tested. This would be an increase of less than 1 millimole (mM) per liter of blood; it is known as lactate threshold.

The second, marked by a blood lactate level of 4 mM per liter of blood, is known as onset of blood lactate accumulation. Both of these methods involve a graded exercise test on a cycle ergometer. Resistance is increased every two to three minutes until the cyclist is exhausted. The cyclist's finger is pricked and blood is taken for analysis of blood lactate at every workload.

The body copes with increased levels of lactic acid by buffering and lowering the acidity through a chemical process called bicarbonate buffering. The process of buffering causes an increasing amount of CO_2 to build up in the tissue. The CO_2 must be removed from the body, a process that causes ventilation (breathing) to increase exponentially. At this

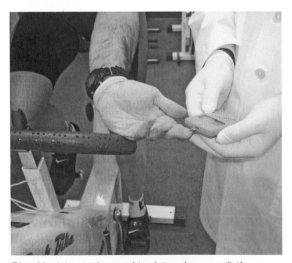

Blood lactate can be used to determine a cyclist's anaerobic threshold for a training prescription.

point, known as the ventilatory threshold (VT), you are breathing hard enough that you will not be able to say more than one or two words easily.

The VT is usually determined during a graded exercise test on a cycle ergometer. When a metabolic cart is being used and gas exchange is recorded, it is usually easy to plot and determine a corresponding heart rate at VT.

The VT is usually expressed as a percentage of VO₂ max, but the most useful information is the corresponding heart rate. If you know that your VT occurs at 180 bpm, you can better determine your training zones—the levels of training intensity that will produce the greatest gains in endurance. I consider this the most important measure that can be obtained from a graded exercise protocol—even more important than VO₂ max—because this is the precise point beyond which you want to extend your limits.

It's possible to determine VT by completing a graded exercise test without a metabolic cart. As your exercise intensity increases, note the heart rate where your breathing increases exponentially. This is the point at which rate and depth of breathing greatly increase. Conduct this test on more than one occasion to ensure that you're recording the same heart rate. This method is not as accurate, but it will give you a ballpark figure.

Although the anaerobic threshold, lactate threshold, onset of blood lactate accumulation, and ventilatory threshold are technically different, they are basically interchangeable. To keep things simple below, I use the term *anaerobic threshold*.

Once you reach the anaerobic threshold—the point at which lactic acid production exceeds removal—it will not be long before you have to slow down. The closer your anaerobic threshold is to your VO₂ max, the better you will be able to perform.

Take, for example, two cyclists with VO₂ max readings of 65 ml/kg/min and 70 ml/kg/min, respectively. One might initially assume that in a time trial, the second cyclist would win. This may not be the case, though, if the first cyclist's anaerobic threshold occurs at 90 percent of VO₂ max and the second cyclist's occurs at 70 percent of VO₂ max. In this case, the first cyclist is more likely to win.

Your greatest improvements in performance can come through increasing your anaerobic threshold. Although there can be a considerable increase in VO₂ max through training, there can be an even larger increase in anaerobic threshold. Untrained riders typically have an anaerobic threshold of 50 to 60 percent of VO₂ max, whereas elite cyclists' thresholds are about 90 percent of VO₂ max. Two ways to increase anaerobic threshold—tempo and interval training—are discussed in Chapter 10. Before you attempt that, however, you must have a solid endurance base.

Another important concept is what I call *racing threshold*, which is most apparent in the context of a steady-state race such as a time trial. In a road race, your pace increases and decreases continuously depending on what the riders in the front are doing. But during a time trial, it's you against the clock, and you try to maintain as fast and steady a pace as possible.

For any given distance, your maximum sustainable speed is your race threshold. Although not a scientific concept, race threshold is limited by the buildup of lactic acid and neuromuscular fatigue—feeling extreme tiredness in the working muscles. Naturally, the longer the course, the slower you will ride; the shorter the course, the faster you can ride. Through experience, you learn those limits, beyond which it's all over if you turn the screws. Inexperienced cyclists tend to turn the screws a little too much and fade as the race proceeds.

TRAINING ADAPTATIONS

The body has a surprising ability to adapt to the stress of training. Training is *catabolic*, but with a proper training regimen, the body adapts to this stress to build itself back up stronger than before in many different ways.

Aerobic Adaptations

Much of a cyclist's training is designed to create aerobic adaptations—changes that increase the delivery of oxygen to the muscles—and increase the muscles' ability to utilize that oxygen for energy production. These adaptations lead to improvements in VO$_2$ max, which translate into improvements in performance. The following are among the most important specific adaptations that occur with endurance training:

- Increase in total blood volume. Plasma and hemoglobin concentrations increase. Increases in hemoglobin production usually begin three to four weeks into training. Augmented hemoglobin concentrations in the blood deliver more oxygen to the muscles, allowing them to do more work. Initially, water loss that occurs due to sweating during training lowers plasma volume, but changes occur within the body that promote water retention in general. These changes in the blood in particular result in an increase of plasma volume, which is essential to prevent the blood from becoming too viscous.
- Increase in capillary density within the muscles. There will be a greater number of capillaries in relation to each individual muscle fiber. Gas and nutrient exchange in the muscle tissue occurs at the capillaries, so the more capillaries that exist, the more oxygen and nutrients can be delivered to the working muscles.
- Increase in myoglobin. Put simply, myoglobin is hemoglobin found in muscle tissue. The more myoglobin there is in a muscle, the greater the rate of oxygen transfer from the blood into the mitochondria of the muscle cells.
- Increase in the size and number of mitochondria. All oxidative energy production occurs in the mitochondria, so an increase in their number and size within muscle cells leads to an increased capacity for energy production.
- Increase in glycogen stores. Glycogen stores top out at about 2,000 kCal in endurance-trained individuals. (Untrained individuals store considerably less glycogen.) This provides more ATP through the use of aerobic glycolysis and beta-oxidation, enabling the body to break down fat for energy for longer periods.
- Increase in intramuscular stores of triglycerides (fats) and a decrease in adipose storage of fat. With training, the body begins to move fat from adipose stores (such as love handles) and converts it to triglycerides to store within the muscles, where it can be more quickly utilized for energy.
- Switching to burning fat sooner. The body stores a limited supply of glycogen but a practically unlimited supply of fat (70,000 kCal or greater). To spare glycogen during periods of long activity, the body learns to switch to burning fat sooner.

Another important aerobic training adaptation is a decrease in resting and submaximal heart rate. The average sedentary individual has a resting heart rate of 70 to 80 bpm, compared to figures in the thirties and forties for elite endurance athletes. To understand how this comes about, consider the "cardiac equation":

$$\text{cardiac output} = \text{stroke volume} \times \text{heart rate}$$

Cardiac output is the volume of blood pumped by the heart per minute; stroke volume is the amount of blood pumped per beat; heart rate is the number of beats per minute.

At rest, cardiac output is low due to the body's low energy requirements. As activity increases, cardiac output increases to supply the blood needed to meet the demand. The body cannot greatly alter stroke volume, so the heart rate increases. But over time with training, three key adaptations occur: the heart chambers undergo healthy enlargement, the heart contracts more forcefully, and the blood volume increases. The increase in blood volume allows for greater filling of the heart chambers. Larger heart chambers mean that the heart can take in more blood during diastole, the "filling" portion of the heartbeat. And a more forceful contraction increases the amount of blood ejected from the heart and into the arteries on each beat. All of this means greater stroke volume. Because only a given cardiac output is required by the body for any given submaximal workload, an increase in stroke volume allows the heart to beat more slowly.

Anaerobic Adaptations

Although the main focus of training for cycling is aerobic, anaerobic training cannot be overlooked.

Whenever you sprint for the finish line, power up a steep hill, attack off the front, respond to an attack, or bridge a gap, the anaerobic system is called into play. This occurs off and on frequently throughout a race. To be competitive, you need to be able to respond to these situations.

Interval training and tempo work that is slightly above the anaerobic threshold will improve your body's ability to buffer lactic acid. (These forms of training are described in Chapter 11.) This can result in an increase in anaerobic threshold by up to 40 percent, which will greatly increase your race threshold for any given distance. At the same time, training above the anaerobic threshold will generate even greater benefits in your aerobic performance.

essential principles of training

If one specific training program worked for everyone, there would be no need for more exercise physiologists, coaches, or books such as this one. But research has demonstrated that individuals respond differently to training.

Many collegiate and professional training programs, however, do not individualize their training to each athlete, using instead a cookie-cutter approach involving extremely high-volume workouts. Unfortunately, this type of training results in chronic overtraining and overuse injuries and destroys many good athletes whose bodies need more time to recover than others.

Genetics play an important role in determining one's potential. Just like hair and eye color, our ultimate ability to perform well in endurance or power events is passed on from parent to child, determined largely by the percentage of slow-twitch and fast-twitch muscle fibers. There are also genetic differences among individuals in the production of hormones, neuromuscular control, metabolism, and body fat percentage and distribution, to name just a few of many additional pertinent variables.

Good genetics, however, are far from a guaranteed ticket to the winner's podium. Lance Armstrong was most certainly born genetically gifted, but so are dozens of cyclists who compete in the Tour de France. Lance also trained as hard as, if not harder than, any of his competitors, using a training program that was ideally suited to his body and his racing objectives. It was the combination of genetics and training (plus attitude, organization, strategy, tactics, sponsorship, and a few other factors) that allowed him to win le Tour seven consecutive times.

We all have a genetic ceiling—the absolute physical limit of how well we can perform—and no matter how hard we train we will not be able to break through it. But the majority of athletes never reach it, and most don't even come close. You may not have the genetic background to win le Tour, but you can become a much better competitive cyclist through dedication to a well-designed training program.

OVERLOAD

Overload is one of the core principles of training. You must regularly overload your body for adaptations to occur. Training breaks down the body, but, given proper recovery, the body builds itself back up stronger than before and better prepared for the next training session. As your body adapts, you gradually increase the stress, and your performance increases as well. If you don't increase the stress, you won't see improvements; if you increase the stress too much or don't permit adequate recovery, you may see a decline in performance due to overtraining.

You can increase stress by increasing duration (time), frequency (number of days), or intensity (speed). When starting a program, it's always better to increase duration and frequency before intensity, and the increase should be gradual. This reduces the risk of injury and overtraining. You must be able to handle the distance before you worry about speed.

RECOVERY

Recovery is one of the most overlooked principles of training. The body needs adequate time between training sessions in order to rebuild. Cyclists worry about whether they trained hard and long enough, but many do not pay attention to how much sleep they get, whether they are fully recovered from their last workout, or whether they're receiving proper nutrition. As a coach, I never have a problem getting my athletes to train hard, but I do have problems getting them to go easy on their easy days.

Proper sleep is a key factor to recovery, and the harder you train, the more sleep you need. You should sleep at least seven hours a night, and as much as ten if you're training many hours a day almost every day. If you often feel drained during the day, you may not be getting enough sleep.

Nutrition is another key recovery factor; it's essential for rebuilding muscles and replenishing energy used during training. Nutrition is important before, during, and after training sessions and races. See Chapter 13 for details.

OVERTRAINING

Overtraining is a syndrome in which a cyclist's performance decreases over time. Everyone has a bad day now and then, which doesn't mean they're overtrained, but a persisting decline can be considered overtraining.

Overtraining may be physiological or psychological in nature, or both. Physiological causes are usually tied to inadequate recovery and/or are brought on by a sudden increase in the volume or intensity of training beyond the body's ability to cope.

When a cyclist says he feels "burned out," he is psychologically overtrained. Psychological overtraining may occur due to the monotony of training itself, or due to stress in everyday life.

Physical and psychological stress can impair the function of the immune system, leaving the body open to illness and decreasing its ability to heal quickly. The good news is that exercise is a good way to relieve psychological stress.

The overload principle affects the body's immune system. Immediately following hard exercise, the immune system is functioning lower than normal, making the athlete particularly susceptible to illness. But the immune system bounces back, and with repeated training it becomes stronger overall, which decreases the risk of illness. With overtraining, however, you run the risk of chronically impairing your immune system and increasing your overall risk of illness.

Here are the main signs of overtraining:

- prolonged decline in cycling performance
- constant fatigue
- chronic illness
- bad attitude toward practice
- resting heart rate persistently higher than normal
- abnormal sleeping patterns
- overuse injuries
- changes in body composition or eating habits

If overtraining is suspected, take a few days to a few weeks to recover. In most cases, you need not take off more than a couple of days, and reducing your training for a short period will be sufficient. If you experience severe fatigue and weight loss, it may be illness and not overtraining; see a physician to make sure.

Overtraining can be avoided easily if the proper precautions are taken:

- Ensure adequate recovery between training sessions.
- Increase training gradually, avoiding large jumps in frequency, intensity, or duration.

- After a layoff period, avoid jumping back in where you left off. Gradually work your way back to the volume and intensity of your previous training.
- Ensure that you receive adequate sleep and nutrition.
- Listen to your body and act accordingly.

The longer you train, the more adept you'll become at determining when something isn't right with your body. One saying that I repeat over and over to my students and athletes is, "It's much better to be 10 percent undertrained for an event or race than 1 percent overtrained."

SPECIFICITY OF TRAINING

Specificity of training means training the way you would like your body to adapt. In other words, to become a better cyclist, you have to ride. The adaptations that occur during aerobic training are specific to the stress placed on particular muscles. With training, the muscles in your legs will learn to fire efficiently in the specific patterns used for pedaling. Although swimming and running will increase your cardiovascular endurance, neither will help your legs adapt as they need to for cycling. It's OK to do a little cross training during the off-season to maintain cardiovascular fitness, but you still need to spend most of your training time on the bike.

There is also specificity among different forms of cycling. Track cyclists cover short distances as quickly as possible, without concern for energy conservation. They should train to maximize anaerobic power, concentrating on short distances and sprinting. Stage cyclists should spend hours and hours riding to build a strong aerobic base of endurance.

There is also specificity to bike setup. Your body adapts to your bike's seat tube angle, saddle height and fore-and-aft position, top tube length, crank-arm length, and stem length. Riding a bike with a different setup can negatively affect performance and even lead to overuse injuries.

If you have to make changes to your setup, do so slowly over a period of time. It takes a few weeks for your body to adapt. If the changes are drastic, you may experience a drop in performance for a short period.

A cyclist who had chronic knee pain asked me to evaluate his setup. I found that his saddle was far too low, which increased pressure on his knees. We raised his seat to obtain a 25-degree knee angle. His knee pain was relieved, but his performance declined. I advised him to stay with it, and after three weeks he was riding stronger than ever.

My colleagues and I conducted a study at the University of Alabama that found there is specificity between training on upright and aero handlebars. Triathletes who always ride in the aero position were found to be more economical and powerful in that position, and less so in an upright position, whereas pure cyclists who always ride with upright bars were found to be more economical and powerful in that position.

DETRAINING

"Use it or lose it" succinctly defines the important training principle of detraining. All of the training adaptations discussed in Chapter 10 are reversed without adequate stimulus to keep them in place. It takes a long time to gain your current level of fitness, but detraining occurs relatively quickly.

Among the many physiological changes that occur during detraining are losses in the following:

- Muscle strength and endurance. Known as muscle atrophy, this affects the speed and power you can produce in a sprint.
- Cardiorespiratory endurance. You won't be able to put in the long miles that you could before a layoff.
- Agility and coordination. This may affect your bike-handling skills.

The length of time that a cyclist is unable to train determines the amount of detraining that occurs. On occasion, not training for a couple of days, or training at a lower workload for a week or so, may be beneficial, allowing the body to recover from months of rigorous training. But after about a week of no training, a cyclist will start feeling the effects.

Detraining also is affected by the level of activity during the layoff. If you're injured but can cross train, you may be able to limit the severity of detraining. If you're completely immobilized due to injury, however, changes will begin within a few days. It's not unusual for a broken limb to lose half its muscle mass by the time the cast is removed.

The duration of the layoff determines the length of time it will take to come back. You may be able to bounce back relatively quickly from a layoff of a few weeks, but one of a few months will take longer. Of course this also varies from individual to individual. In any such situation, don't attempt to resume where you left off. Build back gradually to avoid overtraining and overuse injury.

CONSISTENCY

It is important to train consistently to achieve your potential. Inconsistency leads to poor performance and possible injury. Establishing a rigid training schedule can be difficult because it involves changing many aspects of your home, work, and social routines, but once established it becomes part of your daily routine and is easy to maintain. Once a routine is established, many cyclists feel guilty if they miss their workout.

As discussed in Chapter 9, writing down your training program will help you establish a routine and maintain consistency.

FREQUENCY

How many days a week should you train? You need to ride at least three days a week to see significant gains; greater frequency leads to greater gains. For most cyclists, three to five days a week is sufficient. The most successful competitive amateurs and virtually all professionals train six or seven days a week, with one or two of those days being "active recovery."

It is important to slowly work your way up to the desired frequency and refrain from doing too much at once. Beginners should start with easy rides two or three days a week, with a recovery day between each ride.

DURATION

Duration is how long or how far you ride during each session; it is measured either in time or distance (miles or kilometers). Gradually increasing duration is known as "building a base." As an endurance sport, cycling is built on an endurance base. You must be able to complete the mileage of a race comfortably before you can work at becoming competitive.

Duration and intensity are inversely related. You cannot ride a 50-mile race at the same intensity as a 10-mile one. As distance goes up, intensity must go down. If intensity is increased before a strong base is established, cyclists leave themselves open to injury.

Duration should be increased gradually—no more than 5 to 10 percent per week. If your "long" ride is 30 miles and you want to increase it to 60 miles, add 5 to 10 percent to your distance each week until you reach your goal.

The appropriate duration of training varies with a cyclist's goals. For racers, follow the 25 percent rule: your training distance should be at least 25 percent longer than your longest race. If your longest race is 60 miles, your long rides should be at least 75 miles. If your long rides are 100 miles instead of 75 miles, so much the better. On the other hand, if the longest race you will ever do is 30 miles, then 100-mile rides, although definitely beneficial, may be overkill. Your main concern is to ensure against having an inadequate base. Can you imagine competing in a 60-mile race when your longest ride during the season was 40 miles? Although you may be able to complete the distance, you're looking at a very bad day off the back of the pack.

For recreational cyclists who want to participate in charity rides, the 25 percent rule is recommended, although it may not be necessary. If you want to complete your first "official" century, the fact that you can do 100 miles without hurting yourself should be sufficient, provided you maintain the same pace during the ride and don't start feeling competitive. That said, if you can do 125 miles without trouble, the century will be that much easier and possibly more enjoyable. It's possible to complete a century when your longest ride has been 60 miles, but you'll be hurting severely when you do. By completing at least one 100-mile ride prior to your first century, you'll know that your body is physically ready, and you'll have the psychological boost of knowing that you can finish.

Intensity

Intensity is the "how hard" of training. As mentioned, you should establish a good endurance base before you work on intensity.

Physiologically, there are only three intensity levels: below, at, and above anaerobic threshold. Training below threshold should consist of long slow distance (LSD) rides and recovery rides, to build and maintain your endurance base. An LSD ride for a beginner may be one to three hours; for a pro it may be six to eight hours. Recovery rides promote active recovery and should be short and easy. Don't use your largest chainring on recovery days; stay in your small ring (or middle ring if you have a triple) to ensure that you don't overdo it. You should finish a recovery ride feeling as though you could have done twice the work.

Training at anaerobic threshold is also known as tempo or race-pace training. After a warm-up, you hold a steady pace right at threshold for the

desired distance, similar to a time trial. In the absence of competition, it's difficult to accurately simulate a race pace in practice. This is why scheduling races as "training" is an ideal way to improve performance. It also gives you an opportunity to work on tactics.

Training above threshold, also known as interval training, involves periods of high intensity followed by periods of recovery—for example, high intensity for 5 minutes followed by 5 minutes of soft pedaling, repeated five to ten times. You can also do longer high-intensity intervals—for instance, hard cycling for 10 to 20 minutes followed by 5 to 10 minutes of soft pedaling, repeated three to five times.

These are examples of structured intervals, but you can also train with nonstructured intervals, such as when answering attacks. A group rides at an easy pace, then a rider attacks by sprinting off the front of the group. The others respond by bringing the attacker back into the group. The attacks happen randomly throughout the ride. At the end of an interval session on a hard day, you should be pretty thoroughly exhausted.

Most of your training—90 to 95 percent of total volume—should be below threshold, with the majority of that being LSD. Too many cyclists train at threshold almost every day. They may become good racing at that intensity but will never become great without a balanced combination of LSD and interval training to raise their threshold. They become chronically tired and frustrated by their lack of improvement, and eventually their performance declines.

I once coached a mountain biker who trained hard every day. He consistently finished in the top three in the sport class but could not improve beyond that. For a year I tried to convince him that he was training too hard. When his performance began to decrease, he finally took my advice and, by the following year, he had moved up from sport to expert class and was consistently finishing in the top ten.

In general, cyclists should have no more than one or two "hard" days a week at or above threshold. Beginners should not worry about hard days at all until they build a strong base. In the beginning, cyclists will see increases in speed without high-intensity workouts. Building a base strong enough to support a serious high-intensity program may take one to two years. With specific periodization, professional cyclists can have three or more hard days a week, but average riders cannot handle that amount of intensity.

Determining Intensity Using Speed

Because intensity plays a key role in a training regimen, it's important to measure it. Four methods of measurement are common—using speed, heart rate, power, and "feel"—but only the latter three are really effective.

Speed is not an effective measure of intensity because it's so easily affected by wind and terrain. The intensity of a cyclist maintaining a given speed will be decreased by a strong tailwind or a downhill, and vice versa for headwinds and uphill. Speed is also influenced by whether a cyclist is riding alone or sheltered in a group.

Speed can be used as a marker set by riding a familiar course at race pace, but this is a measure of performance, not intensity per se. To use speed as a marker, record the temperature, the wind speed and direction, the time it takes to complete the course, and the average speed. Given equivalent conditions, it should be easy to monitor improvements in performance. But don't try for a personal best every time you ride the course. Remember that most of your training should be at a slower pace.

Determining Intensity Using Heart Rate

Heart rate is a better indicator of intensity, but it must be measured accurately. It's possible to count your heart rate while riding by finding your pulse at the carotid artery (in your neck) or the radial artery (in your wrist), but this is difficult, possibly unsafe, and often inaccurate. And as intensity increases, these factors become even more problematic. Nonetheless, beginners who need only a rough guide may find it acceptable. Once you find your pulse, count for six seconds and multiply by ten to get your heart rate in beats per minute. If you miss just one beat while counting, you may be off by 10 to 20 beats per minute (bpm)—a large discrepancy.

Using a heart-rate monitor while riding is easier, safer, and much more accurate. Heart-rate monitors are available for as little as $40 at bike shops and general sports retailers and online. Get one that allows you to program in training zones, or pairs of upper and lower heart-rate limits. An alarm sounds when your heart rate is outside the zone you have selected.

Determining Maximum Heart Rate

To use heart rate as a training tool, first you must know your maximum (max) heart rate. Several methods to find this are described below; all of them involve the use of a heart-rate monitor. In all methods, conduct the test when you're well rested and well hydrated, and be sure to spend 10 to 20 minutes warming up and 10 to 20 minutes cooling down. To capture your true max heart rate, you need to give everything you have during the test. It can be helpful to have friends along to encourage you.

- Indoor cycle ergometer. After your warm-up, begin pedaling at your normal training cadence. Then increase resistance on the ergometer by 0.5 kp (kilopond; 1 kp represents the force applied by the mass of 1 kg) every three minutes while maintaining your pace. When you can no longer continue, you will have reached your max heart rate.
- Hill repeats. Find a hill a half mile to a mile long. After warming up, pedal up the hill as hard and fast as possible. Repeat three to

five times with a two-minute break between each set. By the last climb you should have reached your max heart rate.

■ Repeated sprints on flat ground. After a warm-up, complete three to five sprints at an all-out effort. The sprints should last two to three minutes. Watch your heart rate after completing the sprint because it may continue to rise before it begins to fall. By the last sprint you should have reached your max heart rate.

■ Monitoring during a race. You had better believe that if you're sprinting to the finish line, you will know your true max heart rate.

Repeat these processes more than once to eliminate spurious readings. These methods are demanding, and beginners should approach them with caution. If you've been sedentary up to this point, it's best to get medical clearance prior to starting.

I mention one more method to determine your max heart rate simply because it's out there as "common knowledge": subtract your age from 220 (for example, 220–35 years = 185 bpm). I discourage the use of this method because sometimes it's not even in the ballpark. According to the equation, my max heart rate would be 184 bpm, but my actual max heart rate is 201 bpm: I've seen it there on numerous occasions.

Using a Heart-Rate Monitor

A simple but acceptable approach to establishing your training zones relies strictly on heart rate max. Set the heart-rate monitor's zones to between 50 and 65 percent of your heart rate max for recovery rides, and between 60 and 80 percent for LSD rides. (Beginners should stay closer to 60 percent during LSD.)

If you know the heart rate that corresponds to your current anaerobic threshold, you can get even better results. Setting the bottom end of the zone at 60 percent of heart rate max and the top

end at 10 percent below the heart rate that corresponds with your anaerobic threshold ensures that you stay below threshold on your easy days (LSD and recovery rides).

Heart-rate monitors are useful on hard days as well. If you know your heart rate that corresponds to your anaerobic threshold, you can ensure against going too hard early in a tempo ride or a race. Keep in mind, though, that during a race you'll have to respond to attacks and hills regardless of heart rate. The monitor is, therefore, more useful when competing in a self-paced event, such as a time trial. You need to know your corresponding heart rate for the given distance of the event. Heart-rate monitoring can also be useful during interval training by ensuring that you receive adequate recovery between sets, which will allow for a more potent training session.

But the best use of a heart-rate monitor is to keep you easy on your easy days. Every time the alarm sounds, you know you need to back off. The exception is when climbing a steep hill, where it's usually unrealistic to stay below your heart-rate limit for LSD and recovery rides.

It is better to train within zones rather than attempt to maintain one specific target heart rate because heart rate at any given level of intensity can be somewhat variable. It can vary on a daily basis due to various factors such as hydration levels, and even during a ride. This latter phenomenon, known as cardiac drift, is marked by a slow heart-rate increase throughout the ride even though intensity has not changed. As a ride progresses, the body loses water through sweat. This draws down the volume of plasma in the blood, leading to a reduced blood volume. To keep cardiac output the same, the heart rate must increase to compensate for the lower stroke volume. The longer the ride and the hotter the day, the more the heart rate will drift.

One of the hardest lessons to learn is to let your cycling buddies go on ahead when they're riding harder than you should for that day. Too often, a ride that has been represented as an easy

day turns into a hammer fest, involving easy riding for the first mile or two, followed by an increase to race pace, attacks on every hill, and a series of sprints thrown in for good measure. My definition of an easy ride is one that allows you to hold a conversation and enjoy the scenery. Keep in mind that "easy" is relative, and one rider's easy conversational ride at 18 mph may be another's threshold.

Determining Intensity Using Power

Power is defined as force multiplied by distance and divided by time. In cycling, power deals with the amount of force that the cyclist applies to the pedals. Power is a good way to determine intensity because it can directly measure the cyclist's work during training. With the proper equipment, a cyclist who wants to train at 250 watts (W) can

MORE ABOUT HEART-RATE MONITORS

Athletic heart-rate monitors consist of two components, a transmitter and a receiver. The transmitter, a strap that's worn around the chest, contains a sensor that detects heart rate and a wireless transmitter that sends a signal. This signal is received and displayed by the receiver, which is worn on the wrist like a watch. (Earlier models used a wire between the two.) It's best to avoid pulse meters, in which the transmitter attaches to the finger or earlobe, because they're not as accurate. Entry-level heart-rate monitors cost about $35, but you should spend a bit more to obtain at least two additional features not present on the cheapest units.

The first feature, discussed above, is programmable training zones that trigger an audible beep when you stray outside the set range. This saves you the trouble of constantly looking at the receiver. The other feature is a coded analog or digital signal between the transmitter and the receiver. When you ride with a group, chances are that more than one person is wearing a heart-rate monitor. If the heart-rate monitors are not coded, they may "cross-talk," or interfere with other signals. Your readings may be sporadic, or you might even pick up someone else's heart rate on your display. Heart-rate monitors with coded analog or digital signals eliminate this problem, as well as interference from overhead power lines that occasionally disrupts uncoded signals.

Two other useful features include:

A heart-rate monitor consists of a transmitter, which is worn around the chest, and a display receiver, which is worn on the wrist or on the handlebars.

- Energy expenditure measurement. This feature helps you track calories used while riding and resting. Awareness of calories used can help you refuel adequately before your next bout, and assist in weight management. This measurement is only an estimate.
- Data downloads. Garmin and Polar offer cycle computers that allow you to download heart rate and other cycling data, such as speed, duration, distance, and pace, for analysis on a home computer.

monitor and maintain that power level to elicit the desired intensity regardless of headwinds or tailwinds that may significantly affect speed.

A 30-second Wingate test is often used to determine a cyclist's peak and mean power. The resistance on the cycle ergometer is set at 7.5 percent of the rider's weight in kilograms. The cyclist warms up for 10 to 20 minutes, then sprints as hard as possible for 30 seconds. Both peak and mean power, represented in watts, are recorded and can be used to calculate a power-to-weight ratio.

For example, an 80 kilogram (176 pound) individual produces peak power of 1,364 W and mean power of 530 W during a Wingate test. This equates to peak power of 17.05 W/kg (7.75 W/lb.) and mean power of 6.62 W/kg (3.01 W/lb.). Although these numbers are often used to compare cyclists, they are better markers of individual performance. Monitor peak and mean power throughout your training season; if you can increase them, you will ride faster.

Both variables in this equation can be manipulated to increase your numbers, and most beginning cyclists need to work on both. Many cyclists, however, devote too much effort to losing weight and not enough to increasing power production. Power production can be increased through specialized training on the bike and weight training in the off-season (discussed in Chapter 12).

Determining Intensity by Feel

Some cyclists prefer to train by feel. Although this is a viable approach, it's a little more complex than it sounds. Cyclists who have been training for a while are so in tune with their bodies that they know their limits by the way they feel. During a race they push right up to their threshold and not beyond. This method is hard for beginning cyclists who don't yet have the base of experience to make these judgments. Accurately adjusting pace based on how you feel can be learned only through trial and error.

Paying attention to your breathing can help you determine intensity. During recovery rides your breathing should allow you to carry on a conversation easily; if not, you're riding too hard. During LSD training you should still be able to hold a conversation with nothing more than slight problems during longer sentences. During tempo training you should be able to get only a few words out. If you can say more than one or two words during your intervals, you're definitely not pedaling hard enough.

You can also determine intensity by using a rating of perceived exertion (RPE) scale. The Borg scale, the most commonly used one, ranges from 6 to 20. A rating of 6 is equivalent to soft pedaling down a hill. At a rating of 13 to 15, you will be at your threshold. At a rating of 20, you would feel as though your legs were breaking off and you were about to puke and black out. Although it takes some time to be able to dial in this scale to your own intensity levels, research has demonstrated that, with practice, most people can reproduce the scale on command, as long as the conditions are the same. The best way to dial in the Borg scale is with a graded exercise test on a cycle ergometer, beginning at 6 or 8 and ending at 20.

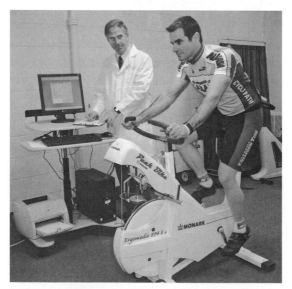

A 30-second Wingate test is used in laboratories to determine a cyclist's power-to-weight ratio.

POWER METERS

There are currently four methods of measuring power available to the consumer. All of them measure power on the bike and send the information to a handlebar-mounted computer for interpretation and display:

- ◼ SRM crankset. Measures power through strain gauges in the crank arms.
- ◼ Power Tap hub. Relies on a strain gauge and replaces the regular rear-wheel hub.
- ◼ Ergomo Sport bottom bracket. Measures force applied to the bottom-bracket spindle.
- ◼ Polar Power System. Measures chain speed and tension, and can be used in conjunction with specific models of the company's heart-rate monitors. This appears to be the least accurate and reliable method of the four.

By the time this book is in print, a new power system should be available from MicroSport Technologies. The Revolution Power System measures power at the pedal/shoe interface. In theory this system should be relatively accurate, but the product had not yet been tested independently when this book was being written.

For more details on setting intensity using power, read *Training and Racing with a Power Meter*, by Hunter Allen and Andrew Coggan. The authors explain the importance of measuring power for training, detail

SRM cranksets are used to monitor power output while cycling.

methods of measuring power, and suggest how to put the information to good use.

Using heart rate and power output in combination is probably the best method of monitoring intensity. Power Tap hubs and SRM cranks allow you to measure heart rate and power, and download the data to a PC. These units are somewhat costly, but if your goal is to reach your true genetic ceiling, I can think of no better tool.

Keep in mind, though, that these are all just tools to assist you in your training. They won't make you a better cyclist if you don't train. And if you don't use them to analyze your training and make adjustments accordingly, they are nothing more than expensive gadgets.

FLEXIBILITY

Flexibility is the ability to move each joint through its full and proper range of motion—something that many cyclists overlook as an essential aspect of fitness. Lack of flexibility cannot only limit performance, but it can also lead to injury. A cyclist riding at a pace of 90 rpm makes 21,600 pedal strokes over four hours. Other than standing out of the saddle once in a while and shifting slightly fore or aft on the saddle, cyclists maintain a relatively fixed position with a relatively small range of motion over long periods. Without an active flexibility program to counteract this, cyclists inevitably lose flexibility.

Stop reading right now and see whether you can touch your toes without difficulty. How tight are your hamstrings? I'm willing to bet that most readers will not get even close. (It doesn't count if you bend your knees.)

Following are the essential stretches you should do to improve your flexibility for cycling. When performing them, do not stretch to the point of pain; that will lead to injury. (If you want to feel burning and pain in your legs, do intervals or hill repeats.) Instead, stretch until the muscle is tight and you feel mild discomfort. Hold it there for 15 to 30 seconds; relax, then repeat two to four times.

This is known as static stretching. Learn to relax into the stretch and let gravity do the work for you. Do not use ballistic stretching, in which you bounce or otherwise use momentum to stretch further; this can lead to injury.

Quadriceps Stretch

One of the biggest mistakes people make when stretching the quadriceps (thigh muscles) is to push the heel of the foot into the gluteus maximus. This places too much pressure on the knee. Instead, while standing, hold your left ankle with your right hand and pull up and back. This stretches the quadricep muscles without putting excessive strain on the knee. Repeat with the opposite ankle and hand.

Hamstrings Stretch

This movement should be conducted seated. (If done standing, you risk becoming light-headed and falling on your face.) Sit on the floor with both legs stretched out in front of you. Relax, lean forward, and with both hands grasp as low as possible on your legs. This movement also stretches your back. If you can, grip your toes and pull back to stretch the calves as well.

Adductors Stretch

This movement stretches the adductors (muscles located on the inside of the leg). Sit on the floor and bend your knees so you can place the bottoms of your feet together in front of you. Pull your feet

toward your body and push down on your knees with your elbows.

Calf Stretch

To stretch the gastrocnemius muscle (one of two muscles that make up the calf, see page 162), stand on a low, stable platform and place the toes and ball of one foot on the edge of the platform with the heel hanging off. While keeping the knee straight, drop the heel of that foot downward until you feel a slight stretch. Repeat with the other leg. To stretch the soleus (the other muscle in the calf), put a slight bend in the knee. Do this exercise both ways to fully stretch the calves.

Hip Stretch

Sit on the floor with your right leg out straight in front of you and your left leg bent at 90 degrees. Cross your left leg over your right leg, placing your left foot on the floor on the outside of your right knee. Place your right arm over your left knee and apply pressure to the left leg at the knee. You should feel the stretch in your left hip. Repeat with the opposite side.

Here's a second method. While lying flat on your back, bend your right knee and place your hands on your right shin just below the knee. Bring your knee toward the chest and stretch. Leave your left leg extended. Repeat on the opposite side.

Quadriceps stretch.

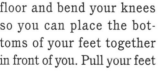

Hamstring stretch.

Adductors stretch.

Calf stretch.

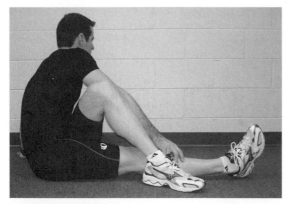

Hip stretch seated.

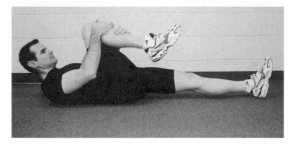

Hip stretch supine.

Tensor fasciae latae and iliotibial tract stretch.

Tensor Fasciae Latae and Iliotibial Tract Stretch

The tensor fasciae latae runs down the lateral aspect (outside) of the leg. This muscle is important in directing the leg forward and resisting external rotation as the hip is flexed. Cycling can cause this muscle to become tight, which can lead to biomechanical errors at the hip and knee.

To stretch this muscle, stand perpendicular to a wall a little less than an arm's length away. Cross the leg that's closest to the wall well behind the other leg, then extend your arm fully and push your hip toward the wall. You will need to adjust your position until you can feel a slight stretch along the outside of the back leg. Repeat with the other side.

Abdominal Stretch

Lie facedown on the floor and place your palms on the floor at shoulder level and shoulder width apart. Slowly push your upper body upward while leaving your lower body on the floor. Do this carefully; too much hyperextension can cause the spinous processes (boney protrusions of the vertebrae) to rub together and can lead to lower-back problems over time.

Abdominal stretch.

Lower-back stretch.

Neck stretch.

Lower-Back Stretch

Lower-back flexibility is important in cycling, especially when trying to achieve a comfortable aero position. For this stretch, lie on your back on the floor; bring up your legs and hips, and roll your body to shift your weight onto your shoulder blades. Continue to bring your lower body up and over your head until you feel a light stretch in your lower back. You can place your hands on your hips or keep them on the ground for support, whichever is more comfortable.

Neck Stretch

During cycling the neck remains in a slightly extended forward position, with little movement, for a prolonged period. This makes it extremely important to work on neck flexibility. Do all three of these stretches for three different ranges of movement:

1. Rotate your head to the left; hold for 15 to 30 seconds, then repeat to the right.
2. Flex your head toward your chest and hold for 15 to 30 seconds, then extend your head back and hold for the same amount of time.
3. Tilt your head to the left and hold for 15 to 30 seconds, then repeat to the right.

You can perform these stretches with no assistance, or you can use your hands, a towel, or a partner to assist. If you do use any assistance, be gentle and move slowly to prevent injury.

off-season training

The common conception that the off-season is a time to relax and rejuvenate is only partially true. The off-season is not a time to stop training; rather it's the time to change your training to prepare for the following year. It's also a time to take a mental and physical break from long grueling hours on the bike and high-intensity workouts. But if you stop training completely, you'll enter the upcoming season with a poor base. Seasons can be won and lost based on off-season training.

Although you will not ride as long or as hard during the off-season, you must not stop riding entirely. If you do, your fitness level will drop dramatically and it will take a long time to rebuild for the next season. The off-season is ideal for building strength on and off the bike. Your four main goals for the off-season should be the following:

- Recover from a hard race season (both mentally and physically).
- Maintain a sufficient endurance base.
- Develop strength through resistance training.
- Improve technical and tactical aspects of riding and racing.

In the off-season cyclists need to lower the intensity of training to allow the body to recover. It can even be beneficial to park the bike in the garage for anywhere from a few days to two weeks. Don't park it longer than two weeks, though, or you'll lose a lot of your base conditioning. Instead of taking two weeks completely off, you could take a couple of weeks off from a structured workout program, continuing to ride but not worrying about how hard you're riding. Don't worry about interval training or threshold training during this period. Most of your training (with the exception of hill training, discussed below) should be at a conversational pace. You should also reduce the volume of training by 20 to 40 percent. You can do this by decreasing the duration and the frequency of your rides.

The off-season also gives you the opportunity to recover mentally from the rigorous training and racing that occurs during the season. This includes recovering from high levels of mental stress, which can leave the body susceptible to illness and cause it to heal more slowly than normal. And it provides a break from what can be the mind-numbing monotony of training. This is a chance to ride simply because you love to ride—something that's easy to forget during the racing season. If you're feeling burned out at the end of the season, your motivation is probably waning and you really need a break. By the end of the off-season, you should feel mentally rested and be looking forward to resuming the rigorous, goal-oriented discipline of high-volume, high-intensity training.

INDOOR TRAINING

Depending upon where you live, road riding in winter may be perfectly reasonable, somewhat uncomfortable, or out of the question. But it's not just a matter of cold weather and poor road conditions; available daylight can be in short supply in winter. So even if you live in a climate that's warm year-round, indoor training can be an important part of your off-season training.

Trainers, Rollers, Spin Bikes

To maintain your cycling-specific adaptations, you should maintain your endurance base with an exercise that involves pedaling. For indoor training, you have three choices:

- Trainers. These are small metal frames that hold the bike upright, with the rear wheel off the floor, and provide some means of applying resistance to the rear wheel as you pedal.
- Rollers. These consist of three or four cylinder-shaped rollers, each about a foot wide, held in a flat framework. They do not have adjustable resistance and they do not hold the bike in place, so the rider must maintain balance while "riding."
- Spin bikes. These are stationary bikes specially designed for bike training rather than general fitness exercise.

Physiologically, a trainer is often the best option because you use your own bike—the setup to which your body has adapted. Trainers are also far less expensive than spin bikes.

The problem with trainers, however, is that they lock the back wheel and frame into a fixed position, preventing the side-to-side rocking that's typical when pedaling on the road. This places an extraordinary amount of force on the back wheel and the frame, which can cause early fatigue and failure of both. This is also tough on the rear tire, which can develop a flat spot after just a few rides

A stationary trainer locks the rear axle in place and provides resistance at the rear wheel.

on the trainer. (Continental has a tire designed specifically for use on trainers; it dissipates heat better than normal tires and lasts twice as long.)

To avoid damage to your one and only race bike, you may wish to use an old bike or a training bike on a trainer. It may even be worthwhile to buy a used bike with similar geometry specifically for that purpose.

Rollers do not lock the rear wheel in place, so they do not place unusual stress on a bike. But because the bike just sits on top of the rollers, and you don't have the benefit of forward momentum to assist you in maintaining your balance, rollers require a greater amount of skill and a highly developed sense of balance to use. Falling off rollers can cause serious injury and damage to any object located nearby. And you cannot adequately adjust the tension on a roller, which may limit your ability to train optimally. On the other hand, using rollers improves your balance and pedaling skills.

Because rollers don't lock the bike in position, they require much more skill to ride.

Spin bikes allow the cyclist to adjust resistance by increasing or decreasing the force applied to the flywheel.

Spin bikes have a fixed gear and a flywheel (which may weigh 30 to 50 pounds), so you can't just stop pedaling as you would on a road bike. During my first spin class, we were spinning pretty hard during an interval session. The seat was bothering me, so I decided to stand slightly to readjust my bottom. Not realizing that the gear was "fixed," I stopped pedaling as I would on the road, and before I knew it I almost flew over the handlebars. My right knee was sore for a week.

Indoor training can quickly become boring, producing a tendency to find other things to do besides getting on the trainer. Videos that provide structured workouts for indoor training are one way to break the monotony. Because the majority of these videos are for interval training, you should be careful not to train hard every day.

Another option is to invite friends over and have an indoor ride together. Socializing with your training buddies helps the time pass quickly, and establishing a "training date" with your friends on certain days each week provides

the discipline to make sure you do it. You can ride casually as you watch your favorite cycling movie (the movie doesn't have to be about cycling), or the group can train hard while watching a training video.

One of my favorite products for indoor training is CompuTrainer, a computer-driven trainer from RacerMate Inc. (see the Appendix for their website). The software displays a route on the monitor using realistic, computer-game-like graphics, and changes resistance on the trainer as the terrain changes. As you ride, the system captures training data such as cadence and power output. You can specify various courses—even the route for an upcoming race on your schedule—and change the view on the monitor to keep things interesting.

Many facilities offer spin classes, where a certified instructor leads you through an organized workout on spin bikes. A good spinning class can give you an effective workout as well as entertain you. To find a good spinning program, call around to your local gyms.

CROSS TRAINING

It's best to stay away from the trap of cross training. Running, swimming, and other noncycling cardiovascular exercises are not valid off-season substitutes for cycling because they lack the training specificity of cycling. Running and swimming improve your ability to run and swim, not your ability to cycle. Compare an elite marathon runner's legs with a professional cyclist's, and you'll notice that the runner's legs are smaller. This is due to the training specificity that occurs in these very different sports. Having said that, a little running, snowshoeing, or cross-country skiing added to your program will not hurt; in fact they can be beneficial by providing a mental break from cycling while helping you maintain cardiovascular fitness.

Cyclo-cross and mountain biking are better forms of off-season cross training. Both provide cycling-specific benefits, and both can often be conducted more comfortably in the cold than can road riding; they are done at lower speeds, and many trails are sheltered from the wind. Riding on narrow, twisting, bumpy trails also improves your bike-handling skills, and the scenery is a pleasant change from long hours on the road.

RESISTANCE TRAINING

Developing strength during the off-season gives you the ability to put more power into every pedal stroke during the "on" season. Through resistance training on and off the bike, you increase your average power output and peak power, boosting your overall speed and your hill-climbing and sprinting abilities. I use the term *resistance training* as opposed to *weight training* or *strength training* because it's a broader term. (Because weight training does little or nothing to improve cardiovascular fitness, however, it's important not to neglect aerobic training.)

Resistance training may decrease your performance in the beginning of the following race season. It may take a short period for your newly strengthened leg muscles to relearn the proper

Mountain bikes have thicker frames, wider tires, and (usually) smaller-diameter wheels than road bikes, in addition to different shifters, handlebars, and brakes. Most mountain bikes also have shock absorbers.

Cyclo-cross bikes are similar to road bikes. The main differences are wider tires, cantilever brakes (to provide clearance for mud), and minor frame and fork details to accept cantilever brakes.

firing sequence, and you may feel a little sluggish at first. That will change as your training switches to increased endurance and interval training. Then you'll see the improvements from your off-season resistance training.

Cyclo-cross is an excellent way to train during the off-season.

Design your program so you gain "useful" muscle mass, concentrating on the lower body. Although you want to avoid developing an overly muscular upper body that adds weight and isn't helpful for cycling, you don't want to ignore your upper body either. Upper-body strength is extremely important for cyclists—to support your upper body on the bike, to assist in bike control, to establish a strong base of support that will aid in power production, and possibly help prevent injury.

Lifting correctly for three months during the off-season will not make you overly large for three reasons:

- You'll keep your repetitions high (20 to 30 reps per set, see page 159) with low weight.
- A portion of the resistance training will be conducted on the bike.
- You'll spend only an appropriate amount of time developing your upper body.

DELAYED ONSET OF MUSCLE SORENESS

Concentric movement, or loading, occurs when active muscles shorten during contraction (for example, during the upward phase of squats). Eccentric loading occurs when the muscles lengthen during contraction (for example, during the downward movement of the squat). A condition known as delayed onset of muscle soreness (DOMS) occurs only as a result of eccentric loading. DOMS is the feeling of muscle soreness that occurs one or two days after a workout and can persist for one to three days.

The circular pedaling motion of riding is concentric, so DOMS does not result. (A cyclist's legs may be tired after a long day in the saddle, but they won't be sore. The exception occurs when riding a fixed-gear bike such as a track bike, in which you use eccentric movement to slow down.) Weight training, however, involves equal amounts of concentric and eccentric movements. You will feel sore the day after you lift. And if you really overdo it on Day 1, the amount of soreness that hits you one to three days later can be truly debilitating.

A friend called to tell me he had started his off-season weight-training program and had a hard workout on his first day. I asked him to call me the next day and let me know how he felt. The following day, he informed me that he could barely get out of a chair and walk across the room. It took him almost a week before he felt like riding, and almost two weeks to return to the weight room.

You can limit DOMS by starting with very light weights for the first week or two, and gradually increasing. After a few weeks of training, you will scarcely notice any soreness.

Although your body may be used to punishing workouts on the bike, it's not used to weight training. Start your program slowly to avoid injury. Doing too much too soon can damage muscles and ligaments, which will keep you out of the weight room and off your bike until you recover. It can also make you so sore that you won't be able to exercise again for days or weeks, as described in the sidebar.

Adaptations to Resistance Training

During the first eight weeks or so of resistance training, increases in strength come from three neuromuscular adaptations, without any increase in muscle-fiber size:

- Recruitment of more motor units. When you start lifting, your body recruits motor units that you have not been using.
- Better coordination of motor units. The muscles' contractions will be better synchronized, enabling them to work together more effectively.
- Extended golgi tendon organ threshold. The golgi tendon organ (GTO) is located at the junction of the muscle tendon and bone. As a muscle contraction increases in intensity, a greater amount of stress is placed on the tendon and its place of attachment to the bone. At a specific threshold, the GTO activates to inhibit the muscle contraction. With training, the threshold of the GTO increases.

After about eight weeks, following these neuromuscular adaptations, further increases in strength will come from hypertrophy of the muscle—an increase in the size of the muscle fibers. Although these increases in strength occur more slowly than the three neuromuscular adaptations, these are the changes that will make the biggest difference in your upcoming season. So be patient and don't get frustrated if your increases slow after the first few weeks of strength training.

DESIGNING A STRENGTH-TRAINING PROGRAM

A properly designed strength-training program incorporates these variables: frequency of exercise, number of sets and number of repetitions of each exercise within each set, the weight or other resistance used, and the type of exercise.

Frequency

The first thing to determine is frequency. During the off-season, you should do strength training two or three days a week. Take at least one day off between each resistance day to prevent overtraining and allow time for recovery. (I like to use Monday and Friday for weight training and Wednesday for on-the-bike resistance training.) Lower the frequency during preseason to about once a week for maintenance until race season starts. Once the season starts, discontinue resistance training.

Reps and Sets

A repetition (rep) is a single movement against the weight or other form of resistance—for example, lifting a dumbbell a single time. A set is a specified number of repetitions done continuously. The combination of reps and sets determines the volume of training. Start with only one set, then slowly work up to as many as four. Because cycling is an endurance sport, reps should be fairly high—between 20 and 30 reps per set. Once you can achieve 30 reps for every set, it's time to move up in weight.

Determining Resistance

For the first couple of weeks, restrict your lifting to extremely light weights to help prevent injury and limit the effects of DOMS. You should finish each set feeling that you could have lifted a much heavier weight. After a couple of weeks, slowly increase intensity by lifting heavier weights. Choose a weight that allows you to complete 20 to 30 repetitions, reaching exhaustion at the end of every set.

Type of Exercise

In selecting exercises from those described here, concentrate on the lower body, choosing at least one exercise that works the major muscle groups in the legs, such as squats or the hip sled. Also select exercises that work individual leg muscles, including the quadriceps, hamstrings, gastrocnemius, and soleus. For the upper body, make sure you cover each major body part with one exercise, such as a bench press and a lat pull-down. Choose core exercises that will strengthen your lower back and abdominals. Be sure to include at least one day of on-the-bike resistance training weekly.

The order in which you do exercises is important. Because small muscle groups assist large ones, you should start with the large muscle groups to avoid fatiguing the small muscle groups too early. During a bench press, for example, the triceps assist the pectoralis major. If you have worked the triceps first in another exercise, you may be unable to work the pectoralis major to full potential in a bench press. The same thing would occur if you worked the biceps prior to the latissimus dorsi in a lat pull-down or a seated row. Use the chart below to determine which large movement to perform before the corresponding small movement. Shoulders and core movements should be your last exercises of the day.

The goal of the following section is to give you the tools to develop an adequate weight-training program for cycling. It is by no means an exhaustive list of weight-training movements. You can add and switch out exercises. For example, if you don't

LARGE- AND SMALL-MOVEMENT EXERCISE	
Large Movement	**Small Movement**
Bench press	Triceps movements
Lat pull-down	Biceps movements
Seated row	Biceps movements
Squat	Quadriceps, hamstrings, gastrocnemius, and soleus

like triceps push-downs, you can replace them with triceps extensions, and you can replace the overhead press with lateral dumbbell raises. Although you can add to the leg workout, I would not remove any of the suggested exercises. For a full list of exercises, I highly recommend *Anatomy for Strength and Fitness Training*, by Mark Vella (see Appendix). This book explains how to correctly conduct all movements and shows all muscles involved.

Weight-Training Log

It's important to keep track of your progress in a weight-training log. This will also help you organize your workout, so you know what exercises to do in what order. Your log should include the date, list the exercises you will do and in what order, and have space to fill in the weight or resistance and the number of reps and sets. Feel free to make

copies of the accompanying sample log or modify it to meet your needs.

Machines or Free Weights?

Weight machines and free weights both have benefits and drawbacks. Although the choice is a personal one, I recommend that beginners start on machines, then move to free weights later if they choose.

Because using free weights necessitates stabilizing the weight as you move it, it requires more skill to use. Machines limit the weights' ranges of motion, so there is less risk of injury. For example, when bench-pressing free weights, there's a tendency for the weight to move back and forth. If you were to lose control of the weight, a serious injury could result. When using a chest press machine, no back-and-forth movement is possible, so there's less chance of injury. For this reason,

WEIGHT-TRAINING LOG							
Date:							
Exercise	**Weight**	**Set 1**	**Set 2**	**Set 3**	**Set 4**	**Set 5**	**Set 6**
Squat or hip sled							
Lunge							
Leg extension							
Leg curl							
Seated calf raise							
Bench press							
Triceps push-down							
Lat pull-down							
Seated row							
Biceps curl							
Overhead press							
Shrug							
Crunch	N/A						
Twisting crunch	N/A						
Leg raise	N/A						
Back extension	N/A						

most machines do not require a spotter—another advantage—and changing weights is faster and easier than with free weights. However, some machines may not work well for individuals who are significantly shorter or taller than average.

Some of the liabilities of free weights can be considered benefits. When you begin, a free-weight bench press will feel a little wobbly; but as you continue to work out and strengthen your stabilizing muscles, it will feel more stable. Free weights are more true to life as well. When we lift objects outside the gym, we must stabilize them as they travel through their path of motion.

So although I recommend machines for beginning lifters, choose whichever you feel more comfortable with. Most individuals use a combination of the two based on experience and personal preference.

WEIGHT-TRAINING TECHNIQUES

Learning the general guidelines for weight training, as well as the proper technique for each lift, is important. Improper technique can lead to injury and time away from training. If you have never lifted before, I recommend hiring a personal trainer or a coach. (Many gyms provide trainers for this purpose.)

Follow these general guidelines for lifting:

- Never "throw" the weights around. Maintain proper technique throughout the movements.
- Always use slow and controlled movements.
- Keep a strong and controlled grip on the bar at all times. Always wrap your thumb around the bar, and never use a thumbless grip.
- Do not lift beyond your ability. Ignore how much your workout partners can lift and pay attention to your own workout needs. Leave your ego at home.
- Listen to your body. Know the difference between discomfort and pain. You'll feel discomfort when lifting, which is commonly known as the "burn." If you feel sharp or

shooting pain, you have caused damage that, if ignored, can lead to serious injury.

- Work large muscle groups before you work small muscle groups.
- Never hold your breath. This can lead to dizziness and fainting, which is bad if you have a hundred pounds or more on your shoulders.
- Always use a spotter with free weights. It takes only one slip to end your cycling career.
- Always use collars with free weights to keep the weights on the bars.
- Ensure that the equipment you're using is functioning correctly, and don't ignore "out of order" signs.
- Pay attention to your surroundings and don't goof off in the weight room. Most injuries that occur in weight rooms are due to carelessness and horseplay.

Exercising the Lower Body

This section covers the primary muscles involved in the lower extremities during cycling. This is not a complete discussion of all the lower-body muscles, but it does cover the ones that you need to pay the most attention to as a cyclist.

You usually hear the terms *quadriceps* and *hamstrings* in reference to the muscles located in the upper leg. Because some of the muscles that make up these groups have different jobs depending on the action of the joint, the groups are broken down into their individual muscles for this discussion. (The quadriceps consist of the rectus femoris, vastus medialis, vastus lateralis, and vastus intermedius. The hamstrings consist of the biceps femoris, the semitendinosus, and the semimembranosus.)

A muscle that crosses more than one joint is responsible for movement at more than one joint. The rectus femoris, for example, crosses the knee and the hip and is used during knee extension and hip flexion. The remaining muscles of the quadriceps are responsible only for knee extension.

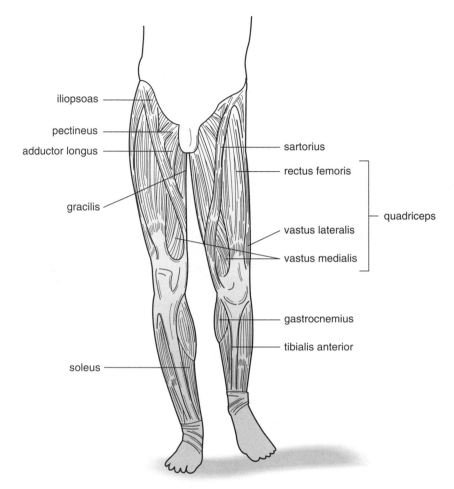

Leg muscles, front view.

Hip extension occurs during the downstroke of the pedal (from twelve o'clock to six o'clock). The muscles involved in hip extension are the gluteus maximus, the biceps femoris, the semitendinosus, and the semimembranosus. Also during this phase of the pedaling motion, extension occurs at the knee joint; it involves the rectus femoris, vastus medialis, vastus lateralis, and vastus intermedius. Plantar flexion (pointing the toes down and away from the leg) occurs at the ankle; it involves primarily the gastrocnemius and the soleus—usually referred to together as the calf muscle.

Hip flexion occurs as the pedal moves from six o'clock back to twelve o'clock. The muscles responsible for hip flexion are the rectus femoris, iliopsoas, pectineus, and sartorius. Flexion also occurs at the knee; it involves the biceps femoris, semitendinosus, and semimembranosus. The tibialis anterior and the extensor digitorum are the primary muscles responsible for dorsiflexion (pulling the toes upward toward the lower leg) during this portion of the pedal stroke.

Squat

Squats are good for developing leg strength. The main muscles used are the quadriceps, hamstrings, gluteus maximus, gastrocnemius, and soleus. The core muscles are also used.

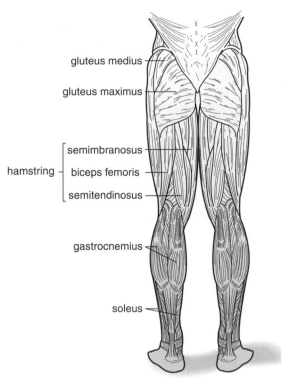

gluteus medius

gluteus maximus

hamstring
- semimbranosus
- biceps femoris
- semitendinosus

gastrocnemius

soleus

Leg muscles, back view.

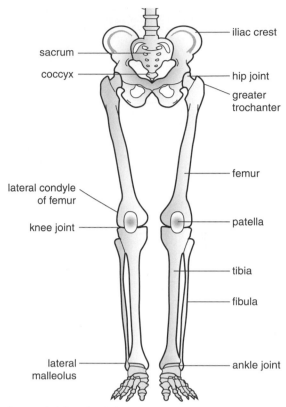

sacrum

coccyx

iliac crest

hip joint

greater trochanter

lateral condyle of femur

knee joint

femur

patella

tibia

fibula

lateral malleolus

ankle joint

Lower skeleton, front view

Down position of the squat.

Up position of the squat.

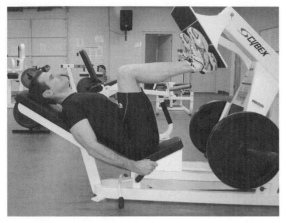

Down position of the hip sled.

Up position of the hip sled.

Place the bar centered at the base of the neck and across the back and shoulders. Keep a strong, full grip on the bar, and position your feet shoulder width apart. During the lowering phase, stay centered and don't allow your knees to move forward beyond your feet. Lower your body into a seated position until your thighs are parallel to the floor, not beyond. (Going too low puts unnecessary strain on the knees.) When returning to the standing position, stop just before the knees lock. (Locking your knees can lead to injury.) Keep your head up throughout the entire movement.

Hip Sled

Lifting with the hip sled exercises the quadriceps, hamstrings, gluteus maximus, gastrocnemius, and soleus. I recommend the hip sled over the squat for beginners because it requires less skill to perform, thus reducing the chance of injury while working the same muscles. All hip sleds are different, so make sure you know how to operate the equipment before you begin.

Place your feet shoulder width apart. Push the weight up to the point just prior to your knees locking, then lower the weight until your knees are at a 90-degree angle to the floor. Do not lower beyond 90 degrees.

Lunge

The lunge involves the quadriceps, hamstrings, gluteus maximus, gastrocnemius, and soleus. You can do lunges in any of three positions: with a bar across your back (similar to the position for the squat), or while holding a dumbbell in each hand, or with no weight at all. I recommend starting

Alternating leg lunge.

with no weight and working your way up as your body adapts.

Stand with your feet about hip width apart. Step forward with one leg, then lower your body until the thigh of the leading leg is parallel to the floor and the knee of the back leg is almost touching the floor. Return to the starting position and repeat with the other leg. Continue to alternate legs until you have reached the desired number of reps.

Standing Calf Raise

A standing calf raise, which works the gastrocnemius and the soleus, can be done with or without weights. If using weights, you can place a bar across your shoulders, hold dumbbells in your hands, or use a machine designed for calf raises. Although calf raises can be done on flat ground,

they are usually done on a raised platform, which allows for a wider range of motion.

If conducting heel raises on the floor, stand flat footed, then rise up onto the balls of your feet and toes, then lower the heels back to the floor. If using a platform, stand with the back half of your feet off the platform. Rise up onto the balls of the feet and toes, then lower your body so the heels go just below the top of the platform.

Seated Calf Raise

The seated calf raise works the gastrocnemius and soleus. Because the knees are bent during this exercise, the gastrocnemius is put on slack, reducing its ability to fully contract and allowing you to concentrate more on the soleus. When cycling, the knee is constantly bent and the soleus is brought into play.

Most gyms have a machine designed for seated calf raises. If a machine is not available, you can use a bench and weights. Place one or two 45 lb. weights on the floor in front of the bench. Sit on the bench, place a barbell across your legs, and position your feet so the balls of your feet are on the weights with the back portion of your feet hanging off. Movement at the ankle is the same as for standing calf raises.

Standing calf raise.

Seated calf raise.

Down position of the leg extension.

Up position of the leg extension.

Leg Extension

Leg extensions work the quadriceps muscles. Adjust the bench seat so your lower legs just hang down, and adjust the bar so it goes across your lower legs at your ankles. Extend your lower legs, stopping just before they lock, then lower the weight back to the start position—just prior to the weights touching down on the remainder of the weights located on the stack.

Leg Curl

Leg curls work the hamstrings primarily but also the gastrocnemius. Most leg-curl machines require you to lie prone. Adjust the bar so it crosses your legs at about ankle level. Move your heels toward your gluteus maximus, then lower the weight to the start position—just prior to the weights touching down on the remainder of the weights located on the stack.

Working the Upper Body

The upper-body muscles support the weight of your torso during cycling, are used to control the bike, and provide increased power when climbing or sprinting out of the saddle. Upper-body strength really comes into play if you do cyclo-cross, mountain biking, or anything similar to Paris-Roubaix,

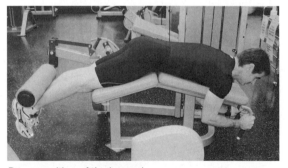

Down position of the leg curl.

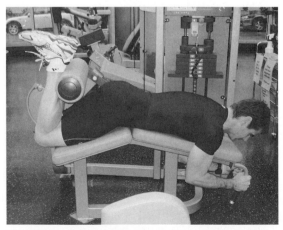

Up position of the leg curl.

where you are riding over rough cobblestone roads. Upper-body strength can also be beneficial in a crash. The stronger the muscles are that surround a joint, the more stable that joint will be and therefore the less likely to dislocate.

Bench Press

The main muscles worked during the bench press are the pectoralis major and the triceps brachii. The anterior deltoids, serratus anterior, and coracobrachialis muscles are also used.

Lie flat on your back and grasp the bar with your hands about shoulder width apart. Lower the weight to about an inch from your chest, then push it back up to the start position. Keep the weight controlled throughout the movement, and do not bounce the weight off your chest.

Up position of the lat pull-down.

Lat Pull-Down

This movement exercises the latissimus dorsi, teres major, and biceps brachii. Sit on a lat pull-down machine with your legs placed under the

Up position of the bench press.

Down position of the bench press.

Down position of the lat pull-down.

Seated row.

padded bar and your hands grasping the bar more than shoulder width apart. Pull the bar down toward your chest, then allow it to go back up. Do not pull the bar behind your head; this can cause injury.

Seated Rows

Seated rows work many of the muscles in the back, including the latissimus dorsi, trapezius, rhomboid (major and minor), teres major, posterior deltoids, and biceps brachii. Sit with your arms extended and grip the bar of the seated rowing machine. Keeping your back arched, bring the bar to your chest and squeeze your shoulder blades together, then return to the start.

Arm Curl

This movement exercises the biceps brachii. Grip the barbell with your hands shoulder width apart. Keeping your back straight, curl the bar toward your

Down position of the arm curl.

Up position of the arm curl.

upper body, then return to the start. Don't use your back to help lift the weight, and be careful not to "throw" the weight up: both actions can lead to injury.

Triceps Push-Down

This movement, which works the triceps brachii, can be done on a lat pull-down or similar machine. Facing the bar, place your hands on it less than shoulder width apart. Start with the bar about chest level, then push down until your arms are straight. Return to the start position and repeat. To focus on the triceps brachii, make sure to keep your elbows close to your body.

Overhead Press (Military Press)

This movement, which can be performed seated or standing, works the deltoid, pectoralis major (clavicular head only), and triceps. Conduct this exercise with the bar in front of your head. Performing this exercise with the bar behind the head places too much strain on the shoulder joint. Grasp the bar where your hands comfortably fall, a bit more than shoulder width apart. Start with the bar across your chest at the base of your neck. Push the bar up to full extension, then lower it back down.

Shrug

This exercise works the upper trapezius and the levator scapula, muscles used to help hold your head up as you ride. The more aerodynamic the position, the more you use these muscles. You can conduct this exercise using dumbbells, barbells, or a machine.

Stand with your feet shoulder width apart. Grasp two dumbbells of the same weight, one in each hand, and let your arms hang at your sides. Shrug your shoulders in an upward manner. Get a good contraction at the top of the shrug, then return to the start position.

Up position of the triceps push-down.

Down position of the triceps push-down.

Down position of the overhead press.

Up position of the overhead press.

Down position of the shrug.

Up position of the shrug.

Core

Core muscles are important for almost all movements, but many times they are ignored. In cycling they are important for maintaining upper-body posture while in the saddle and for stabilizing the pelvic region while pedaling. Weak core muscles can lead to a sore back due to their inability to support the spine, pelvis, and general thoracic region.

Do not use weights or weighted machines when conducting core exercises; use body weight only. You do not want to increase the strength or size of these muscles by increasing resistance (weight). The objective of core exercise work is to increase muscular endurance by increasing the number of repetitions.

Crunch

There are many different ways to do crunches, which strengthen the rectus abdominis and the oblique abdominals, but only one method is described here. Regardless of the method you use, never pull on your head with your hands. I usually recommend crossing your arms in front of your chest and placing your hands on the opposite shoulders. This position greatly reduces the risk of neck injury. If you do place your hands behind your head, make sure you don't apply force with your arms.

Lie on the floor with your legs in the air with a 90-degree bend at the hips and knees. Cross your arms across your chest and raise your body until your elbows just touch your knees. Repeat for as many reps as possible.

Take a 10- to 20-second break, then put your left foot on the ground and place your right ankle on your left knee. Place your right arm straight alongside your body and your left hand on your left shoulder. Move up with a slight twist and touch your left elbow to your right knee, then return to the start position. Repeat this movement the same number of times as you did the first set.

Crunch.

Take another 10- to 20-second break and repeat this movement on the opposite side.

Leg Raise

This movement is designed mainly to work the abdominal muscles, but it also works the rectus femoris and the tensor fasciae latae. You can perform this flat or on an incline bench.

Lie flat on your back with your arms alongside your body, your hands just beside or under your bottom, and your chin tucked to your chest. Start with your feet 6 inches off the ground, then raise your legs until they are just past vertical. To further work the abdominals, lift your hips off the floor. Return to the start position with your feet 6 inches off the floor and repeat as many times as you can.

Back Extension

This exercise is designed primarily for the gluteus maximus and part of the hamstrings (semitendinosus and semimembranosus), but it is also good for

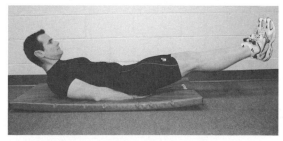

Leg raise.

working the muscles of the lower back (quadratus lumborum, iliocostalis lumborum, longissimus thoracis, and iliocostalis thoracis). Conduct the exercise using a machine built specifically for this purpose. With your lower body locked into position, lower your upper body toward the floor, then raise your upper body back to the start position.

On-the-Bike Resistance Training

Resistance training on the bike is good for building strength specific to riding. Hill repeats, using a much harder gear ratio and a much slower cadence than normal, are one of the best ways to do this. For example, on a hill that you would normally climb using your 23-tooth gear in the back, drop to 18 or 15. This will force you to slow your cadence and put more power into each pedal stroke. Conduct most of your repetitions seated, but do some standing as well.

You can accomplish the same effect by riding large gears at low rpm on flat ground. When doing this, be careful not to put too much torque into the knees, which could lead to an overuse injury. This method of pedaling is not economical, and you do not want to race this way, but it helps build strength during the off-season.

Overgeared hill repeats are a good way to conduct on-the-bike resistance training.

Back extension.

STADIUM WORKOUT

Stadium workouts are good for increasing "explosive" strength—the kind you need when attacking. The type of training designed for this purpose is known as plyometrics.

This type of training must be started very slowly. Heavy eccentric loading that occurs during plyometrics can lead to a severe case of DOMS. If you jump right into it, you'll be lucky if you can walk for the next three to seven days. As with weight training, however, the negative effects will decrease as your body adapts.

Go to a stadium or find a set of stairs where you can go up and down without hurting yourself or getting in people's way. Warm up by stretching and walking up and down the stairs a few times, then run up at a comfortable pace and come back down. Once you're warmed up, you're ready to start your sets. Each set should consist of the following:

1. Run up hitting every step, then walk back down at a safe pace.
2. Run up hitting every other step, then walk back down.
3. Slowly lunge, as mentioned earlier, up every other step, then walk back down.
4. Hop up every step on both legs at a time, then walk back down.

After you complete the sets, cool down and stretch. Start with no more than two or three sets during the first week. After that, slowly increase to the desired number of sets. Be careful; as you tire you increase the risk of making a mistake, which, if done on concrete stairs, can make for a very bad day. It may be a good idea to have a friend with you in case of an emergency.

nutrition

Proper nutrition is important both on and off the bike. On the bike during a long training ride or race, it keeps fuel levels up. Off the bike, it refuels the body and allows it to rebuild between workouts.

This chapter covers the basics of general nutrition. If you want to read in greater detail, check out any number of good nutrition books, some written specifically for endurance athletes. (I recommend *Sports Nutrition for Endurance Athletes*, by Monique Ryan.) You can also work with a registered dietitian to develop a nutritional program that suits your needs. Dietitians can provide insight and advice that's hard to obtain from a book. Almost all professional riders and teams work with a nutritionist.

NUTRIENTS

Six categories of nutrients are necessary for the human body to function: carbohydrates, fats, protein, vitamins, minerals, and water. These nutrients are responsible for every action in the body, including producing energy, building tissue, catalyzing chemical reactions, transporting oxygen and nutrients, and maintaining body temperature (thermoregulation).

Much research has gone into determining the optimal amount of each nutrient necessary to sustain and improve endurance performance. Too little or too much of any one may be detrimental to performance, so the nutritional goal of an endurance athlete is to get the right amount of each.

Carbohydrates

Carbohydrates are an extremely important fuel source for the human body. They are the only source of energy that the central nervous system can use. (It's a shortage of carbohydrates that causes the feeling of light-headedness and disorientation when you "bonk.") Carbohydrates are converted to glycogen and stored in the liver for later use, and in the muscles for on-site energy production. (The glycogen that's stored in the liver is transformed into glucose for transport in the bloodstream; it's commonly referred to as blood sugar.) Glycogen is essential in metabolizing fat as fuel.

You want to optimize your carbohydrate intake by consuming the right type, as well as the correct amount, of carbohydrates. Fruits, grains, and vegetables are good sources of carbohydrates. When choosing grains, select unrefined whole grains whenever possible. When grains are refined, they lose important nutrients, which makes them less beneficial. Choose complex carbohydrates (starches and dietary fibers) over simple carbohydrates (simple sugars).

The glycemic index measures the ability of carbohydrates to affect blood glucose levels due to their rate of absorption into the bloodstream. Foods that are low on the glycemic index (below 50) are slower to digest and do not greatly affect blood sugar levels (large changes in blood glucose levels have a negative impact on the human body). Low-glycemic-index foods include pasta, beans, oatmeal (not instant), peaches, and grapefruit. Foods that are moderate on the glycemic index (50 to 70) have only a slight effect on blood glucose. Examples include cream of wheat, pineapple, pears, and whole-grain bread. Foods that are high on the glycemic index (above 70) can cause a spike in blood glucose levels. This spike causes a release of insulin beyond what is necessary (hyperinsulinemia). This spike in insulin causes a reduction in blood glucose (hypoglycemia) that can negatively affect the performance of the central nervous system. Foods high on the glycemic index include soft drinks, white bread, sports drinks, and energy gels. Foods high on the glycemic index do have a place in an athlete's nutritional strategy, however, which is discussed below.

Complex carbohydrates are usually, but not always, lower on the glycemic index than simple carbohydrates. Although many unhealthy foods fall into the high-glycemic category, not all foods with a high glycemic index are bad for you. Carrots, watermelon, and potatoes are healthy foods that have a high glycemic index.

Average individuals should consume about 50 percent of their total daily caloric intake in the form of carbohydrates. For endurance athletes, the recommended figure is 60 to 70 percent, depending on the volume of training. Endurance athletes deplete glycogen stores much more rapidly than sedentary individuals and therefore must take in larger amounts of carbohydrates to replenish those stores after every workout.

Endurance athletes should therefore stay away from low-carbohydrate diets. Some "experts" claim that endurance athletes should drop their carbohydrate intake to 40 percent of their total caloric intake and increase protein intake accord-ingly, but there is no substantial body of scientific evidence that even remotely supports this.

Fats

Fats (or lipids) are utilized by the body in the following ways: to assist in the production of hormones, as insulation, for carrying fat-soluble vitamins, to protect vital organs from trauma, and as an energy source. Fat stores provide a virtually unlimited supply of energy (70,000 to 80,000 kCal in most people), restricted only by the availability of glycogen. On long, low-intensity rides, fat is utilized as a main source of energy.

Fat stored in the body can be categorized as "essential" fat (the amount required to maintain normal daily functions) and "nonessential" (storage beyond that amount). Fat that you consume can be categorized based on the number of chemical bonds between the carbon atoms in the fat molecule. Unsaturated fats contain one or more double carbon bonds, whereas saturated fats contain no double carbon bonds. You want to limit the amount of saturated fats that you consume and keep the majority of your fat intake as unsaturated fats. This will help keep down your bad cholesterol (LDL, or low-density lipoproteins). Canola, sunflower, safflower, and olive oils are high in unsaturated fats. Butter, lard, shortening, and coconut oil are high in saturated fats and should be avoided.

Trans-fatty acids, or trans fats, do not occur naturally but are created when food processors add hydrogen to oils, through the process of hydrogenation, to increase the shelf life of products and keep oils from separating. This greatly increases the saturation of the fat, making trans fats among the unhealthiest of nutrients. Packaged foods must currently list all trans fats on the label, and there is a move toward eliminating all trans fat from foods.

Staying away from foods high in saturated and trans fats is more a life-and-death issue than a matter of cycling performance. There is a strong link between diets high in saturated and trans fats and cardiovascular disease. Both types of fat increase the amount of low-density lipoproteins in the blood. This is the "bad" cholesterol that leaves plaque deposits on artery walls.

The attraction of fats is that they make food taste better, which is probably why the diet of the average American includes much more fat than necessary. About 20 to 25 percent of an endurance athlete's caloric intake should consist of fats, and these should be mainly unsaturated. Meat, fish, and healthy oils are good sources of fat in an athlete's diet.

Proteins

Proteins are used primarily for building muscle tissue and other components in the body. Although proteins can be broken down for energy, the body does not store excess protein, so if you're using protein as your main energy source, you have placed your body in a "starvation" situation and are breaking down tissue (primarily muscle) in order to form glycogen for energy.

Proteins are made of amino acids, of which there are twenty in the body. Eight of these amino acids are considered essential in adults (ten in children). This does not mean that the remaining, nonessential amino acids are not important; rather, the nonessential amino acids can be produced by the body. The essential ones, therefore, are an essential part of your diet. A complete protein is one that contains all the essential amino acids, of which animal foods such as lean meat, eggs, and milk are good sources. Vegetarians need to monitor their diets carefully to ensure that they consume sufficient quantities of essential amino acids.

When we hear about the importance of protein in an athlete's diet, it is usually in reference to power sports such as power lifting, bodybuilding, or American football. But proteins are extremely important to the endurance athlete as well. Long, high-intensity training sessions and races place a major strain on the body, and protein is essential in repairing the damage. Therefore, the dietary reference intake (DRI) recommendation of 0.8 gram of protein per kilogram of body weight may not be adequate for most endurance athletes. Most research suggests that endurance athletes need about 75 percent more, or about 1.4 grams of protein per kilogram of body weight daily. This should account for about 15 percent of your daily caloric intake, with some give or take based on the intensity and duration of exercise.

Most Americans receive more than the recommended amount of protein in their diets. The body cannot store protein for later use; excess is excreted or stored as fat. Taking in overly large quantities of protein can place unnecessary strain on the liver and kidneys.

Vitamins

Vitamins do not provide energy directly, but niacin, B vitamins, and pantothenic acid play key roles in the chemical processes that produce ATP (adenosine triphosphate), which is the only substance that can be used as energy in the body. Vitamin D is important for maintaining bone density. Vitamin C plays an important role in the synthesis of collagen (connective tissue) and in iron absorption. Vitamin E acts as an antioxidant. These are just a few of the reasons why vitamins are essential for athletic performance.

Adequate vitamin intake can be obtained through a well-balanced diet. Individuals on insufficient diets may not receive adequate amounts of all vitamins and may need to take supplements. Because of the increased demands on the body due to exercise, endurance athletes may need to supplement as well. Keep in mind that insufficient amounts of specific vitamins can be detrimental to development and health, and that too much of certain vitamins can be toxic. To determine the amount of each vitamin needed, consult the published list of dietary reference intake (see Appendix).

Antioxidants

Free radicals are unstable molecules that are missing an electron. They are formed through the body's interaction with the environment and through its normal oxidative metabolic processes. Free radicals "steal" electrons from other molecules to stabilize. When this occurs, the other molecules are damaged or destroyed. Free radicals are linked to tissue degeneration and the development of coronary artery disease. Because metabolism increases with exercise, free-radical production also increases.

Antioxidants play an important role in preventing free radicals from damaging the body, so it's important to consume adequate amounts. Antioxidants fight damage caused by free radicals by donating electrons to the unstable free radical and by repairing damage caused by the free radical. Three of the most important antioxidants are the vitamins C, E, and β-carotene (hereafter called beta-carotene). Fruits and vegetables are ideal sources of antioxidants; if you're eating a well-balanced diet, you should be getting enough antioxidants to handle free radicals.

Minerals

Nutritionally speaking, minerals are inorganic substances required for numerous chemical processes in the body. Some minerals, such as calcium, are needed in large quantities, whereas others, including zinc, are required only in small amounts. Minerals are obtained through eating meats, dairy products, and plants. Three of the most important minerals—calcium, iron, and phosphorus—are discussed below.

Calcium

Calcium, by far the most abundant mineral in the human body, plays a key role in many of its chemical processes. Calcium is essential in building and maintaining healthy bones, which are 60 to 70 percent calcium. Throughout life we continually resorb old bone and construct new bone. Calcium deficiency can lead to low bone density, and prolonged deficiency leads to osteoporosis, in which the bones become brittle and susceptible to fractures. (Osteoporosis is discussed further in Chapter 15.) Calcium also plays an important role in muscle contraction.

Calcium can be obtained from dairy products and some plants, but few diets meet the minimum requirement of about 1,000 mg per day— the equivalent of 30 to 40 oz. of milk. You need to examine your diet and possibly consult a registered dietitian to ensure that you are taking in enough calcium. If you're not getting enough calcium through your diet, you may want to consider supplementing, even though your body has more difficulty absorbing calcium from supplements in comparison to natural sources. Women are more susceptible to osteoporosis than men and need to be extremely vigilant.

Iron

Although essential, iron is required by the body only in small amounts. The majority of iron is used to make hemoglobin and myoglobin; the remainder is stored for later use. In order for oxygen to be transported in the blood, it must bind to the iron located on hemoglobin. A common sign of iron deficiency (also known as iron-deficiency anemia) is a feeling of constant fatigue, which severely limits your ability to function on a day-to-day basis, much less train or race.

Meat, particularly red meat, is the largest source of dietary iron. Liver is the richest source because the liver is where iron is stored in the body. Nonetheless, it's better to eat lean meats to avoid excessive cholesterol intake. Iron can also be obtained from some plants, such as potatoes and beans, but absorption from these sources is limited.

Three categories of people are at high risk of developing iron deficiencies. Women are at risk due to blood loss during the menstrual cycle, coupled with frequently inadequate dietary intake of iron in their diets. Athletes are at risk due to iron loss through sweat and because of the increased turnover rate of hemoglobin and increased hemoglobin production that occur due to training. Vegetarians are at risk because plant foods in general are not high in iron, and even the iron that is contained in some plant foods is not absorbed well. Anyone reading this book is presumably an athlete, so if you are in one of these three high-risk categories, you need to be concerned with iron intake (and particularly so if you're a female vegetarian athlete).

Be careful if you choose to take supplements because high levels of iron can be toxic. If you think you suffer from iron-deficiency anemia, consult your doctor, who will advise you on whether and how much to supplement.

Phosphorus

Calcium binds with phosphorus to make calcium phosphate, an essential component in bones. Phosphorus also plays an important role in energy production by assisting in the formation of ATP, ADP, and PC_r (see Chapter 10). Phosphorus can be obtained from meats, dairy products, and cereals and is provided in more than adequate amounts by the average diet.

Fluids

Because our body consists of 60 to 70 percent water, it is vital to existence. About 75 percent of the weight of muscles is water. Water acts as a transport medium for gases, nutrients, and other compounds. Water is also vital in thermoregulation, cooling the body by providing fluid for sweat and absorbing heat in the body's core and moving it to the skin, where it can be cooled through the evaporation of sweat. Water does not compress and therefore helps provides structure to cells in the body.

Water is lost from the body mainly through respiration, urination, defecation, and sweating.

Exercise increases losses due to respiration and sweating, and inadequate hydration can negatively affect health and performance. When training in hot conditions, it becomes even more imperative to monitor water loss and intake.

NUTRITION AND EXERCISE

To perform optimally and stay healthy throughout the season, it's important to develop a dietary strategy that covers nutrition before, during, and after training.

Individuals' reactions to type, quantity, and timing of fueling are highly variable, so no single program suits everyone. For example, "normal" insulin levels vary from individual to individual and affect the storage and transport of carbohydrates; rates of digestion vary, so the timing of intake must vary; and some individuals' sweat contains higher levels of sodium, so they need to ingest more salt. Because a proscriptive approach isn't feasible, here are some general guidelines that will help you develop a dietary strategy to meet your specific needs.

Before Training and Events

Make sure you are well hydrated before training or racing. Monitor your weight to ensure that you're replacing water lost during exercise. You do not want to start a road trip with your radiator half empty.

Through trial and error you will determine how much and how soon to eat before a ride. If you're planning an easy ride, you probably need not be overly concerned with amounts and timing. However, it wouldn't be wise to go to your favorite all-you-can-eat buffet and jump on the bike five minutes later.

Harder days require more planning. Through the process of autoregulation (see Chapter 10), blood is directed where it's needed most—to working muscles and skin during exercise, and to the digestive organs after eating. If you eat too soon before exercising, your working muscles and digestive system will compete for blood flow, and this will decrease your ability to perform and may lead to gastrointestinal distress.

Some athletes cannot function without a "healthy" breakfast. To make sure this does not interfere with competition, these individuals need to get up early in order to have 2 to 4 hours in which to digest the meal. Other individuals are better served by eating a small meal 1½ to 2 hours before the race starts. Find out by trial and error during training so you know how your digestive system normally functions and thus avoid an upset stomach during an event.

Stay away from meats just before competing because they take a long time to digest. Eat carbohydrates that are low on the glycemic index, such as slow-cooked oatmeal, and avoid high-fat, heavy foods such as bacon-egg-and-cheese croissants. Many cyclists eat an energy gel just prior to a long event to reduce the rate of glycogen depletion. This is a good idea as long as you time it correctly. Energy gels are high on the glycemic index and lead to low blood sugar levels and fatigue if they're taken 15 to 30 minutes prior to exercise. Instead take the gel 5 minutes before starting to exercise. This will help keep blood glucose levels up, spare glycogen stored in the liver for later use, and not have a negative effect.

During Training and Events

On rides longer than 1½ to 2 hours, it's important to reduce the rate of glycogen loss. I use the phrase "reduce the rate of glycogen loss" for a reason. When you ingest glycogen during strenuous exercise, it does not go to the liver for storage, so you are not replenishing glycogen stores. Instead you're increasing blood glucose levels. The glycogen is taken up by the working muscle, thus sparing glycogen stored in the liver.

Research has demonstrated that ingesting carbohydrates during endurance activities increases performance by delaying the onset of fatigue. This is where carbohydrates that are high on the glycemic index become important. Because of the immediate energy demands while cycling, ingesting carbohydrates during the activity avoids the cascade effect—normally associated with high-glycemic carbohydrates—that leads to low blood sugar. Make sure you have enough gas in the tank when you sprint for the finish line. If your glycogen supplies fall short, so will your race.

Cyclists should ingest 30 to 60 grams of carbohydrates per hour during rides lasting longer than two hours. This recommendation depends on three factors:

- Intensity. At low-intensity workouts (less than 60 percent of VO_2 max), supplementing carbohydrates is usually not necessary due to the low percentage of glycogen and the high percentage of fat being used for energy. At moderate intensities, 30 grams per hour is sufficient, and at high intensities you will need up to 60 grams per hour.
- Distance. Longer races require much larger amounts of glycogen.
- Body size and muscle mass. The larger the body and the greater the muscle mass, the more glycogen will be required.

In general, sports drinks and gels work better than energy bars and "normal" food during high-intensity activities. They are easier to digest and they enter the bloodstream faster. At lower intensities, solid foods work just as well. Typical sports gels contain about 25 grams of carbohydrate; sports bars contain about 45 grams; and a 12-ounce sports drink contains 60 to 80 grams. If you use energy gels, take one every 40 to 60 minutes, depending on intensity and duration.

Never try a new food strategy during a race. If energy bars, gels, or drinks will be offered on the course, find out the brand and flavors in advance

Sports gels consumed during exercise can help limit glycogen depletion.

and try them in training to determine how your body reacts.

Most individuals ride centuries at moderate to low intensities, finishing in five to seven hours. That's a long time to go without "real" food. If gels don't keep hunger at bay, you may need to eat some fruit or a sandwich.

It is imperative to stay well hydrated during an event, drinking 15 to 35 ounces of water for every hour ridden, and not waiting until you feel thirsty. The distance of the event and the environmental conditions (heat and humidity) will affect the amount of water you lose. Keep in mind that you sweat the same amount in a hot, dry environment as in a hot, humid environment, although

it may seem quite different due to the rate of evaporation.

Thirst is a defense mechanism reminding us that we need to drink when hydration levels are low. Note the present tense: when hydration levels are low. Cycling is a relatively steady-state exercise with a long duration, placing a large amount of stress on the circulatory and cooling systems. When you start feeling thirsty, it's already too late and you're on a downward spiral. When water loss equals 2 to 3 percent of body weight, the plasma volume is reduced enough to negatively impact performance. Your health will begin to be affected at a water loss of about 5 percent of body weight. At a loss in excess of 8 percent, plasma volume has dropped so low as to impair the body's ability to cool itself, leading to serious health implications including heat stress and/or heatstroke (see Chapter 5).

Water is sufficient for your fluid needs on rides less than two hours and on days that are not excessively hot. On longer rides or extremely hot days, you should use sports drinks as well. These will replace sodium lost in sweat and help support glycogen stores.

As bad as dehydration is, overhydration, or hyponatremia, is also dangerous. It usually occurs during rides of 70 miles or longer, where individuals are worried about becoming dehydrated. A combination of three factors usually leads to hyponatremia:

- The athlete drinks more water than is lost.
- There is a decrease in sodium levels through sweat. (The athlete may have insufficient sodium levels to begin with due to poor diet.)
- During exercise, autoregulation leads to decreased renal blood flow, resulting in a decrease in urine production and an increase in water retention.

The imbalance created by a high concentration of water and a low concentration of sodium can cause headache, nausea, cramping, seizures, coma, heart attack, and death. Unfortunately, many of these symptoms also apply to dehydration. Many times, hyponatremic athletes think they are dehydrated, causing them to increase their water intake, which makes the situation worse.

After Training and Events

Nutrition is an essential component of recovery. After a hard day in the saddle, you need to replenish glycogen stores in the muscles and liver. After a moderate- to high-intensity workout lasting longer than two hours, it will take about twenty-four hours to fully replenish glycogen stores with proper nutrition. You have a small window of opportunity, occurring within the first two hours post exercise, to maximize your recovery potential. For optimal results you should attempt to replenish within the first thirty minutes. Most athletes do not refuel properly and thus enter their next training bout with low glycogen stores.

For quick absorption, replenish with foods that are high on the glycemic index. Add protein to your recovery meal to aid in muscle recuperation. Also, it is theorized that because protein influences insulin levels, it will assist in glucose and amino acid uptake into the muscle. A 4:1 ratio of carbohydrate to protein (4 grams of carbohydrates for every gram of protein) is recommended.

For some people, eating a meal of solid food during the first two hours after a hard workout can cause gastrointestinal distress, and at times it may be simply inconvenient. "Recovery drinks" are available with the correct 4:1 ratio of carbohydrates and protein. Beyond the two-hour window, continue replenishing glycogen stores by consuming carbohydrates that are low on the glycemic index to prepare for the following day's workout.

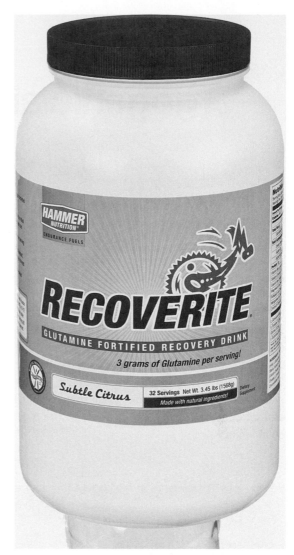

Recovery drinks containing a 4:1 ratio of carbohydrates and protein can increase recovery after an intense workout.

ergogenic aids

Ergogenic means "work enhancing." In competitive sports, an ergogenic aid is any substance or method that has the capacity to enhance athletic ability. It does so by increasing performance during an event, aiding recovery between workouts, or aiding during a workout to increase later performance. Performance enhancers may be legal or illegal—anything from supplementing glycogen during a ride to blood doping. This chapter addresses the ethical and legal considerations for the use of ergogenic aids in cycling and examines the efficacy of a few of the most common ones.

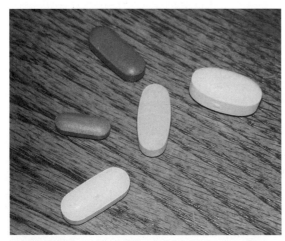

Ergogenic aids, such as these in tablet form, are often employed in an attempt to increase performance.

ETHICS AND LEGALITY

Cyclists are continually striving to improve their performance, looking for that one thing that will make them just a little faster. If someone offered you a magic pill that would increase your performance, would you take it? If I told you it was a *legal* magic pill with no negative side effects, it would probably make your decision easier. But what if it were illegal and had serious side effects, including possible death? That too seems like an easy decision, but a surprising number of people say yes. Balancing the risks of legal actions and serious health complications against improved prospects of winning is a decision that many athletes make every day.

Throughout history, athletes have competed to determine who is best. There is an assumption that victory is gained on the bases of genetics, discipline, training, and skill and not through the application of some advantage that is unavailable to other competitors. It's an appalling period in our sport when we have to wait for the results of drug tests to determine the *true* winner of the race. As I write this, the 2006 winner of the Tour de France is still up in the air due to a positive drug test of overall winner Floyd Landis, and in the 2007 Tour de France, two teams were disqualified for the same reason. Le Tour—by far the most visible bike race in the world—has become virtually synonymous with cheating, and the sponsor of the most successful team in Tour history withdrew because of the bad publicity. If we want to see our sport flourish, we must not tolerate unethical or illegal behavior. It's not just the responsibility of the sport's governing bodies; it behooves every athlete, coach, trainer, and team sponsor to keep the sport clean.

The World Anti-Doping Agency (WADA) was created by the International Olympic Training Committee to develop a list of banned substances, draft rules governing their use, test for the banned substances, and enforce the rules. Testing and enforcement in the United States is handled by the United States Anti-Doping Agency (USADA). Substances are usually banned for one or more of the following reasons:

- The substance is illegal to buy or sell.
- The substance has side effects that endanger the cyclist's health.
- The substance gives an unfair advantage to the cyclist.

The list of banned substances is modified from time to time (see the Appendix for the website), and competitors need to check it periodically to stay current. Ignorance is not a valid argument if you are found using a banned substance. Be careful when taking over-the-counter medications because many contain banned substances. If you need to use a medication that contains a banned substance to treat an illness, you can file for a therapeutic-use exemption. Be cautious of nutritional supplements because some contain banned substances that may not be listed on the label. Athletes are held accountable regardless of how the substance entered their body.

Not all ergogenic aids are illegal. There may be a gray area in which certain legal aids could be unethical, such as a hypothetical new drug that would artificially increase your hemoglobin count but is not yet banned. In those instances you need to consult your conscience. As an athlete, your goal should be to perform to the best of your ability within the rules of the game. As an exercise physiologist, I spend a lot of time researching ways to improve performance, and although I despise any form of cheating, I fully support the use of ergogenic aids that fall within the sport's legal guidelines, are ethically sound, and do not endanger the athlete's health.

SUPPLEMENTS

I have a hard time coming to terms with the way in which nutritional supplements are allowed to be manufactured and sold in the United States. Because supplements are not considered drugs, they are not required to undergo safety testing. Except for the one limitation that supplement companies cannot make claims regarding curing or affecting a disease state, the companies are allowed to make any claims they wish, regardless of the truthfulness of the statements. They are not required to show independent scientific evidence supporting their claims, and the listed ingredients and their amounts need not be accurate or truthful.

The drug ephedrine is an excellent example of the negative effect of this lack of regulation. Ephedrine is a stimulant that was used in supplements that promoted weight loss and increased athletic performance. Over many years, adverse side effects were reported that included arrhythmias, cardiovascular disease, stroke, heat-related illness, seizures, and death. These effects were well documented, but it took until 2004 and more than eighty deaths before the Federal Drug Administration (FDA) finally banned the use of ephedrine in supplements.

Many supplements are asserted to be healthful because they are "natural" herbs. Although many natural herbs have valuable properties, the fact that a substance is natural is in no way related to its healthfulness. Ma huang is a natural herb used as a stimulant in many supplements. It contains ephedrine and has been shown to cause heart arrhythmias, psychotic events, and death.

Some supplements can be beneficial, some can be detrimental, and some will only cost you money. Before taking any supplement, research it. First let's look at where you should *not* obtain information:

- Celebrity endorsements. These are always strongly suspect because the celebrity is being paid to promote the product, may have no personal experience with it, and didn't write the advertisement (and may not care what it says).
- Athlete's unsolicited testimonials. Even if the athlete is not trying to mislead, these testimonials are questionable because the number of variables surrounding athletic success makes it difficult to accurately assign credit to any one factor. Though an athlete may truly believe that the supplement is the secret to his or her success, few athletes have the expertise of nutritionists or physiologists to make these judgments accurately. The "success" could also be due to a placebo effect, whereby the athlete trains harder because he or she believes that the supplement is effective.
- Magazine articles. Consumer health and "enthusiast" magazines are a poor source of information on supplements, especially if the supplement companies advertise in the magazine. Magazines often run well-intentioned articles on supplements, but many magazine writers lack the expertise to properly interpret the results of scientific research. Articles may be based on a single study in a peer-reviewed journal. This is problematic because even careful research results often contradict one another. Even worse are articles based on news releases from a single researcher that fail to mention the conflicting results of other tests, or from supplement manufacturers themselves that may be based on no sound research whatsoever.
- Magazine advertisements. As noted above, supplement companies can make virtually any claims they wish, regardless of truth or accuracy. Beware especially of advertisements designed to look and read like objective magazine articles or product reviews. Most magazines require that these pseudo-articles carry a disclaimer stating "paid advertisement," but these words are usually run so small as to go unnoticed. The intention of these ads is to mislead the reader, and I think they damage the credibility and integrity of any magazine that runs them.

Now pardon me while I contradict myself. I stated that athletes and magazines are not accurate sources of information on the effects of supplements. Nevertheless, these sources can be a good place to start your research. Although many important discoveries occur in a lab, often it is athletes and coaches who first discover what works, after which we science geeks conduct the research necessary to validate or disprove those claims. Few cyclists read peer-reviewed scientific journals, often getting their tips instead from other athletes or magazines. If many professional cyclists are using a specific supplement, it's possible that there is some benefit to its use. The key is to investigate the scientific literature.

Sound scientific research is conducted in an independent lab in a manner designed to obtain unbiased results. (Many supplement companies claim that their products have been scientifically proven, but the majority of these claims are unfounded: the labs may not be independent, and the research, if it was conducted at all, is not intended to be unbiased but, rather, to generate a desired result.) The best database for exercise science and sports medicine literature is Pub Med; see the Appendix for the website.

Scientific literature does have drawbacks, however. Because the articles are written for scientists, they may be difficult for the average individual to understand. Although the Pub Med database is available to everyone, full articles may be hard to obtain outside of a university library. (You might try interlibrary loan.) When perusing the literature, read beyond whether the substance seems to "work" and look for known and possible side effects. Most importantly, read *all* of the studies relevant to the substance of interest. One positive result doth not scientific consensus make.

If the scientific literature is too cumbersome and the popular magazines are unreliable, where do you go for sound information? Exercise physiologists, nutritionists, qualified coaches, and sports physicians are knowledgeable sources for information on supplements.

If you decide that an ergogenic aid is worth trying, be cautious with it and learn how your body reacts before you make it part of your training regimen. Different individuals may respond differently, which is why the scientific literature can be equivocal at times.

Ginseng

Touted as an energy booster, ginseng root is probably one of the most widely used supplements in the world. It is sold as a supplement and added to a vast number of other products. Ginseng theoretically enhances athletic performance by reducing fatigue and providing more energy.

Current scientific research shows no benefit to taking ginseng as an ergogenic aid. Anecdotal evidence of increased performance may be due to stimulants present in some ginseng products.

Phosphate Loading

In theory, ingesting sodium phosphate increases available phosphate for ATP production, which in turn leads to increased performance. It is also thought that increased phosphate stores lead to increased synthesis of 2,3-diphosphoglycerate. This compound stimulates the release of oxygen from hemoglobin so it can be more readily transported to the muscle.

Although little research has been conducted, the current evidence is equivocal and does not support an increase in performance from ingesting sodium phosphate as an ergogenic aid. There appear to be no adverse reactions to ingesting phosphate, but at high doses gastrointestinal distress is common.

Creatine

Creatine has been one of the most talked-about and disputed supplements in recent history. In the ATP-PC$_r$ system of short-burst (3 to 15 seconds) energy production, creatine binds a phosphate with ADP to create ATP (see Chapter 10). In theory, if creatine stores are increased, more energy is produced through the ATP-PC$_r$ system.

Research as to whether creatine actually works during short-term anaerobic exercise is equivocal (roughly twenty-five articles for and eighteen against). This could be due to differences among individual test subjects. There is no strong scientific evidence that creatine enhances endurance performance. However, there may be some benefit to using creatine during off-season weight training or interval training.

The most common short-term side effects linked to supplementing with creatine are muscle cramping, dehydration, and gastrointestinal distress. Long-term effects are not known. Due to the known side effects and the absence of conclusive benefits, I do not recommend creatine use for cyclists.

Ribose

Ribose is a naturally occurring sugar that affects performance in three ways:

- assists in glucose production
- can be converted to pyruvate for energy production through the oxidative pathway
- is a key compound in adenosine, an important component of ATP

In theory, increased stores of ribose lead to increased ATP production and increased performance. The first studies conducted on ribose were in clinical settings, where ribose infusions increased ATP stores in cardiac patients suffering from ischemic heart disease (heart disease marked by a reduction in blood flow to the myocardium). In studies using animals with induced ischemia, ATP levels also increased after ribose infusions.

Research on ribose as an ergogenic aid, however, has been less promising, and current studies do not support its use. In the clinical studies, ATP levels were initially low due to an ischemic condition, whereas in the ergogenic studies, ATP levels began at normal levels. In the clinical trials, large doses were administered intravenously, whereas in the ergogenic trials, smaller doses were administered orally. (Ribose may have been degraded in the stomach during oral dosing.) The only known side effect is the possibility of gastrointestinal distress at high oral doses.

Caffeine

Caffeine is a natural stimulant commonly found in coffee, tea, chocolate, and most sodas. Research has demonstrated conclusively that caffeine can boost athletic performance.

Caffeine can depress feelings of fatigue and discomfort during exercise, enabling the athlete to perform at a higher intensity level and/or for a longer period. Caffeine also increases the mobilization of free fatty acids, making them more available for energy production and thus conserving glycogen stores. In addition, caffeine increases activity at the junctions between nerves and muscles,

Caffeine is the most widely used stimulant in the world. Drinking coffee, in the correct amount and situation, can increase performance.

and increases the recruitment of motor units, both of which increase the muscles' ability to contract.

Caffeine's side effects are also well known. It can cause muscle tremors, gastrointestinal distress, headache, nervousness, elevated heart rate, arrhythmia, and high blood pressure. In hot conditions it can lead to thermoregulatory complications. These symptoms are more likely to occur at high doses and in individuals who do not usually consume caffeine.

If you normally take in caffeine and it does not negatively affect you, consuming responsible quantities before a race should not lead to adverse conditions. If you do not normally consume caffeine, don't consume any prior to an important race because you don't know how it will affect you in those circumstances. You really don't want to spend the race in the port-a-john. Experiment during training and low-priority events.

I cannot make the following statement strong enough: *Stay away from caffeine pills!* The amount of caffeine in pills is not regulated, and most contain

CAFFEINE CASE STUDIES

Here are two examples of individuals who took caffeine pills to increase their athletic performance.

I used to teach a jogging class in which students were required to run 5 kilometers in 28 minutes in order to pass. The students knew this from day one and had all semester to prepare. One female student chose to walk and talk with friends during class instead of training. When it came time for the 5k, she was worried about passing and took caffeine pills to help her performance. By the second lap she was shaking and having heart palpitations. We quickly took her off the track and brought her in for medical treatment, which was successful. Fortunately there were no lasting complications.

The second example involved a male exercise physiology student who was a moderately to highly trained triathlete. During exercise physiology class, I discussed the benefits and side effects of caffeine as an ergogenic aid and told the story of the lady from my jogging class. This student asked questions about exactly what form of caffeine pills she had taken. A few weeks later, I conducted a 1.5-mile run/walk test in the class. Being an overachiever, the male student wanted to outperform everyone in the class and took caffeine pills. Not only did he end up visiting the doctor with heart palpitations, he had to wear a portable electrocardiogram (ECG) for two weeks and could not consume any caffeine for a much longer time. He later said that because he was fit and regularly drank coffee, he thought the caffeine pills would not affect him in that manner.

The point I want to drive home is that just because caffeine is sold over the counter does not mean it's harmless. If you plan to use caffeine as an ergogenic aid, do it responsibly. Everyone responds differently, and what may be safe for one individual may cause distress in another.

---

larger amounts than you would obtain from drinking even *a lot* of coffee.

In the past, cycling limited the amount of caffeine that could be in your system during competition. But most individuals would experience negative effects below the legal limit of six to eight cups of coffee. The ideal amount for performance enhancement is usually considered to be about three or four cups of coffee.

WADA recently removed caffeine from the prohibited-substance list and placed it on their "watch" list, meaning that there is no legal limit, but they are monitoring its use for possible later regulation. The National Collegiate Athletic Association (NCAA) still has an upper limit of allowable caffeine, but collegiate cycling in the United States is governed by the National Collegiate Cycling Association (NCCA), which has no caffeine limit.

ILLEGAL AIDS

Two illegal and unethical ergogenic aids are so prevalent in cycling that I must address them here. Because their use constitutes cheating, you should be aware that discovery inevitably results in disciplinary action. (And your conscience should inform you that any "win" due to their undiscovered use is no win at all.) More importantly, these ergogenic aids pose serious health risks.

Anabolic Steroids

Anabolic steroids are synthetic testosterone. Research has demonstrated unequivocally that steroids increase muscle mass and performance. It is theorized that they speed recovery by repairing damaged tissue, and they reduce the catabolic effects of exercise. These benefits enable the athlete to make larger gains faster. There is also evidence that steroids stimulate increased levels of red blood cells. Steroids can be administered through injection, oral doses, patches, and creams.

Although cyclists usually don't want to gain large quantities of muscle mass, steroids can still improve their performance by aiding in the recovery process.

Steroids are banned by WADA, USADA, UCI, and the International Olympic Committee (IOC). A cyclist caught using steroids will be suspended or banned from the sport. In the United States, steroids are illegal to buy, sell, or possess, any of which can lead to a prison term. Being illegal, steroids are sold on the black market, making them extremely expensive and precluding any guarantee of purity.

Serious side effects accompany steroid use, some reversible, others not. Reversible side effects include acne, depression, "roid rage" (uncontrollable fits of anger), infections at injection sites, and an unhealthy cholesterol profile. After cessation of steroid use, these effects tend to disappear.

The list of irreversible side effects is longer and more serious. Side effects affecting males and females include cancer, liver disease, cardiovascular disease (all of which can cause death), and baldness. Male users run risks of testicular atrophy, impotence, developing mammary glands (breasts), and a permanent decrease in natural testosterone production. Women users may develop male traits (facial hair and deep voice). Steroid use in women has also been linked to serious birth defects. Steroid use in adolescence can lead to stunted growth due to early closure of the epiphyseal plates (growth plates in the bones).

Let's do the math. On the negative side: steroids have a negative impact on health; they are extremely costly; and users could be banned from cycling, sent to prison, or die. On the positive side: users might cross the finish line first (but they'll know it doesn't count). Time to choose, math wiz!

Blood Doping

Blood doping is more prevalent in cycling than in any other sport, and its rampant use has left the sport with a black eye. Blood doping is the act of artificially increasing hemoglobin (red blood cells) in the body to increase the oxygen-carrying capacity of the blood. This increases the amount of oxygen delivered to the working muscles, which in turn increases the amount of work the muscles can perform. Current research demonstrates unequivocally that blood doping improves endurance performance.

Blood doping takes three forms:

- Autologous blood doping. The athlete's own blood is drawn; the plasma and hemoglobin are separated; the plasma is reinfused; and the hemoglobin is frozen for later use. Over the course of a month or two, the athlete naturally rebuilds his normal level of hemoglobin. The stored hemoglobin is reinfused just before competition to further increase the body's hemoglobin. During the time that hemoglobin levels are returning to normal, however, the athlete feels slightly weak, which affects his training.
- Homologous blood doping. Hemoglobin from a donor is infused into the athlete just prior to competition. This carries the risks of transmitting disease, infection, and an allergic reaction to, or outright rejection of, the hemoglobin (even if the donor and recipient have the same blood type).
- Erythropoietin injection. Erythropoietin (EPO), which is produced in the kidneys and liver, is responsible for stimulating red blood cell production within the bone marrow. In this treatment, synthesized EPO is injected to spur the creation of more red blood cells. This increases the body's demand for iron, which is administered as supplements.

Blood doping has strong negative health consequences; there have been at least eighteen documented deaths linked to blood doping in cycling. By increasing hemoglobin without increasing plasma, doping raises hematocrit to dangerous levels, making the blood too viscous to flow smoothly. The heart has to work harder to push the thickened blood through the body, increasing blood pressure and wreaking havoc on the heart and circulatory system. The thick blood is also prone to clotting in the arteries, which can lead to a heart attack or stroke.

As a cyclist sweats during a long, hard race, the plasma volume drops naturally and hematocrit levels rise. A nondoping cyclist can handle this increase in hematocrit, particularly if he or she pays attention to hydration levels. But when you add blood doping to the mix, hematocrit levels will be much higher than normal, greatly increasing the chances of a cardiovascular incident.

Unfortunately, testing for blood doping is problematic. A higher than normal hematocrit (more than 50 percent for males; more than 47 percent for females) is considered a positive test for blood doping. Although this test catches almost every cyclist who dopes, it also results in occasional false positives. Due to genetics, some individuals naturally have a hematocrit level that is over the limit; if an individual is borderline high, he or she might test positive after a long hot day in the saddle. Training at altitude can also raise hematocrit levels by stimulating increased production of EPO and hemoglobin. WADA and UCI recognize this problem and have developed a procedure to accommodate individuals with naturally high hematocrit levels. Through blood testing, these cyclists can have a blood profile recorded. Paperwork is then submitted to establish the higher-than-normal hematocrit levels and exempt the individual from the normal limits.

It is nearly impossible to directly detect autologous blood doping because the introduced red blood cells are the individual's own. On the other hand, homologous blood doping is easy to detect through genetic differences in the cells, and such tests are reliable and valid. Testing for EPO is more complicated, and the results are still questionable due to difficulties distinguishing between natural and synthesized EPO.

If a governing body decides to end a cyclist's career, it should be positive about the results. Given the difficulties in directly detecting two of the three doping methods, I propose that a complete blood profile be maintained of every rider, and scheduled and random testing be conducted throughout the year (not just during race season). In theory, this should eliminate false positives due to naturally high hematocrit levels, and it would also catch cyclists with naturally low hematocrit levels who dope up to "normal" levels (for example, a cyclist with a normal level of 43 percent who artificially raises it to 49 percent). This program would involve high costs and difficult logistics, but if it can keep the sport clean, it may be worth it.

your unique physique

Body composition plays an important role in a cyclist's health as well as his ability to perform. Regardless of whether your goal is to improve body composition for health or performance, you need to know how to determine body composition and how to obtain your desired body composition in a healthy manner.

Although as a whole, everyone's body adapts to training and racing in a similar manner, there are special considerations for certain populations that affect training adaptations. Age, gender, body composition, and certain medical conditions affect training and racing.

BODY COMPOSITION GOALS

More than 60 percent of Americans are overweight or obese, conditions that have been linked to serious health problems including hypertension, increased LDL ("bad" cholesterol) levels, diabetes, cardiovascular disease, certain types of cancer, gall bladder disease, joint problems, breathing problems, and death.

Cyclists continually talk about weight, but it's really *body composition* that counts—the proportion of fat to fat-free mass in the human body. Fat-free mass consists of everything that is not fat, including bone, teeth, organs, skin, and muscle. Body composition is usually expressed as the percentage of total body mass that consists of fat.

Your body needs some fat to function properly. If your essential fat stores drop below the mini-mum requirements, serious health complications can result. Men require minimum body fat of about 4 percent, and women about 12 percent. Of course these numbers vary somewhat with the individual, and some athletes function well at lower percentages without adverse effects. If you have trouble keeping your body fat above the recommended minimums, you should speak with your doctor. It may be that your body can function properly with lower-than-normal fat stores.

The majority of cyclists reading this book are probably concerned with reaching and maintaining a healthy body fat percentage as opposed to an ideal race weight. The recommended body composition for good health is 8 to 19 percent for men and 17 to 28 percent for women. Overweight is usually classified as a body fat percentage greater than 20 percent for men and 30 percent for women. The higher the body fat percentage above these figures, the greater the risk of health problems, although physically active people who are slightly overweight are healthier overall than sedentary thin ones.

The situation changes for cyclists who wish to compete at the limit of their capabilities. Weight has a dramatic effect on cycling, and excess stores of body fat inevitably slow a cyclist down. Professional cyclists are usually incredibly thin—almost sickly looking—and they walk a fine line maintaining ideal body composition for competition while avoiding a too-low percentage that leads to poor performance and illness.

The recommended body composition for racing is 4 to 10 percent for men and 12 to 20 percent for women. This is hard to achieve and maintain, even for those genetically predisposed toward thinness. The recommended ranges are nonetheless fairly broad due to individual differences. Too often, coaches or trainers emphasize a single, specific number and require all cyclists to reach that goal. Some riders may function optimally at that level; others may merely *be able to* function; and some may be put at serious health risk by this one-size-fits-all approach. Any riders who are close to the lower end of the recommended range should pay close attention to how it affects their health and performance by keeping a record of body fat percentage in their training log. The goal is to be as light as possible while maintaining optimal performance and health.

Measuring Body Composition

If you are serious about training, it's important to keep track of your body composition. There are different ways to measure body fat percentage; some are more accurate than others, and some are a waste of time and money.

Height and Weight Charts, and Body Mass Index

The two most common methods, often seen in gyms and doctor's offices, are based on a simple equation for body mass index (BMI):

$$BMI = 703 \times \text{weight (lb.)} \div \text{height}^2 \text{ (in.}^2)$$

Height-and-weight charts present the results of this calculation in graphic or tabular format for broad ranges of heights and weights: you simply find where your height and weight cross on the chart, which tells you whether you are underweight, normal, overweight, or obese.

Both of these methods utilize only height and weight to estimate body composition. For large-scale population studies, these methods are convenient because they require only two easily obtainable measurements. For individual purposes, however, these methods fall short because they assume that the more you weigh, the higher your percentage of body fat. By failing to take into account that muscle is denser than fat, they completely ignore individual differences; in other words, they do not, in fact, measure body composition. As an extreme example, Arnold Schwarzenegger, in his prime, would have been considered obese according to BMI and height/weight charts.

Bioelectrical Impedance

Bioelectrical impedance systems use a very low-voltage electric current to measure electrical resistance in the body. Water is a good conductor of electricity, so fat-free mass, which contains a high percentage of water, acts as a good conductor, whereas fat, which contains little water, acts as a resistor. The more fat in the body, the greater the electrical resistance.

To measure the body's electrical resistance, bioelectrical impedance systems require that you hold onto or stand barefoot on two electrical contacts. Bathroom weight scales that have these electrical contacts built in are commonly referred to as body fat scales or body composition scales.

Hydration levels have a large effect on bioelectrical impedance readings. As hydration fluctuates, so do the readings, to such an extent that inexpensive, off-the-shelf systems are thoroughly unreliable for measuring body composition. (One of my mentors, Dr. Phil Bishop, described them as "random number generators.") Save yourself some money and stay away from these systems. More expensive models can be useful for monitoring fluctuations in hydration levels.

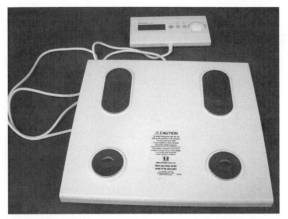

Bioelectrical impedance systems use a very low-voltage electric current to estimate body fat percentage, although most of these systems are not accurate enough to use for training purposes.

Underwater Weighing

Underwater weighing is the most accurate way to determine body composition. Muscle is denser than water and will sink, whereas fat is less dense than water and will float. The ratio of fat to fat-free mass therefore determines how buoyant your body is in water.

This method requires you to sit partially submerged in water in a hydrostatic weighing tank. Once comfortable, you bend at the waist, submerge your head and upper torso, and breathe out as much air as possible. Body weight is measured

before you enter the tank and while you are under water. These measurements, along with others, are placed in a formula to determine the percentage of body fat. Many health clubs and exercise physiology labs have underwater weighing capabilities.

In spite of its superior accuracy, this method has several drawbacks. The equipment is expensive and requires skilled staff to operate it. The subject must exhale as much air as possible and remain still during the reading. Some individuals are not sufficiently comfortable in the water to do this.

Calipers

Calipers are used to measure fat stored directly under the skin at several points on the body. This is an accurate, reliable, affordable, and relatively easy method of estimating body fat percentage.

Calipers cost between $25 and $700, with differences at the lower end of the price range determined by calibration accuracy. Calipers can be used to track body composition in many individuals and would be a worthwhile investment for an individual, a cycling club, a team, or a shop. I recommend Lange skinfold calipers, which cost about

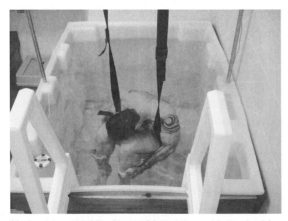

Underwater weighing is considered the gold standard for determining body composition.

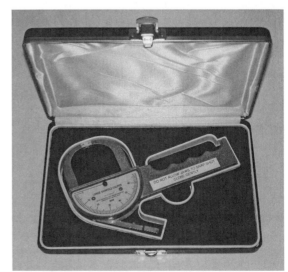

Lange skinfold calipers are an accurate way to measure body fat percentage.

$200. Although not as accurate, $25 calipers are better than not using any at all.

Various protocols are in use that involve caliper measurements at different sites on the body and different formulas to convert the measurements to body fat percentage. The one described here was developed by Jackson and Pollock; I find it accurate and easy to perform. The method involves measuring at three sites on the body, which are known as skin folds and differ by gender. For accurate results, it's important to take measurements at the exact sites specified and to use proper technique every time. Here are other rules for assessing body fat:

- Wear clothing that provides access to skin-fold sites.
- Do not apply lotion to skin prior to performing skin folds.
- Do not work out prior to performing skin folds. No one wants to share your sweat, and it's hard to pinch correctly if the muscles are swollen from the workout.
- Take measurements on the same side of the body every time.
- Stay relaxed and do not "flex" the area being tested.

Men perform measurements at the chest, abdomen, and thigh. Women use the triceps, iliac (hip), and thigh. The exact sites, and how to pinch them, are shown in the photos. Practice finding the sites precisely and consistently; otherwise, your numbers will be useless.

CHEST SITE
Only men use this site, located halfway up the pectoralis major along the outer ridge of the muscle. Pinch the skin in line with the muscle as shown.

ABDOMEN SITE
Only men use this site, located 1 inch directly to the side of the navel. Choose the same side that

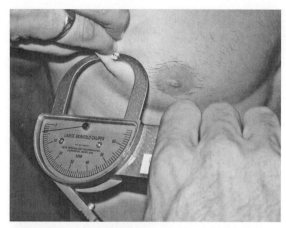

Chest site, used by men only.

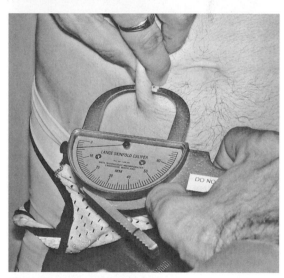

Abdomen site, used by men only.

you are using for the chest and thigh. Pinch vertically, not horizontally.

ILIAC SITE
Only women use this site, located just above the iliac crest (hip bone). After locating the hip bone, pinch a fold of skin just above and in line with the iliac crest.

TRICEPS SITE
Only women use this site. Pinch a fold of skin vertically along the back of the arm, halfway between the elbow and the shoulder.

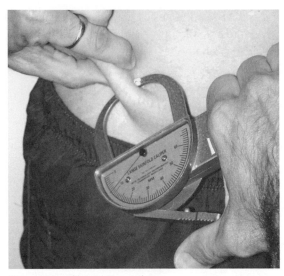

Iliac site, used by women only.

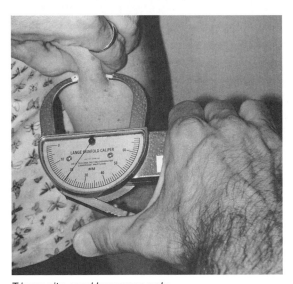

Triceps site, used by women only.

THIGH SITE

Men and women use this site, centered on the thigh halfway between the iliac crest and the patella (kneecap). Pinch the skin vertically.

As shown, pinch a fold of skin between the thumb and index finger with the fingers pointing down. This allows you to place the calipers just below

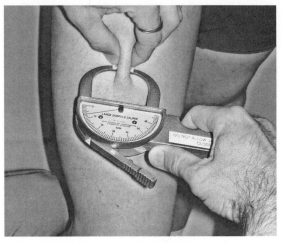

Thigh site, used by men and women.

the finger and thumb. Pinch skin and fat only; avoid pinching the muscle. Place the caliper contacts directly below your fingers on the pinched area, then release the lever, allowing the calipers to close. Do not let go of the skin. Read the calipers and record your findings in millimeters. Remove the calipers *before* you release the skin fold. (It can be a little painful otherwise.) Repeat three or four times to ensure consistent readings. Repeat this process for all three sites. Then take the readings from all three sites, add them together, and plug them into the appropriate equation for body density, by gender, as follows:

MEN

$$\text{body density} = 1.10938 - (0.0008267 \times \text{sum of skin folds}) + (0.0000016 \times [\text{sum of skin folds}]^2) - (0.0002574 \times \text{age})$$

WOMEN

$$\text{body density} = 1.0994921 - (0.0009929 \times \text{sum of skin folds}) + (0.0000023 \times [\text{sum of skin folds}]^2) - (0.0001392 \times \text{age})$$

After determining body density using one of the formulas above, determine body fat percentage using the following formula, developed by Siri:

$$\text{body fat \%} = (4.95 \div \text{body density}) - 4.50 \times 100$$

EXAMPLE

Male: age = 20; chest = 8, abdomen = 15,
thigh = 10 (total = 33)

body density = 1.10938 − (0.0008267 × 33)
+ (0.0000016 × [33]²) − (0.0002574 × 20)
= 1.0786933

body fat % = (4.95 ÷ 1.0786933) − 4.50 × 100
= 8.89%

This method enables you to determine your current body composition and track changes over time as you work toward your goal. This is discussed further later in the chapter.

WEIGHT MANAGEMENT

I wish I could give you the secret to quick and easy weight loss. (If I could I would become an instant billionaire.) Unfortunately, there is none. There are no magical methods or pills that lose weight for you, and you can't do it sitting on the couch and wishing the pounds away. Weight loss and weight management require hard work, commitment, and patience.

As mentioned earlier, your body-composition goal depends on your personal objectives. Everyone will travel the same road, although some people must travel farther, depending on where they're starting from and their destination. The difficulty of the road is determined by genetic makeup and lifestyle choices.

Patience is essential in weight management. Remember that you did not gain weight overnight. It took you years to get where you are today, and you cannot reasonably expect to take off extra weight in a few days or weeks. But don't get discouraged by a lack of immediate visible results. Be patient and stick with your program, and the weight will drop off with time and effort.

Genetics

Physical makeup is largely determined by genetics. If you do not have the physical characteristics of an elite cyclist, blame your parents.

There is a genetic component to overweight and obesity—no different from inheriting brown eyes or blond hair. A child with one or two overweight parents has a much greater chance of becoming overweight than one whose parents are slender. There is also a genetic component to fat distribution within the body. Inherited traits often include a paunch, or a large behind or thighs.

Some individuals can lose and maintain their lower weight more easily than others. This too is based on genetics. But don't use your genetic predisposition as an excuse; instead, use it to motivate yourself to try harder. A genetic predisposition toward overweight is not a sentence to that fate. All it means is that you must pay closer attention to the amount and types of food you eat and the amount of exercise you do.

Lifestyle

Lifestyle has as large an effect on body composition as genetics, if not more. Genetics is merely predisposition; the choices that we make in everyday life are what actually determine how many calories our bodies need and how much they get, and that is really the whole key to weight management. Do you choose to eat a half-pound cheeseburger or a low-fat turkey burger? Ice cream or fresh fruit for dessert? Stairs or elevator? Workout or video game?

The majority of Americans are so inactive that they are classified as sedentary. Because you're reading this book, I assume that your physical activity level is either not an issue or you're in the process of becoming more active. The physical activity part is taken care of elsewhere in this book, so the focus here is the nutrition side of weight management.

Too many Americans eat a diet consisting of unhealthy foods, foods that are extremely high in cholesterol, and portion sizes that are way too large. Many individuals eat out on a regular basis. Fast foods are extremely high in calories and unhealthy in other respects. A McDonald's double quarter pounder hamburger, a large fries, and a 20 oz Coke contains 1,430 kCal and 445 mg of cholesterol (kCal [kilocalories] is the correct terminology for what we commonly refer to as calories [Cal]). This is about three-quarters of the recommended daily caloric intake for many men (almost 100 percent for many women) and, to add insult to injury, cholesterol blocks your arteries. Most main courses at sit-down restaurants contain 2,000 kCal or more; this doesn't include bread, salad, appetizer, or dessert. Most chain restaurants post nutritional information for their meals on their websites. They're worth examining.

Part of the problem is portion size. Meals at many sit-down restaurants are big enough to serve two or three people; often, by the time the main dish arrives, you have already eaten a lot of bread as well as a salad and possibly an appetizer. Unless you possess outstanding willpower, there are a couple of things you can do to avoid overeating. Split a meal with someone else, or box up a portion of your meal as soon as it arrives. (Out of sight, out of mouth.) Watch portion sizes at home, too, by measuring or weighing portions. Dish up servings at the counter and bring only your allotted portion to the table.

The simplest way to eat healthy meals is to buy healthy foods and avoid junk foods. If it's not in the house, you're less likely to want it. Keep fruit around to satisfy your craving for sweets.

To effectively manage your body composition, weight-management strategies must be incorporated into your everyday activities. It is not about dieting and exercise. It's about implementing healthy changes to your eating habits and physical activity levels so they become habits rather than chores.

Setting Goals

Setting goals is one of the most important steps in developing a weight-management program. You need to establish short- and long-term goals to help you achieve your desired body composition. Research has shown that people are more likely to attain goals when they're written down, so do it.

Let's say you want to lose twenty pounds to get down to an optimal race weight. This is a large amount of weight, and you won't be successful in a short time. That lack of success could be discouraging, so you must establish short-term goals to encourage yourself along the way. Your short-term goals could be increments of five pounds, which you might achieve over the course of a month or two. It is recommended to lose no more than a pound per week.

Once you determine your current and target body compositions, use the formulas below to calculate how much weight loss is required to reach your goal.

$$(\text{current weight}) \times (\text{current body fat \%})$$
$$= \text{weight of fat in the body}$$

$$\text{current weight} - \text{weight of fat in the body}$$
$$= \text{weight of fat-free mass}$$

$$1 - \text{desired body fat \%} = \text{\% fat-free mass}$$

$$\text{weight of fat-free mass} \div \text{\% fat-free mass}$$
$$= \text{desired body weight}$$

$$\text{current body weight} - \text{desired body weight}$$
$$= \text{desired weight loss}$$

EXAMPLE

Male: 190 lb.: currently 20% body fat; desires 10% body fat

$$190 \times 0.20 = 38$$
$$190 - 38 = 152$$
$$1 - 0.10 = 0.90$$
$$152 \div 0.90 = 168.89$$
$$190 - 168.89 = 21.11$$

In this example, a male cyclist who wants to drop from 20 percent body fat to 10 percent body fat needs to lose 21 pounds. This will drop his weight from 190 pounds to 169 pounds, assuming that there will be no change in fat-free mass. In reality, this is rarely the case. As your training progresses, you will more than likely increase muscle mass. This will cause a corresponding increase in overall weight and an increase in the weight of your fat-free mass. Due to this phenomenon, you may want to periodically check your body fat and rerun the numbers to enable you to more accurately reach your desired body composition. This is especially true for individuals who are attempting to lose a lot of weight, and individuals who have been sedentary up to this point. Don't rerun the numbers every week or you'll drive yourself crazy, but do recheck the numbers after you have lost significant weight, or once a month.

Continuing the example above: After training for a while and losing ten pounds, the cyclist measures his body density and runs the numbers again. Because of the increase in muscle mass that has occurred, he finds he needs to lose only eight pounds to reach his goal of 10 percent body fat, not eleven pounds as anticipated. He's suddenly three pounds closer to his goal and stronger to boot! Remember, the goal is about body composition, not weight.

Caloric Balance

Weight management can be boiled down to a simple equation: calories consumed minus calories used per day. If you take in as many calories as you burn, your weight will not change and you will be replenished for your next bout of exercise. If you do not replace what is lost, you have a negative balance, which may be good or bad. A small negative balance is OK if you're trying to lose weight to get to your optimal race weight. A large negative balance can lead to poor performance and adverse health outcomes. If you take in more than you burn, you will gain weight, and the more you weigh, the more effort you'll have to put into each pedal stroke, especially when climbing.

To maintain health within a normal lifestyle, the average male needs to consume about 2,000 to 2,500 calories a day and the average female about 1,500 to 1,800 calories. This range is based more on body size than gender, and men are larger on average. A 6-foot-tall woman (well above the average height) will probably need to consume nearly as much as 6-foot-tall man.

These ranges, however, apply to average individuals and represent insufficient calories for endurance athletes. An endurance cyclist can burn up to 6,500 calories during a long race. If that's what you use, that's what you need to replenish.

The first step in determining caloric balance, therefore, is to estimate the calories your body uses. Start by determining your basal metabolic rate (BMR), the minimum energy required for your body to sustain life and function properly at rest. BMR usually ranges from around 1,100 to 2,100 kCal per day.

The most accurate way to measure BMR is with a metabolic cart such as the one used for a VO_2 max test (see Chapter 10). After a good night's sleep, no exercise for 24 hours, and a 12-hour fast, you are connected to the cart and lie relaxed for 20 to 30 minutes. Measurements are taken for 10 minutes, and the results are used to calculate BMR.

Because there is a linear relationship between heart rate and VO_2, heart rate can be used to estimate basal metabolic rate. You will need a heart-rate monitor that estimates kilocalories while at rest. Use the same procedures as when measuring BMR with the metabolic cart. Record the estimated kilocalories for 10 minutes and multiply by 6 to get kilocalories per hour. Multiply the resultant number by 24 to determine caloric expenditure from BMR for an entire day.

The last method to determine BMR uses generalized formulas, such as the ones given next that were developed by Stanely P. Brown et al. These formulas are not as accurate as the two methods listed earlier, but they will get you in the ballpark if your rate is close to average. Like the body mass index, however, they tell you nothing about your individual needs.

MALE

kCal/day = 66 + (13.7 × body weight in kg)
+ (5 × height in cm) − (6.9 × age)

FEMALE

kCal/day = 665 + (9.6 × body weight in kg)
+ (1.7 × height in cm) − (4.7 × age)

EXAMPLE

Male, 170 lb. (77.112 kg), 72 in. tall
(182.88 cm), age 22

kCal/day = 66 + (13.7 × 77.112) + (5 × 182.88)
− (6.9 × 22) = 1,885.03

After determining your BMR, you need to estimate the amount of energy you expend beyond your BMR each day. This is largely dependent on the energy used during exercise and is most easily estimated with a heart-rate monitor. Simply add energy expenditure during exercise to BMR to determine caloric consumption. If the cyclist in the example above burned 800 kCal during a ride, his total expenditure for the day would be 2,685.03 kCal.

Keep in mind that any activity over BMR will increase caloric requirements. Just adding exercise expenditure to BMR will therefore underestimate your daily calorie requirements, unless you lie on the couch all day. This methodology, therefore, will give you only a best guess or a good place to start. If you're losing or gaining too much weight, adjust your daily intake accordingly.

Replenishing

Now that you know how many calories you expend per day, you need to replenish them. This requires

Nutrition Facts
Serv. Size 1/2 cup (120mL) condensed soup
Servings about 2.5
Calories 100
Fat Cal. 15
*Percent Daily Values (DV) are based on a 2,000 calorie diet.

Amount/serving	%DV*	Amount/serving	%DV*
Total Fat 1.5g	**2%**	**Potassium** 160mg	**5%**
Sat. Fat 0.5g	**3%**	**Total Carb.** 17g	**6%**
Trans Fat 0g		Fiber 2g	**8%**
Cholest. 10mg	**3%**	Sugars 2g	
Sodium 620mg	**26%**	**Protein** 4g	

Vitamin A 20% • Vitamin C 0% • Calcium 0% • Iron 4%

It's important to read food labels to help monitor caloric intake.

that you read food labels and determine the number of calories in each meal. Don't be misled by the serving sizes listed on the packaging; measure and take into account the actual servings you consume, and be sure to count extras and sides, such as crackers with your soup and dressing on your salad.

Keep a log to track calories, writing down all foods and drinks consumed during a 24-hour period. Make sure to include snacks and beverages. (Soda drinkers may consume hundreds of calories daily from that source alone.) At the end of the day, compare calories consumed against calories utilized to determine your caloric balance. Many of you will be surprised at just how many calories you take in during one day.

Consuming your caloric intake goal of 2,500 kCal/day solely by eating candy bars may be fun but it's not advisable. It is far better to reach your goal with a healthy, well-balanced diet, as explained in Chapter 13. Keep in mind that you're only estimating the calories used during a day, not measuring them directly, so your numbers may be off. Keep a close watch on changes in body composition, and make adjustments in your diet if you're losing weight too quickly (more than one pound per week), gaining instead of losing, or not changing at all after a reasonable amount of time. Keep in mind that if you're gaining muscle mass, you may actually gain weight, so you may need to measure changes in body fat instead of weight.

All this may seem tedious, but it will pay off in the long run. Keeping a log will allow you to adjust your caloric intake to reach your specific goals.

Fad Diets—Bad Diets

Because you did not gain weight overnight, you will not lose it overnight, although many companies promise you just that. Among the nearly endless number of fad diets and diet products are two that have serious potential negative effects: over-the-counter weight-loss pills and low- and no-carbohydrate diets.

Diet Pills

Over-the-counter weight-loss pills are a multimillion-dollar industry. Like dietary supplements, these products are not FDA tested or approved; as long as they don't claim to cure disease, illness, or injury, their manufacturers can make any claims they wish, to the extent of exaggerating or even fabricating the effectiveness of the product. As a whole, we are an instant-gratification society, and the assertions of the manufacturers often promise the sought-after instant results.

Cyclists should not use weight-loss pills. Most contain stimulants that greatly increase resting heart rate and can cause, among other medical conditions, heart palpitations and death. Combined with the increased heart rate that occurs naturally during exercise, the heart can be seriously overworked. This is especially true when riding on hot, humid days, when blood plasma volume drops significantly due to sweating. This puts excessive strain on the heart that can lead to cardiovascular complications.

Low-Carb Diets

You can lose weight on a low- or no-carbohydrate diet, but it will have a strongly negative effect on your performance and health. Carbohydrates are the primary source of glycogen. If the body's glycogen supplies run low and are not replenished, the body creates its own glycogen through a process known as gluconeogenesis, in which the protein in muscle cells is converted to glycogen. This process is slow, does not produce large amounts of glycogen, and breaks down the muscles. Most of the weight loss generated by low- and no-carbohydrate diets comes not from the loss of fat but from the loss of water and muscle mass—undesirable for any individual but especially for an athlete.

Carbohydrates play several essential roles in the human body. Glycogen is the only substance that the brain and central nervous system can use for fuel, and a shortage can lead to mental confusion and fatigue. Without an adequate supply of glycogen from carbohydrates, fat cannot be properly oxidized for energy production. This results in incomplete fat breakdown, which causes an increase in the body's acidity. That, combined with the high intake of protein common to low-carb diets, overworks the liver and kidneys. These diets also lead to a chronic state of dehydration and electrolyte imbalance, both of which can lead to heart arrhythmias.

Most popular low-carb diets do not distinguish between healthy and unhealthy foods and commonly lead to increased cholesterol intake. (Many foods advertised as low-/no-carbohydrate foods are extremely high in cholesterol.) A high-cholesterol diet greatly increases the risk of developing coronary artery disease.

WOMEN

Although women's cycling is growing every year and promises to continue, there is still much room for improvement in institutional support. Professional female cyclists do not make nearly as much money as men, largely because the races and endorsement opportunities are not in place yet. As women's involvement continues to increase, hopefully the opportunities will too. Given the strong interest recently shown by some manufacturers in designing gear specifically for women (see Chapter 1), there is reason for optimism that other areas of the sport will soon catch up and the field will become more equitable.

Women's cycling has grown rapidly in recent years and looks as though it will continue to grow.

Gender Differences

Physiological differences between males and females must be taken into consideration. First, I want to clear up the common fallacy that men's muscles are stronger than women's. There are no real differences between male and female muscle tissue. In general men have more muscle mass to begin with and produce much larger amounts of testosterone than women, which enables them to produce even more muscle mass through training more effectively. Additionally, due to a higher speed of signaling, males are able to contract muscle slightly faster.

Women are also at a slight cardiovascular disadvantage. Given the same training status, women tend to have VO_2 max measurements 5 to 10 ml/kg/min lower than those of men. In general, women have a smaller heart than men and therefore a smaller stroke volume. Women also have lower levels of hemoglobin. Both of these factors reduce the body's ability to transport oxygen and tend to produce a slightly higher heart rate at any given submaximal intensity. On the other hand, women tend to have slightly higher levels of 2,3-DPG, which binds with hemoglobin and increases oxygen disassociation for better uptake into muscle, and this helps to offset the lower hemoglobin levels.

Female Athlete Triad

Women are uniquely susceptible to three interconnected physiological factors that constitute a serious health risk known as the female athlete triad.

Eating Disorders

The first component of the triad is the failure to maintain a healthy body composition. As discussed above, excess weight is counterproductive to performance, but so are inadequate stores of body fat. As a general rule, women should not drop below 12 percent body fat because doing so may expose them to a health risk. Thinner is not always better.

Anorexia is the failure to consume enough food to maintain a healthy body composition. Many people mistakenly believe that anorexics do not eat, or eat only rarely or only small amounts. In reality, an individual can eat "reasonable" quantities at every meal and still be anorexic if her energy demands exceed her intake. Cycling expends a great deal of energy, and cyclists who consistently fail to replenish with sufficient calories find themselves on a downward spiral leading to unhealthy body composition. An aspiration to reach a desired body composition can also push athletes to become bulimic. Bulimia is marked by binge eating followed by purging by inducing vomiting, using laxatives, or both.

Eating disorders can be life threatening. It is essential that coaches not ignore the situation if they think an athlete (regardless of gender) has an eating disorder. Some athletes may only need advice on how to eat correctly, whereas others may need psychological counseling. Coaches are not typically trained to handle this situation and should seek help from qualified professionals. But coaches can make sure, at least, that they are not part of the problem by pushing cyclists to become too thin or to obsess about body composition. Cycling coaches must monitor their riders' body composition for optimal race weight, avoiding both overweight and underweight.

Amenorrhea

The second part of the female athlete triad is marked by fluctuations in the menstrual cycle and eventually amenorrhea, the cessation of the menstrual cycle. This is thought to be caused by a prolonged negative energy balance leading to unhealthy body composition. Most women with eating disorders eventually develop amenorrhea. However, female athletes who maintain a healthy body composition have also been known to have irregular cycles.

Bone Density Loss

The last component of the female athlete triad is a significant decrease in bone density. Prolonged menstrual irregularities lead to a decrease in estrogen production. Estrogen plays a key role in the absorption and retention of calcium in the bones. With low levels of estrogen, less calcium is absorbed and maintained, leading to a decrease in bone density. This leads to osteoporosis, in which bone strength is reduced and bones tend to fracture. In younger female athletes, it can also lead to stunted growth.

Female cyclists should watch for signs of the female athlete triad. If you think you're experiencing any of these signs, consult your doctor. Eating disorders are extremely difficult, if not impossible, to overcome on your own.

Yeast and Urinary Tract Infections

An increase in yeast infections and urinary tract infections are reported in women who cycle. Yeast and bacteria flourish in moist, warm conditions, such as found in sweaty cycling shorts. To limit infections, change out of your shorts as soon as possible after a ride, and wash them before wearing them again. Don't sit around for hours in your cycling shorts. If you intend to go with your group for coffee or a meal after your ride, bring along a change of clothing. Drinking plenty of water increases urination, which can also decrease the risk of urinary tract infections.

Menstrual Cycle

Whether you ride during your menstrual cycle is a personal decision. If you can function normally during your period, then ride normally. If you have trouble functioning normally, you may want to schedule easier rides during that time. But be careful not to rationalize easy training days when it may not be necessary. Over-the-counter nonsteroidal anti-inflammatory drugs such as ibuprofen (for example, Motrin or Advil) may help with menstrual cramps, but talk to your doctor before using them. (Keep in mind this advice is coming from a male who has never experienced this.)

Pregnancy

Exercise can be beneficial in healthy women going through a normal pregnancy. Here are some of the known benefits:

- reduction in excessive weight gain
- increased energy
- better psychological well-being
- improved ability to cope with the extra weight of pregnancy
- decreased risk of gestational diabetes
- decreased labor pain
- lower, but healthy, birth weight of baby
- accelerated return to pre-pregnancy weight
- accelerated return to pre-pregnancy fitness level

You should, however, seek medical clearance before beginning or continuing an exercise program during pregnancy. Advise your doctor of your training program and work with her to ensure that you and your baby remain safe. Ask what signs you should look for that would indicate an adverse reaction to exercise, and maintain an ongoing dialogue with your doctor about your training and the changes occurring to your body.

Although exercise during pregnancy can be beneficial, do not try to maintain a high level of fitness compatible with racing. Research has demonstrated that blood flow to the fetus is not compromised during mild to moderate exercise. Vigorous exercise, however, is strongly discouraged due to possible competition between mother and fetus for blood supply, among other issues.

Because blood flow is redirected to the fetus, heart rate is not a reliable tool for measuring exercise intensity during pregnancy. It is better to determine intensity using a rating of perceived exertion (see Chapter 11)—that is, feel. Refrain from long strenuous workouts, and do not exercise to exhaustion.

Outdoor cycling is not recommended during pregnancy. One of the biggest dangers to the infant during pregnancy is impact. Even on your best days, there is a risk of crashing. As your pregnancy progresses, your center of gravity shifts, which greatly compromises your balance and increases the risk of a fall. So it is advisable to move to a stationary trainer during pregnancy.

The body's thermoregulatory system is compromised during pregnancy due to increased insulation (added fat deposits) and the redirection of blood flow to the fetus, making less blood available for cooling at the skin. Given the importance of maintaining a healthy core temperature during pregnancy, the cooler training environment that is possible to attain indoors during warm months is another argument in favor of using an indoor trainer.

After pregnancy, you can return to full training as soon as your doctor and your body deem it safe. It will take a little while before hormone levels return to normal. As with any layoff from training, start at lower intensities and progress slowly to prevent injury while rebuilding your base.

AGING

We are all on a physiological curve. We grow stronger from birth until about 25 to 30 years old, when our abilities peak. Sometime between the ages of 35 and 40 we begin a gradual decline that continues for the rest of our lives. Everyone, regardless of being sedentary or active, is on the curve, although 60-year-olds who have been physically active their whole life may well be stronger than sedentary individuals at 35 years.

Research has demonstrated that physical activity enhances health on several levels, and a sedentary lifestyle is associated with many different disease states. Unfortunately, you can't bank exercise; research has shown that there is no protective effect from prior physical activity. Stop training and your fitness level will drop over time until it reaches that of a sedentary individual, with all the associated risks.

Cycling is beneficial for all ages, and you are never too old to begin. Individuals can see improvement in their physical abilities at any age,

Cycling is a valuable lifetime activity that can maintain and/or increase the quality of life as we age.

and prior inactivity is no impediment. Older individuals who begin exercising can realize gains in general fitness that improve the overall quality of life.

Age does, however, impose special considerations on training. After the peak age of 25 to 30 years of age, there is usually a decrease in VO2 max of about 1 percent per year—slightly more for sedentary individuals, slightly less for active ones. As the body ages, there is typically a loss of muscle mass and an increase in body fat—again, more pronounced in sedentary individuals than in active ones. With age it takes longer to recover between training bouts, making it important to closely monitor how your body reacts to training and adapt your program accordingly. This does not mean you must remove high-intensity training from your program, but you may need to alter its type and frequency. By keeping your training level as high as possible, you will be able to ride aggressively and race into your later years.

As we age there is a loss in bone density, which can lead to osteoporosis. Osteoporosis is more common in postmenopausal women than any other group.

Two measures can help offset the effects of aging on bone density. Make sure you take adequate amounts of calcium. This will not increase bone density, but it will help prevent a decrease in bone density. Like muscles, bone needs to be placed under stress to get stronger. To accomplish this you need to engage in a weight-bearing activity. Because cycling is not a weight-bearing activity, and research has shown that cyclists have bone densities equivalent to those of sedentary individuals, it's important for cyclists to enhance their workout with some weight-bearing activities, such as jogging, weight training, or plyometrics. Of course, if you think you have osteoporosis or are at risk of developing it, speak with your doctor before beginning a workout program.

YOUTH

Cycling is an excellent way to involve your child in physical activity. Cycling not only increases physical activity levels but also teaches balance and coordination. Even so, we must be careful when "training" our youth in cycling.

Sports-related injuries in youth are on the rise, and overuse injuries that were formerly found only in collegiate and professional athletes are now being diagnosed in middle-school and high-school athletes. This has come about because young athletes are being trained as if they were adults. But physiologically and psychologically, children are not adults and cannot handle adult-size training intensities and volumes.

Compared to adults, prepubescent children produce small amounts of hormones, preventing their bodies from repairing damage as efficiently

Although cycling is an excellent activity for children, keep in mind that children are not small adults and should not be trained as such.

and adapting to physical stress in the same manner as adults. High-intensity and high-volume training can have a negative impact on the development of young bones, muscles, and tendons. Children may not be psychologically equipped to make safe decisions on training, especially in contradiction to their coach's instructions, and may not accurately follow coaching instructions in the first place.

Training does not increase VO₂ max in prepubescent children. With training there is an increase in endurance performance, but this is due to improved coordination rather than adaptations that lead to increased VO₂ max. Strength gains in children are also due primarily to increased coordination, and few or none to hypertrophy (increased muscle size). Adaptations to anaerobic training are minimal in prepubescent children.

There is no scientific support for high-volume and high-intensity training in children; in fact, scientific research and anecdotal evidence have demonstrated that it can have a strong adverse effect on a child's health, growth, and development. High-impact training, such as plyometrics and weight training, can stunt growth if conducted incorrectly and are not recommended for children under the age of sixteen.

As children grow, the ligaments that surround and support the joints are developing as well. Too much torque applied at the knee joint can weaken and damage these ligaments. For this reason, the USCF has limited the gear ratio allowed for youth during races. Race officials use a roll-out (how far the bike rolls during one revolution of the pedal) to determine whether the bike is in compliance with the current rules. For the most current regulations, check the latest version of the USA Cycling rule book (see the Appendix for the website). The use of spin bikes by children should also be avoided because the act of slowing down a 45 lb. flywheel can place too much stress on the knee.

Don't take the fun out of cycling. When coaching children under sixteen years, focus on developing technique rather than performance. This age is a good time to work on bike-handling skills and tactics. Don't worry about a structured workout program; instead, let them enjoy themselves, ride the way they feel, and decide how long they want to ride. They'll tell you when they're tired.

Children sixteen and older can begin an entry-level adult-style training program. At this age, most youth can handle increased workloads and adapt accordingly. Keep in mind that they are still growing physiologically and psychologically, so you should still be cautious. A coach with specific background in working with youth can structure a program suited to your child's capabilities and health needs.

OVERWEIGHT AND OBESITY

Cycling is an excellent form of exercise for someone who wants to lose weight and become healthier. Because overweight and obesity are risk factors in the development of cardiovascular disease and type 2 diabetes, it's important to have a medical exam and clearance before beginning an exercise program.

With excess layers of fat, the body has difficulty with heat dissipation, which drives up core temperature during exercise. This is compounded when exercising in hot, humid weather. Make sure that you acclimatize to the heat before you begin exercising, and slowly work into your program.

Overweight individuals may have to pay special attention to equipment choices. The wheel sets on road bikes are light for better performance but are not designed to handle large amounts of weight and may buckle when placed under stress. Larger individuals may prefer a mountain bike or a cyclo-cross bike, which have sturdier wheels that will not buckle under heavy loads. As the weight comes off, you can move to a road bike. Another option is road wheels designed specifically for "Clydesdale" riders—those weighing 200 pounds or more.

DIABETES

This section is more for coaches than for athletes. Diabetics are usually well educated on the pathology, treatment, and symptoms of their condition.

Diabetes is a metabolic disorder that affects the regulation of glucose in the body. Due to the nature of diabetes and because it's a risk factor for developing cardiovascular disease, it is important to seek medical clearance before beginning an exercise program. Diabetics should not participate in an exercise program until they have their diabetes under control and are cleared by their doctor, with whom an ongoing dialogue should be maintained.

For proper functioning, the body requires that blood glucose levels remain at a nearly constant level. Insulin, produced by special cells in the pancreas, is a hormone that regulates blood glucose by controlling its release from the liver to the blood and from blood to the tissues. Two basic pathologies, both involving insulin, lead to diabetes.

The first involves an autoimmune dysfunction in which the body attacks the cells in the pancreas where insulin is produced. This causes a significant decrease in the production of insulin, which in turn leads to poor regulation of blood glucose. This is generally referred to as type 1 diabetes and usually requires insulin injections to regulate blood glucose.

The second pathology, associated with type 2 diabetes, involves a reduced effectiveness of insulin due to desensitization. In this case the production of insulin is not affected, but its ability to function is impaired. This is often associated with a sedentary lifestyle and overweight or obesity. Exercise increases the body's sensitivity to insulin and improves glucose regulation, thereby helping to prevent and reduce the severity of type 2 diabetes. Exercise does not have a large direct effect on type 1 diabetes.

One of the biggest risks of exercise for diabetics is hypoglycemia (low blood sugar), which can have serious neurological implications. It is important to recognize the symptoms of hypoglycemia:

- "the shakes"
- increased heart rate, possibly leading to palpitations
- headache
- extreme hunger
- confusion and irrational behavior
- extreme fatigue
- convulsions
- unconsciousness
- coma

Hypoglycemia can proceed from bad to worse very quickly and can, in severe cases, cause death. At the first sign of symptoms, athletes should stop training and measure their blood glucose level. If it is low, they should eat carbohydrates high on the glycemic index to spike blood sugar levels. After eating, they should remeasure their blood glucose level to confirm that it is normal, then decide whether to continue training. Diabetics should keep foods that are high on the glycemic index readily available at all times.

Cycling utilizes large amounts of glycogen for fuel, making it important for diabetics to carefully monitor their blood glucose level before, during, and after a ride. Because of the increased use of glucose, insulin-dependent diabetics may need to adjust doses accordingly.

Because diabetes impairs peripheral circulation and causes peripheral neuropathy (loss of nerves), it is one of the leading causes of nontraumatic amputations. Cycling shoes are designed to be rigid and fit snugly, but this can be problematic for diabetics, who should opt for more flexible and less constricting footgear.

Many diabetics cycle without incident. If they monitor their diabetes, keep it under control, and have realistic goals, cycling can be beneficial. Exercise is an important factor for improved health in type 1 and type 2 diabetes. With type 2 diabetes, exercise is an important tool for prevention and management.

ASTHMA

Asthma is the most common chronic disease in the world; many cyclists have some form of it. Asthma is marked by the following symptoms:

- swelling of the airway passages
- bronchial spasms
- increased mucus production
- difficulty breathing
- coughing

Asthma attacks can be light and barely no-ticeable or severe enough to completely block air-way passages. If you are asthmatic, it is important to carry an inhaler with you at all times. It's better to have it and not need it than to need it and not have it, especially in the sport of cycling where you're often a long way from home. Coaches should always confirm that their athletes have their inhal-ers with them.

In some individuals, asthma is brought on by physical exertion. The symptoms of exercise-induced asthma usually do not appear until 5 to 10 minutes after the cessation of exercise. Exer-cising outside when the pollen count is high, and in heavy traffic areas around exhaust fumes, can aggravate breathing and instigate an attack. Exer-cising in a cold, dry environment greatly increases the risk of an attack, whereas warm, humid envi-ronments decrease the risk.

If you have asthma, it's important to take a little extra time to warm up before an event. This allows your body to adapt to the stress of exercise in that particular environment. You can also use an inhaler prior to exercise as a preventive meas-ure. You must obtain a waiver to use an inhaler prior to a race because bronchodilators are consid-ered a banned substance.

training log

TRAINING LOG

DAY _____ DATE _____

MORNING HEART RATE _____

WEIGHT _____

HOURS OF SLEEP _____

QUALITY OF SLEEP _____

FATIGUE AND SORENESS _____

_____

_____

RIDE

TYPE OF WORKOUT _____

WEATHER _____

DURATION _____

DISTANCE _____

ROUTE _____

_____

_____

_____

_____

_____

_____

_____

AVERAGE SPEED _____

AVERAGE POWER _____

AVERAGE HEART RATE _____

WORKOUT RATING _____

1   2   3   4   5   6   7   8   9   10

COMMENTS

_____

_____

_____

_____

_____

_____

_____

_____

_____

_____

_____

_____

_____

_____

resources

CYCLING BOOKS

General Cycling

Allen, H., and A. Coggan. 2006. *Training and Racing with a Power Meter*. Boulder, CO: VeloPress.

Burke, E. 2003. *High-Tech Cycling: The Science of Riding*. 2d ed. Champaign, IL: Human Kinetics.

———. 2002. *Serious Cycling*. 2d ed. Champaign, IL: Human Kinetics.

Jeukendrup, A. 2002. *High-Performance Cycling*. Champaign, IL: Human Kinetics.

Bike Maintenance

Downs, T. 2005. *The Bicycling Guide to Complete Bicycle Maintenance and Repair for Road and Mountain Bikes*. Emmaus, PA: Rodale Inc.

Jones, C. 2005. *Big Blue Book of Bicycle Repair: A Do-It-Yourself Bicycle Repair Guide from Park Tool*. St. Paul, MN: Park Tool Company.

Zinn, L. 2005. *Zinn and the Art of Road Bike Maintenance*. 2d ed. Boulder, CO: VeloPress.

Health, Disease, and Fitness

Baker, A. *Bicycling Medicine*. 1998. New York: Simon and Schuster.

Pruitt, A. L., and F. Matheny. 2006. *Andy Pruitt's Complete Medical Guide for Cyclists*. Boulder, CO: VeloPress.

Ross, M. J. 2003. *Maximum Performance: Sports Medicine for Endurance Athletes*. Boulder, CO: VeloPress.

Physiology and Nutrition

McArdle, W., F. Katch, and V. Katch. 2006. *Exercise Physiology: Energy, Nutrition, and Human Performance*. 6th ed. Baltimore, MD: Lippincott Williams and Wilkins.

Powers, S., and T. Howley. 2004. *Exercise Physiology: Theory and Application to Fitness and Performance*. New York: McGraw-Hill.

Ryan, M. 2002. *Sports Nutrition for Endurance Athletes*. Boulder, CO: VeloPress.

Vella, M. 2006. *Anatomy for Strength and Fitness Training*. New York: McGraw-Hill.

Wilmore, H., and D. Costill. 2007. *Physiology of Sport and Exercise*. 4th ed. Champaign, IL: Human Kinetics.

CYCLING MAGAZINES

Bicycling (www.bicycling.com)
VeloNews (www.velonews.com)
Cycle Sport (cyclesportmag.com)

WEBSITES

Products and Services

www.campagnolo.com
www.cannondale.com
www.cateye.com
www.chrisking.com
www.ciclosportusa.com
www.ergomo-online.de
www.fujibikes.com
www.garmin.com
www.hammernutrition.com

www.jitteryjoes.com
www.mavic.com
www.microsporttech.com
www.parktool.com
www.pearlizumi.com
www.polarusa.com
www.racermateinc.com
www.rudyprojectusa.com
www.saris.com
www.shimano.com
www.sram.com
www.srm.de
www.toyota-united.com
www.trainingpeaks.com
www.trainright.com
www.tufonorthamerica.com

Organizations for Disabled Cyclists

www.dsusa.org
www.ncpad.org
www.ndsaonline.org
www.usaba.org
www.usolympicteam.com/paralympics
www.wsusa.org

Finding a Coach and Internet Coaching Services

www.trainingpeaks.com
www.trainright.com
www.usacycling.org/coaches/search.php

Miscellaneous

Collegiate Cycling

www.usacycling.org

Racing and Noncompetitive Cycling Events

www.active.com
www.livestrong.org
www.nationalmssociety.org
www.teamintraining.org
www.usacycling.org

Velodromes in the United States

www.americantrackracing.com

USCF Rule Book

www.usacycling.org/forms/RdTrkCx_rulebook.pdf

List of Banned Substances

www.wada-ama.org/en

Determining Vitamin Intake

www.iom.edu/object.file/master/21/372/0.pdf

Database for Exercise Science and Sports Medicine Literature

www.pubmed.gov

index